Teaching with Text Sets

Authors

Mary Ann Cappiello, Ed.D.
Erika Thulin Dawes, Ed.D.

SHELL EDUCATION

Publishing Credits

Dona Herweck Rice, *Editor-in-Chief*; Robin Erickson, *Production Director*;
Lee Aucoin, *Creative Director*; Sara Johnson, M.S.Ed., *Senior Editor*;
Tracy Edmunds, *Editor*; Leah Quillian, *Assistant Editor*; Grace Alba, *Production Artist*;
Corinne Burton, M.A.Ed., *Publisher*

Image Credits

Shell Education

5301 Oceanus Drive
Huntington Beach, CA 92649-1030
http://www.shelleducation.com

ISBN 978-1-4258-0688-0

© 2013 Shell Educational Publishing, Inc.

Table of Contents

#50688: *Teaching with Text Sets*   ©*Shell Education*

Foreword

The book you are about to read is a book about *possibilities* for teaching—*choices* you can make, *options* you can pick from, and *alternatives* available to you. It's a book I wish I had when I began teaching fifth grade many years ago. I knew I wanted to use more literature in my classroom, but I didn't know how. I loved reading, and I especially loved children's books, but I had lots of questions:

- How do I find out about good books? Once I find out about them, how do I get them?

- What other materials make sense to use with books?

- How do I teach my curriculum in social studies and science using books? (At that time, there was no big push on subject standards and no Common Core State Standards, but today, I would throw a question about that into the mix.)

- What activities should my students do based on their reading?

- What kinds of writing, speaking, or artwork make sense?

If only I had owned a copy of *Teaching with Text Sets*, things would have been much, much easier.

We as teachers are fortunate that the authors Mary Ann Cappiello and Erika Thulin Dawes have provided us with informed, useful, and honest answers to my questions. These answers stem from their own classroom experiences, their professional work with teachers, and their extensive knowledge of literature. Mary Ann and Erika's goal is to show us how and why we should use multimodal, multigenre text sets. "It's a mouthful, isn't it?," they ask. Well, yes, it is. Try saying it six times in a row. But in addition to being a mouthful, text sets are also rich collections of material that go beyond books to include primary source documents, videos, audio recordings, magazine and newspaper articles, and all sorts of other material you can find on the Internet. As Mary Ann and Erika explain, text sets are wide-ranging collections of material that all teachers need in order to teach well. Why? They're interesting, they're informative, they're "good to think with," and they work. In short, text sets are the raw materials of good teaching and learning.

Mary Ann and Erika show us step-by-step how to use text sets as the basis of meeting curriculum goals and required standards. Using the topic of *trees*, they take us through the process of planning, developing the text sets, organizing the material, designing the activities, and assessing student work. They don't just talk about it—they do it! Starting from scratch, they build the unit about trees, pausing to share their work with us and providing us with helpful charts for planning units ourselves. So for example, when Mary Ann and Erika talk about planning the unit to teach vocabulary, incorporating content standards, and meeting Common Core requirements, they actually make a plan for their tree unit and provide a blank chart for us to use. When they discuss gathering materials for text sets, they gather materials for their tree unit, filling in an appropriate chart detailing the characteristics of the material and the possible uses. All along the way, Mary Ann and Erika are *describing* what to do and *showing* readers how to do it. This is powerful.

A major component of this book is Mary Ann and Erika's description of how to organize the material collected in a text set so that it can be used effectively for teaching. They have developed a highly original scheme for grouping materials for instruction that includes models such as *the Duet, the Sunburst, the Tree Ring, the Solar System,* and *the Mountain*. For example, the Duet Model consists of two books that provide the opportunity to make comparisons and contrasts when read together. These reusable models provide a variety of interesting and purposeful ways to use text sets in the classroom.

Mary Ann and Erika take you inside two classrooms that put these models to work. In the first classroom, elementary school children are learning about immigration, while in the second classroom, middle school students are learning about space. Once again, we are treated to the specifics of what was done and why. Mary Ann and Erika share with us the struggles of planning, such as when the materials they hope to find are not available, as well as the joys of planning, such as when the materials they do find provide them with an overwhelming number of options to pursue. Because of their carefully chosen text sets, the learning that results is rich and varied. This is no "here-today-gone-tomorrow" teaching, with teachers racing from topic to topic to cover content as quickly as possible. Instead, these classes engage in in-depth learning—the kind of learning that lasts.

As someone who works with both beginning and experienced teachers, I know that teachers are looking for books that not only tell them about good teaching but also show them how to do it. This book does that. A teacher could simply take some of the units and curriculum presented in this book and make use of it right away. Or, a teacher could use the models described here to prepare original units. *Teaching with Text Sets* is a resource for all teachers, no matter what subjects or grade levels we teach or what our level of classroom experience. If only it were available when I was teaching fifth grade!

—Myra Zarnowski
Queens College, CUNY

Acknowledgments

Writing this book would not have been possible without many people. Each of us has many colleagues to thank from our years in public schools, teachers with whom we initially enacted many of the ideas in this book. Hundreds of former students, both children and Lesley graduate students, allowed us to see what worked and what did not as we refined our practice.

Our understanding of the many roles that children's and young adult literature can play in K–12 schools was shaped by Dr. Barbara Kiefer, with whom we both had the good fortune of studying with in graduate school. Barbara's vision, and that of her mentor, Charlotte Huck, is at the heart of the work that we do.

We are very lucky to work in a collegial and collaborative environment at the Graduate School of Education at Lesley University. As the structure of this book began to take place, we each received a course release—Mary Ann a Faculty Development Grant, Erika a Russell Grant—which gave us additional space and time for our ideas to percolate. Karen Muncaster supported our work with an Academic Technology Grant and continually sent us helpful links and resources to build our digital collections. Our colleagues in the Language and Literacy Division can always be counted on for guidance, constructive feedback, and new ideas, and our division director, Margery Miller, is our strongest advocate.

Throughout this process, we were extremely fortunate to have a very capable graduate assistant, Deirdre Savarese. Deirdre researched, formatted, and annotated the text sets in Chapters Eight through Eleven. We know that many teachers and students will benefit from her hard work, and we are so grateful for her shared vision of teaching with text sets.

We are thankful to the many librarians in the Minute Man system for putting up with our interlibrary loan requests: to librarians Pam Harland, Julie Roach, and Mary Thulin in particular for their guidance along the way and to the staff at Water Street Books in Exeter, NH, who always found a way to get books quickly.

Without Caitlyn, Zoe, Maggie, and Hillary, as well as the support of Jenn and Tracy, this book would not be complete. We are so grateful to these thoughtful teachers and administrators, not only for allowing us to plan curriculum alongside them and wreak havoc on their schedules, but also for trusting in us in the first place.

We are grateful to Linda Dacey, who shepherded us through our work with Shell Education, and to our editor, Tracy Edmunds, for her support. Marc Aronson of Rutgers University has been a strong advocate of the book from the onset, and we have benefitted from many conversations with him about the role of nonfiction literature in the classroom. Myra Zarnowski of Queens College of the city of New York gave us careful feedback on earlier versions of this book and supported us throughout by answering questions and offering guidance. Myra, we could not have done it without you.

Our parents were our first teachers, and they remain our biggest cheerleaders and most patient listeners. Thank you!

Finally, to Tim and Bill, we offer our thanks and our love. We spent a lot of time on the phone or busily writing on the computer. We frequently leapt into the car to race to the library before closing. We ate a lot of pizza. Ella, Will, and Clara, your natural curiosity reminds us that children arrive at school brimming with questions that need to be honored with deep exploration of content, engaging texts of all genres and modalities, and thoughtful curriculum design. You inspired every word on the page.

—Mary Ann and Erika

Introduction

Multimodal, multigenre text sets… It's a mouthful isn't it? So what are they? And how do you use them? This book describes multimodal, multigenre texts sets, including children's literature of all genres, periodicals, and rich digital resources as tools for teaching content across multiple subject areas and grade spans. We'll share our definition of text sets and the models for teaching with texts sets with illustrated examples from various grade levels.

This book evolved from our experiences over time as educators, which jointly span the spectrum of learners from preschool to college students. In our current positions as literacy faculty members at Lesley University, we share an office that is cluttered with children's and young adult books, but that is just the tip of the iceberg. The content of this book is drawn from hours of conversations about our past teaching practices and our current teaching endeavors. Mary Ann has worked as a middle and high school English-language arts and humanities teacher and as a curriculum facilitator for language arts and social studies at the secondary level. Erika has worked as an elementary classroom teacher, a reading specialist, and as a literacy supervisor. We have worked in urban, suburban, and rural areas with diverse student populations. We draw on our preK–12 experiences daily as we now work with preservice and inservice teachers, and we cherish our many opportunities to continue our work in elementary and middle school classrooms. Our teaching lives are not perfect, and we do not expect yours to be, either. We love the messiness of teaching. We learn from our mistakes, and, at our best and at our worst, we learn from the students with whom we share our classrooms. We also cherish the opportunity to collaborate with one another. Neither of us begins a new class, conducts a workshop, or speaks at a conference without first working her ideas through with the other.

We each teach a mix of courses in the Graduate School of Education at Lesley University in Cambridge, Massachusetts, including courses in children's and young adult literature and nonfiction literature, and literacy methods. When we teach our literature courses, we not only teach our students how to find and evaluate books for the classroom but also model the many roles any one book can play in classroom life. When we teach our literacy methods courses, we strive to model methods in the context of vibrant curriculum and interesting, engaging multimodal, multigenre text sets that focus on children's and young adult literature.

Over the past seven years, we have noticed the disconnect teachers experience between the national focus on isolated reading instruction and assessment and the reality of their classrooms. We believe that student-centered curriculum is the context in which successful instruction and assessment takes place, and yet, curriculum has not been a focal point of the national education agenda. Time and time again, we hear teachers tell us their administrators admonish them to cut social studies and science out at the elementary level because more time needs to be spent on literacy and mathematics instruction. This is done despite teachers' knowledge of their students and their understanding that science and social studies are essential fields of study that foster engagement at all levels and even hook some students into reading.

Our development as teachers has been grounded in the fields of reading, English language arts, and literacy, but our perspective on literacy positions us in a larger conversation about content learning. We view literacy (reading, writing, speaking, and listening) as a vehicle for learning content. We believe that one always reads or writes with the goal of learning or communicating about the world around us. The work of reading or writing in school should be no less purposeful than the work of reading and writing outside school. We are not content-area specialists in all fields of study, but we are, by nature, deeply curious. We have learned how to seek the expert resources and have sought integration of literacy and content in our teaching throughout our careers. Our goal is to provide elementary and middle school teachers of all content areas with *models* for using texts in the classroom. In this book, we will help you consider the best books in the field of children's and young adult literature, books that have been vetted by content and literacy experts. Our models will work best when you apply *your* content expertise and *your* knowledge of the children you teach.

As we write this book, educators at all levels are beginning to grapple with the implications of the new Common Core State Standards. We are thrilled that these standards reflect our longstanding belief that it is through the reading of multiple texts representing a diversity of perspectives that students will develop the critical-thinking skills necessary in our information-saturated world. The Common Core State Standards place strong emphasis on reading to learn content information, a focus that has been obscured by the National Reading Panel Report's (2000) emphasis on decontextualized reading skills that has dominated literacy instruction over the past decade. The new standards reflect a shift back to integration in the teaching of language arts and a look forward to the need for multiple literacies for the 21st century. In short, we think it is an incredibly exciting time in the field of education!

This book is a fusion of our teaching lives and an outgrowth of our work with teachers. We want to help you build rich curriculum. We want to help you bring content back into focus in your classroom in order to foster student engagement and increase their sophistication with reading and writing. Our goal is to share the strategies that we have developed for expanding the teaching potential of quality children's literature titles, helping you create a bridge between great books, great digital resources, and the rich undertakings of your classroom.

How to Use This Book

In Part I of this book, we walk you through our processes for curriculum design with multimodal, multigenre text sets using a unit on trees as a concrete example. **Chapter One** defines the concept of the multimodal, multigenre text set and introduces the steps to creating such a set. In **Chapter Two**, we walk you through a process for considering content covered by state and local standards as well as the Common Core State Standards as a starting point for your curriculum planning. In **Chapter Three**, we share some of the best resources that we use for finding and locating texts. In **Chapter Four**, we present several models for organizing and arranging texts within a unit of study. And in **Chapter Five**, we discuss some of the different ways that students respond to texts in a text set and create their own texts to add to the text set.

In Part II, we provide you with snapshots of teaching with text sets in actual classrooms. We share these examples not as "perfect models" but with the intent of sharing the excitement, messiness, surprises, and benefits of integrating texts sets into an existing or new unit of study.

In **Chapter Six**, we describe a social studies unit on immigration that we revamped with a team of three teachers at a suburban PreK–8 school that shares a long history with Lesley University. In **Chapter Seven**, we describe our work with a teacher teaching a unit on the solar system at an urban PreK–8 school, also a partnership school with Lesley University.

Our intent in sharing these unit snapshots in Chapters Six and Seven is to provide you with additional examples of the processes of teaching with text sets that we have described in Chapters One through Five. Rather than providing a running narrative of classroom events, we walk you through the planning sequence that we introduced in Part I. We worked closely with the teachers throughout the planning process—visiting the classrooms frequently, supporting teachers as they made adjustments to their teaching throughout the unit, and reviewing the student work. To make it easier for you to connect the processes in Part I with the units in Part II, we have outlined the chapter headings with the same terminology: "Starting with Content"; "Building Text Sets"; "Organizing Texts for Instruction"; and "Creating and Responding to Texts."

In "Starting with Content," we describe how we worked with the teachers involved to identify the key content of the unit. In "Building Text Sets," we discuss the sources and processes we used to locate the texts that would comprise the text set for the unit of study. In "Organizing Texts for Instruction," we present the text models that were used as the teachers taught the unit and why these models were selected. Finally, in "Creating and Responding to Texts," we describe how students responded to texts and how they expressed their learning through a variety of modalities.

Once you have had an opportunity to see teaching with text sets in action, we hope that you will feel ready to try our planning processes and text models in your own classroom. You might feel a bit intimidated, wondering just how to begin. To help you consider what your first steps may be in teaching with text sets, we have created Part III.

In Part III, **Chapter Eight** through **Chapter Eleven**, we include a chapter on each of the four different text sets we discuss. Two of the topics were presented in Chapters Six and Seven—Immigration and Space. We want you to have a chance to look at the books that we considered for those two units in Part II. You have the opportunity to look at a full K–8 multigenre, multimodal text set on each of these two topics that we have already explored in depth in order to design your own curriculum. You can take our ideas, consider some of the texts and model combinations that we recommend, and create your own in-depth explorations for your students. The other two text sets are on new topics: the Great Depression and honeybees. Why these topics? We think they offer great versatility for integrated classroom explorations, and they can fit into a variety of curriculum frameworks.

In each chapter, you will see the full text set, from children's books to magazine articles to multimodal resources. Next, you will find one example for each of our text models. However, unlike in Chapter Four, where we designed the Tree Ring Models to be used within the same unit, we are instead providing a more impressionistic approach. We share an example of how you can use every text model, but we think broadly and draw from different content areas and grade spans to offer you the greatest array of samples. Think of it as your own curriculum buffet table!

It is our hope that these examples deepen your understanding of the text models, highlight the relationship between content and text in curriculum planning, and illustrate the versatility of instruction with text sets. The combinations of texts that can be used are infinite. The selections are mentor models, launching points to help get you started.

©*Shell Education*

Part I

How to Teach with Text Sets

Understanding Multimodal, Multigenre Text Sets

Imagine peeking through the window of an elementary classroom where students are studying trees. The students and their teacher are in and out of the school doors, walking in a wooded area near school or in a nearby city park, drawing and sketching what they see, binoculars in hand, and documenting their evidence further with digital cameras. Back inside the classroom, they examine their digital photographs of leaves, bark, individual branches, and whole trees in small groups, and as a whole class they use the LCD projector. Once a week for over a month, the class continues to venture out to document the changes in the trees, be it spring or fall, and notice which parts of the tree change and which stay the same, graphing their data to share the results. All the while, seeds are growing inside the classroom, and students are documenting those changes with words and pictures and are generating questions about what they observe.

As students interact with the natural world around them, they also research trees through print. They read survey and concept nonfiction books in small groups, drawing and writing down information that begins to answer the questions that they and their teacher have about trees, and documenting their new questions. Within small groups, students explore texts that are a good fit for where they are as readers—not too hard, not too easy. As they finish one book, they move on to another, adding to their knowledge, comparing information from one book to the next, and synthesizing what they learn in print with what they observe in the natural world. Some students who are not the strongest readers in the class have an immense knowledge of trees and are reading more complex books than they might otherwise. Some of the stronger readers know less about trees and are starting off with easier books to build their knowledge and support what they observe in their data collecting. While in these groups, students receive instruction to strengthen their reading strategies for nonfiction texts in order to both expand their knowledge of trees and bolster their reading capacity.

As students are further immersed in their reading about trees, they start to read about the role of trees in the economic life of the region in which they live, learning about the ways in which the local economy grew as a result of having or not having hardwood trees. For example, students in New England may read books about the role of shipbuilding, mast-making, and colonization in the 17th and 18th centuries. By reading newspaper and magazine articles selected by their teacher, students can compare the role of trees in the past with current logging and paper industries. However, elementary students in the Northwest might be learning about the role of the logging industry and economic development in the 19th century and comparing those events with current debates about the appropriate use of natural resources. They may also start looking at data that the teacher has obtained from federal and state fish and wildlife or natural resources divisions to see what trends they have observed in the local tree population and what threats might exist. In addition, students may use online video-conferencing technology to conduct interviews with staff from one of these departments so that they have access to the most accurate and up-to-date information. Students may also explore historic photographs gathered from a state or local historical society or museum to compare and contrast the tree population from 50 years ago to today. They examine artifacts from the industries of the past, such as employment advertisements, work cards, or accounts of important milestones, in the city's or town's economic history.

To synthesize what students are learning across texts and experiences and to demonstrate their new knowledge and skills to themselves, their teacher, and their community, students are immersed in production. Some students might be working on a mural of local trees that will hang in the public library to educate the community about the role trees play in healthy air. Other students might be using poetry picture books as mentor texts and writing their own illustrated poetry picture books to share with primary grade reading buddies. They might also record and post their creations on the school webpage so that families and community members can be informed. Still other students might be creating local tree guides complete with original digital photographs, illustrations, diagrams, and graphs, to donate to the town's or city's parks department for use in a summer day camp program. A few students may be writing longer works of fiction or nonfiction about the role of trees in their town or city in the past or in the present. These will become books as well. Students may record themselves reading the books so that the audio books can be shared with community members through the local library system.

While this is happening, students are enacting many elements of the Common Core State Standards for English Language Arts and Content Literacy: They are engaged in an exploration of science content standards for the intermediate grades and exploring the natural world with 21st century tools. They are reading well-written, age-appropriate children's books that inform them on the topics they are exploring and serve as mentor texts for their own writing. They are also meaningfully engaged in producing work that allows them to grow as readers, writers, scientists, and historians.

Teaching with Text Sets

By immersing students in a variety of reading experiences and inviting them to explore the natural world through observation and experimentation, the teacher in the trees scenario described harnessed students' natural curiosity, addressed their range of reading needs and interests, and scaffolded learning so that important content standards were learned while the students also improved and expanded their reading capacities. This integrated science, social studies, and literacy curriculum was designed to meet curriculum standards, and the texts that were explored by students were expertly selected and organized by the teacher to meet the content of the standards and the reading needs of individual students. For those varied reading experiences, the teacher used a multimodal, multigenre text set. To create such a text set, she pulled from the world of children's fiction, nonfiction, and poetry. She also used websites, government reports, and newspaper and magazine articles, including those written specifically for children. Also included were primary sources and photographs from a state or local historical society or museum. Students were immersed in both print and digital texts.

At this point, you may be thinking, "Wow, that sounds ideal, but it also sounds pretty challenging." You may be wondering how you can find the time and the resources to teach in this way, given the daily demands of your teaching and personal life. We wrote this book because we know how you feel. You want to offer your students the richest possible curriculum, but you are sometimes overwhelmed by too many choices and you feel as if you do not know where to begin. Or, you have so many curriculum directives and new initiatives that you feel you cannot take on one more thing. We hear you! Our goal in writing this book is to share what we have learned about teaching with multimodal, multigenre text sets and make this kind of planning and teaching manageable so that you and your students can experience the many benefits of teaching with text sets.

In this chapter, we will define what we mean by a multimodal, multigenre text set, and we will share some of the reasons why we think teaching with text sets is so exciting, rewarding, and important. Next, we will discuss our view of teachers' roles as curriculum designers. Finally, we will introduce you to the key processes for curriculum design with multimodal, multigenre text sets that we explore throughout this book.

Defining the Multimodal, Multigenre Text Set

We are certainly not the first educators to teach with text sets. In the past, text sets have been defined in a variety of ways. Back in 1991, when states were just starting to define standards and benchmarks in response to national legislation and the World Wide Web was in its infancy, Linda K. Crafton wrote of the potential of text sets to generate connections, suggesting that "when readers read texts that are conceptually related in some way, they are engaged in an exploration of cognitive and linguistic ties." She defined text sets as "collections of conceptually related materials," including "non-print 'texts' such as audiotapes, filmstrips, videotapes, and art" (1991, 189). Similarly, in 1993, Douglas and Jeanette Hartman proposed the use of text sets, seeking to "expand the role of the reader" through the use of different arrangements of related texts. They defined a text set as including a range of texts on a continuum from linguistic to nonlinguistic, with linguistic texts consisting of written pieces of any genre and nonlinguistic texts as all others, such as song, dance, photographs, and video, etc., each necessary for providing students with sufficient opportunity to read "across texts" (1993, 202).

Both above definitions of a text set stand out because of their early emphasis on diversity in text types. Text sets have been consistently defined over the years as a collection of conceptually related books; however, the role of multimodal texts has not always been a visible component of text set definitions. Opitz defined them as "collections of books related to a common element or topic. Single copies of books are often used to create them, with each student reading a different book related to the topic" (1998, 622). Ward and Young stated that text sets are "a collection of books grouped around a similar topic, theme, genre, or author" (2008, 215). Text sets can also be defined by the number of texts they include, such as when Short, Harste, and Burke suggest that a set is comprised of "five to fifteen texts that relate conceptually in some way, such as similar themes, text types, topics, and so forth" (quoted in Mathis 2002, 127).

More recently, Nichols proposed a broader definition of text sets, emphasizing the role the reading of multiple texts can play in enhancing students' abilities to comprehend and think critically about content. She defines texts sets as "a collection of sources of information that have a commonality; that is, they explore a shared topic, issue, or big idea," further elaborating that "text sets should include a variety of genres, text types, levels, and media forms" (2009, 34–35).

The world of print and technology continues to evolve at a rapid pace; the online environment now allows for extraordinary access to nonlinguistic texts with a simple Internet search. Text sets were never more possible than they are today, and we need a revised definition that includes our new understandings of 21st century texts. Given the ubiquitous nature of digital texts in the lives of even very young students today, we can incorporate a broad range of texts into content study, as Hartman and Hartman (1993) and Crafton (1991) suggested in our pre-Internet age. We are immersed in multimodal texts on a daily basis, moving back and forth between print and digital texts. Print texts are transformed online with new visual and audio components. Many texts are authentically multimodal from the start. Through technology and the use of text sets, we have the ability to create the kind of classroom environment "where students are challenged and surprised often by unexpected, serendipitous linking discoveries in their reading; where students continually revise their understandings and responses to previous texts; where students exploit the rich literary and artistic possibilities within, across, and beyond texts; and where students spend their days waist high in works that can be traversed in one direction, and then in another…and still another" (Hartman and Hartman 1993, 210).

Our Definition

We know our term "multimodal, mutigenre text set" is a mouthful! So, what is really meant by this? A multimodal, multigenre text set is a versatile tool constructed by a teacher or team of teachers and, ideally, a school or public librarian that can be applied at any grade level, from pre-kindergarten through high school, and can be used as a means of achieving the goals of a unit of study. Text sets themselves are not the focal point of the curriculum or unit of study; whatever it is that "holds" the text set together—a topic, concept, theme, or question—is the focal point. For example, in the opening of this chapter, trees were the focal point of the unit of study. A text set is an important tool to help you meet your unit goals.

When we refer to a text set as *multimodal,* we mean that the text set includes information in many modalities, including print, audio, and visual. It includes podcasts and videos of performances, news footage, and live footage via webcams often found on websites. It also includes visual texts, such as photographs, drawings, and paintings, and physical objects, such as artifacts, sculptures, and buildings.

A text set is *multigenre* when it includes texts in a variety of genres. We define *genre* as a form of writing that serves a socially recognizable purpose (Allan, McMackin, Dawes, and Spadorcia 2009). This is a broad definition of genre, one that encompasses forms of writing as diverse as a tweet, a recipe, a baseball card, a traffic citation, or a museum display card. Teachers typically view this broader definition of genre as liberating, opening up new possibilities for student exploration and student writing products.

We also include traditional genres and multigenre works in text sets, such as picture books and chapter books, as well as magazine and newspaper articles and primary source documents.

A Multimodal, Multigenre Text Set

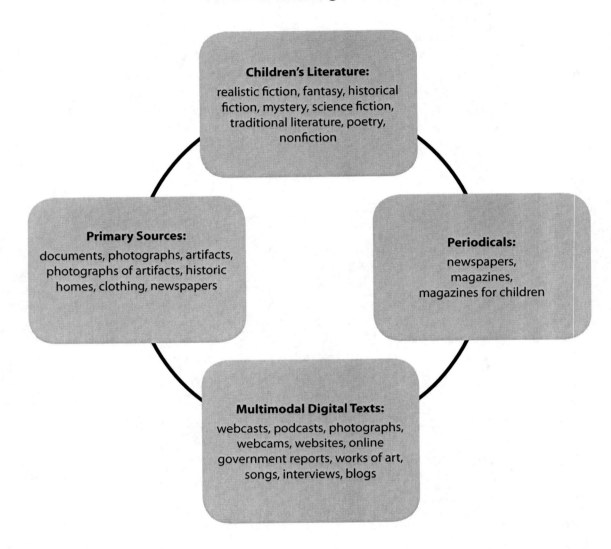

Children's Literature: realistic fiction, fantasy, historical fiction, mystery, science fiction, traditional literature, poetry, nonfiction

Periodicals: newspapers, magazines, magazines for children

Primary Sources: documents, photographs, artifacts, photographs of artifacts, historic homes, clothing, newspapers

Multimodal Digital Texts: webcasts, podcasts, photographs, webcams, websites, online government reports, works of art, songs, interviews, blogs

An Example: Tree Text Set

The students at the beginning of this chapter were working with a multimodal, multigenre text set as part of their study of trees, a required element of curriculum standards for science at the elementary level. When gathering the texts for use in this unit of study, we sought texts that represented a diversity of genres, modalities, and reading levels. We offer you a sampling of the texts that we located to provide a concrete example of a multimodal, multigenre text set. A more complete text set example for trees can be found in Appendix C.

Tree Text Set Sampling

Text	Genre	Modality
Trout Are Made of Trees (Sayre 2008)	nonfiction picture book	print, visual
Poetrees (Florian 2010)	nonfiction poetry	print, visual
The Quest for the Tree Kangaroo (Montgomery 2006)	photo essay	print, visual
Planting the Trees of Kenya: The Story of Wangari Maathai (Nivola 2008)	picture book biography	print, visual
The Greenbelt Movement http://www.greenbeltmovement.org/	website	print, audio, visual
"Growing Trees for Kenya" (Creegan 2009)	magazine feature article	print, visual
Leafsnap (Columbia University, University of Maryland, and Smithsonian Institution)	app	print, visual
Audubon Trees—A Field Guide to North American Trees (Green Mountain Digital)	field guide, app	print, visual
The Lorax (Universal Pictures 2012) (Columbia Broadcasting System 1972)	animated movie	audio, visual

Note: Bibliographic information for titles listed in this chart can be found in the Trees Text Set in Appendix C.

The Reasons for Teaching with Text Sets

Now you know what a text set is. So, why would you want to teach with text sets?

Do you ever wonder why districts spend thousands of dollars on one-size-fits-all curriculum that winds up fitting very few? No teacher has the time to consider, let alone strategically use, all the bells and whistles that accompany most curriculum packages. For far fewer dollars, individual or teams of teachers can construct multimodal, multigenre text sets that use authentic texts in all of their diverse formats, meet the varied needs of students regardless of where they fall on the literacy continuum, utilize 21st century literacies, and ground students in exploring their community and the global community in meaningful ways. We find these possibilities thrilling.

If customizing curriculum to meet the needs and interests of your students was not enticing enough, the Common Core State Standards for Language Arts and Content Literacy are a clarion call for using text sets and diverse literacy practices. The Common Core State Standards suggest that "[t]hrough reading a diverse array of classic and contemporary literature as well as challenging informational texts in a range of subjects, students are expected to build knowledge, gain insights, explore possibilities, and broaden their perspective" (Common Core State Standards 2010). This is a vision of reading we are excited to make a reality.

Capturing Interest and Cultivating Engagement

The world is infinitely interesting, and you want your classroom to reflect the energy and diversity of thought that students bring with them each and every day. You want your students to become more skillful readers, but you also want to cultivate a passionate engagement with reading and the content of science, social studies, literature, and the arts. You also know that when students are engaged with what they are doing, learning occurs more expeditiously and at a deeper level. Teaching with text sets stimulates student interest and motivation by offering them choice and variety.

Prompting Inquiry

One way to channel student interest and engagement is through inquiry. The careful layering of content through the use of multimodal, multigenre texts allows students to generate questions that can guide their learning. One unit of study might start with a song, another with a portrait of someone from the past, yet another with a current newspaper article. As each text is confronted, students' questions can deepen and change. This inquiry also cultivates interest and engagement, allowing students to care deeply about pursuing answers. Ownership of their learning then follows.

Reading for Multiple Perspectives

Teaching with text sets allows teachers to highlight the fluidity of content knowledge and perspectives in any content area, and the interesting connections, contradictions, and questions that naturally arise when texts provide multiple perspectives on an area of study. When texts that represent a diversity of perspectives on an issue are used, students are forced to grapple with conflicting, questionable, or missing information, exactly the kind of thinking skills required of them by the Common Core State Standards.

As students read literature, informational texts, and multimodal texts of increasing complexity and variety across the grade level continuum, they will develop the ability to analyze how texts represent authors' worldviews and to think about the particular choices made by an author as he or she composed the text.

Building Prior Knowledge

When starting a unit of study, it can be difficult to fully understand what knowledge of the topic students in class already bring into the classroom. Often, it can feel difficult to manage the wide range of prior knowledge that exists. Teaching with text sets allows you to carefully layer content by using multimodal, multigenre texts to build prior knowledge for topics of study that are abstract or distant to students. In many cases, short texts have the greatest potential for building prior knowledge on a topic so that students can later tackle longer, more complex texts or ones that are more abstract.

Reading fiction and nonfiction picture storybooks aloud is a wonderful way to introduce background knowledge. Works of art, historic photographs or maps, short videos, or live webcams, such as ones at zoos or animal sanctuaries, are also great introductions to a unit of study that scaffold exposure and provide students with working knowledge of a topic that they can draw upon in future readings.

Encouraging Student Writing: Text Sets as Mentor Texts

Today, new genres of text are being created all the time. For example, apps are considered a new genre of text. Only a few years ago, apps did not exist. Now, even the youngest children know what a phone or tablet app is. When students are provided with multiple genres in multiple modalities, they are given an expanded range of possibilities for both demonstrating learning and selecting the type of writing they want to do.

So often we ask students to read large quantities of fiction in school, particularly in language arts, but we then ask them to write nonfiction in the form of a memoir, a personal response to the text (in terms of the testing world), or a literary essay. We ask them to write these forms over and over again, but rarely do we give them models of authentic memoirs or personal responses from which to learn. To write quality nonfiction, students need to read quality nonfiction, have working models of a variety of nonfiction text structures, and have an understanding of how similes and metaphors are functional in that genre to explain concepts and ideas in ways readers can understand. Only after studying a genre as readers can students write within that genre as authors. Multimodal, multigenre text sets model a world of writing possibilities for students.

Differentiating Instruction

One of the most exciting features of a text set is the opportunity it provides for differentiated instruction. As opposed to the one-size-fits-all model of a basal reader or prescribed program, teaching with text sets allows teachers to select the kinds of texts that are appropriate for scaffolding learning at all levels in the classroom, providing for the range of needs in today's culturally, socially, and linguistically diverse populations. For example, a teacher might use a nonfiction chapter book as part of a whole-class read-aloud because the text has important content but is slightly beyond the reach of many students' individual reading capacities. Through the read-aloud and whole-class discussions, all students can access the content.

Within a unit of study, a teacher can divide students into flexible groups for different purposes on different days. On some days, students may be grouped based on their reading needs so that they can read texts that are an appropriate fit and work on focused reading strategies and content exploration. On other days, students might be grouped based on a subtopic of interest to collectively explore an audio or visual text. As study progresses, students might explore another subtopic or perspective, but within each group, students read different materials selected purposefully by the teacher to meet their reading needs.

Multimodal, multigenre text sets dramatically increase options for differentiating instruction within a unit of study. With a variety of texts related to a chosen content focus, texts can be appropriately selected and layered to make the content more comprehensible for English language learners (Echevarría, Vogt, and Short 2007). The array of modalities in a multimodal, multigenre text set engages a broader spectrum of learning styles, allowing the needs of all students to be met, but in particular addressing the needs of students who have Individual Education Plans. Additionally, a multimodal, multigenre text set will naturally incorporate texts of varying text complexity, which is a key area of attention in the Common Core State Standards. As students read multiple texts about related content, they build their ability to read texts on the topic at increasing levels of complexity; concepts and vocabulary become more familiar with multiple exposures, making texts at higher reading levels more accessible to all students.

Supporting Vocabulary Development

Teaching with text sets expands students' vocabulary development. The fields of social studies, mathematics, and science have particular vocabulary associated with them, and vocabulary instruction is one of the most important aspects of developing content literacy. Students need multiple opportunities to interact with important words and concepts in order for those words and concepts to become a part of their working knowledge and expressive language. When teachers have students read a variety of texts on a topic, view photographs or works of art, graph information, or write narratives on a particular event, students have repeated opportunities to confront and grapple with content vocabulary and hear, read, speak, and write those words. In this language-rich environment, students will develop an understanding of certain words through expert modeling and explaining by the teacher, repeated exposure, and specific meaningful use (Beck, McKeown, and Kucan 2002; Graves 2005), all of which are strategies particularly supportive to English language learners and students with learning difficulties.

Now that you know the benefits of teaching with text sets, we want to share our vision of teachers as curriculum designers to ground you in a vision of teaching with text sets.

Teachers as Curriculum Designers

Our vision of teaching with text sets places you in the driver's seat. Creating curriculum is a deeply creative and intellectual endeavor. It can be fascinating, exhilarating, and, at times, overwhelming! It is certainly messy.

Both of us have always worked in elementary and secondary schools where we had the privilege to design and plan almost all of our curriculum and instruction. When Erika had a mandated program for language arts, she was able to use the program as a base, which she extended and deepened to meet her expectations of what her students needed to know and be able to do.

Certainly, we had state content and skills-based standards to incorporate into our planning and to measure student learning against, but there was no packaged curriculum, product, or textbook that we had to follow. When we entered the teaching profession, we were expected to craft units of study that met the needs and interests of our students as well as the state standards. Because our principals and superintendents trusted us to do this work, we threw ourselves passionately into curriculum design year in and year out. It was a joyful and complex enterprise and also time consuming. However, we found that the benefits of ownership over our curriculum saved us time in the end because we were integrating instruction and teaching what we believed was most important for our students to learn.

Curriculum is not fixed, and creating it is not always a linear process. Planning and designing curriculum is a constant give-and-take as you attempt to balance your goals for your students, the demands of state standards, the opportunities and limitations of your school culture, the books and materials that you have, and the new ones you discover. Sometimes you cannot find the resource that you want for the unit, and so your design changes. Sometimes it is the discovery of a new resource that changes the design because the resource provides such important learning opportunities. You will see examples of both of these instances in this book. In a study of immigration, as discussed in Chapter Six, we struggled to find books that students could read independently and that met our curriculum design goals, and so we altered our vision slightly. In an exploration of the solar system, discussed in Chapter Seven, a nonfiction picture book was the perfect catalyst for the unit, modeling how theories about the solar system have changed over time.

Finally, curriculum work is never really "done." It is always a work in progress, a labor of love. What you experience with one group of students is not the same experience the following year. You recalibrate with each group as students change. You discover new resources, or the content itself changes, and you learn alongside your students, always striving to meet their needs.

Now you may be reading this and thinking, "But that is not *my* world. That is not *my* school. I do not have those choices." We realize that many teachers who entered the field in the past decade have not always had the same opportunities to design curriculum. We think you should. We think you can. *You* are why we are writing this book. We believe that with the advent of the Common Core State Standards and the standards' emphasis on authentic literacy practices, critical-thinking skills, and diverse texts, more and more curriculum can and should be designed at a district and school level.

Now that we have shared our vision of teachers as curriculum designers, we will introduce some of the processes that we will be sharing with you throughout the book so that you, too, can learn to teach or refine your teaching with text sets.

Our Process for Teaching with Text Sets

This book is designed as a "how to" manual for teaching with text sets. Using examples throughout, we'll walk you through the processes that we use when we develop curriculum with multimodal, multigenre texts. These processes include:

1. **Starting with content**—work with your curriculum and standards documents to identify the content that you will teach.

2. **Building a text set**—locate and identify high quality print and digital resources related to your content.

3. **Organizing texts**—make instructional decisions about how the text resources you have identified will be used to scaffold, immerse, and extend content for students.

4. **Creating and responding to texts**—consider how students will read and respond to the texts in the text set, what texts they will create, and how you will assess content and literacy learning.

Step One: Starting with Content

The unifying concept, topic, theme, or question of a multimodal, multigenre text set can be based solely on language arts content or include one or more content areas, such as science or social studies. Content will drive both the text selection and purpose. In Chapter Two, we walk you through a process for considering content covered by state and local standards, as well as the Common Core State Standards, as a starting point for your curriculum planning.

Step Two: Building a Text Set

Once you have established which content standards you think will help scaffold your unit of study, you will search for appropriate texts on the topic in a wide variety of genres and modalities. The kinds of texts you discover may help shape and fine-tune the goals of your study. In Chapter Three, we will share with you some of the best resources that we use for finding and locating texts.

Step Three: Organizing Texts for Instruction

Once you identify texts that could be used in your curriculum, you must figure out how to use them and decide which to include and which to exclude. The goals of the curriculum and the needs of students will determine the role each text has for an individual, a small group, or a whole class. Each text can be considered both on its own and in relation to the other texts. Depending upon the unit of study, one type of text may serve as an introduction or scaffold, such as a nonfiction picture book. In another unit of study, primary source artifacts or photos of those artifacts might be the scaffold that builds prior knowledge and sparks student interest. Other texts might serve as a core portion of the unit, providing important content and modeling writing structures and styles as a mentor text that students return to again and again. Still other texts might be read or viewed by some students to build strategic knowledge about subcategories of information within the unit, thereby extending their knowledge of the content. In Chapter Four, we will walk you through several models for organizing and arranging texts within a unit of study.

Step Four: Creating and Responding to Texts

When exposed to a broad array of different text types in a text set, students develop an understanding that writers shape their texts to match their purposes for writing and the perceived needs of their audiences. This awareness of the subjective nature of texts and the wide array of choices, such as genre, structure, and voice, that an author must make when composing is a necessary component of students' own abilities to produce original texts, which allows for synthesizing and presenting their learning in a content area, another requirement of the Common Core State Standards. In Chapter Five, we will discuss some of the different ways that students respond to texts in a text set and create their own texts to add to the text set.

Summary

This chapter demonstrates how teaching with text sets can:

- Capture student interest and cultivate engagement
- Prompt inquiry
- Provide opportunities to read for multiple perspectives
- Build prior knowledge on a topic
- Encourage authentic student writing practices
- Differentiate instruction to meet the literacy needs of students
- Support vocabulary development

Reflection Questions

1. How does the definition of a text set resonate with your understanding of the kinds of texts students are currently reading in and out of school?

2. What do you think are the most important benefits of teaching with text sets for your students, particularly your culturally and linguistically diverse students?

3. What are some of the ways that you see the Common Core State Standards as an opportunity to use authentic texts and tasks in your classroom?

Starting with Content

Let us return to those elementary students exploring trees in Chapter One. They do not just study trees. They explore many facets of the local environment and of particular ecosystems around the world. They explore deforestation in some parts of the world while simultaneously realizing that their own community may have more trees and forests now than it did a century ago when grazing herds dotted hillsides and fields were covered with crops instead of tree canopy. If these students live in an urban community, they may learn about the significance of urban greenways and clean air. To that end, they may gather data in a tree survey, count and graph the number of trees on the streets surrounding the school, and create an action plan to plant more. They learn about what trees grow locally and globally and explore their community's past and present with an eye towards the future. In short, they learn the necessary content.

We define content broadly as knowledge about the world and how it works. Content is the *who* and the *what* to be studied and the topics and subtopics that you want to explore with your students.

We believe that teaching with text sets begins with content. We see trees as a very concrete topic for elementary students to explore and also one that offers lots of opportunities for more abstract thinking about ecosystems, history, the community, and national and global issues that are related to clean air and the environment. Trees are also beautiful. We can draw and paint them, as many artists have through the ages. We can also play in them and sit in their shade. Perhaps more importantly, we feed ourselves off the fruit and nuts that trees produce. Trees are homes to bugs, birds, and mammals. Squirrels may live inside their trunks and birds may build nests on their limbs, but we cut them down to build our homes. As lumber, trees have been important commodities for hundreds of years. In New England, the King's Pines, which were extremely tall white-pine trees found during the colonial period, are an important part of American history. These white pines sailed the world over as masts on British naval ships and were catalysts for colonization. Where you live, trees may also play an important but different role in your region's history or current landscape. Or, they may not, and you know of better topics with which to explore ecosystems and interrelationships among living things. Transforming content standards into local contexts can maximize student learning opportunities. In our tree unit, we drew on both local and global contexts.

In our years teaching students, we found content to be central to capturing student engagement and fostering a spirit of inquiry. As an elementary teacher tasked with teaching and integrating literacy, mathematics, social studies, and the arts, or a secondary teacher of language arts, mathematics, social studies, or science, you know that you are always teaching skills *and* content. The content looks a little different at each end of the educational spectrum, but it is at the heart of classroom planning.

Before you begin teaching with text sets, we think it is important for you to situate yourself in the content that you want your students to explore as well as the content that they need to investigate based on state and local standards. We articulate this process in the chart below:

Understanding the Unit Planning Process
Identify Standards
• Content standards • Language arts standards
Get Current
• Refresh your content knowledge by reviewing newspapers, magazines, and multimodal texts available online
Select Content and Establish Goals
• Establish unit goals • Confirm standards you are teaching to mastery • Confirm standards you are using but not teaching to mastery • Begin to think about logical ways of "chunking" the content
Determine a General Time Frame
• Construct an approximate time frame for the unit

In the pages that follow, we explore what the Common Core State Standards refer to as content literacy. Next, we discuss how we use state and local content standards for curriculum planning and how we go beyond those standards to explore the content further by incorporating the latest news from the field. Having a strong sense of the content that you and your students will investigate will shape your process of locating and planning instruction with multimodal, multigenre text sets.

Content Literacy

When elementary students study trees, they do not just learn about trees or ecosystems or natural resources. They simultaneously fine-tune their reading, writing, listening, speaking, and viewing strategies in order to grapple with important questions, make connections among different texts, and describe what they observe in the natural world around them. In this context, content is not a separate or isolated learning goal. Skills and strategies are used to access content, and in turn, through the exploration of content, skills and strategies are practiced and refined. We find them to be inextricable. Literacy is both a set of skills and strategies that can be constantly improved as well as a vehicle by which content is learned.

The Common Core State Standards for English Language Arts and Content Literacy require an integration of content and literacy instruction. In the standards, content literacy is blended into one set of standards for language arts in grades K–5, while separate standards exist for language arts and content literacy in grades 6–12 because teachers at the latter levels teach content in more specialized contexts. But what exactly is content literacy?

Elizabeth Moje (2008) suggests that content areas are based on disciplines. Disciplines, such as biology, history, or musicology, exist in the "real world," while content areas mimic the disciplines but exist only in the world of schools. Content areas divide up the day and the knowledge that must be taught in a school-based context organized by mandates such as state and local curriculum standards, time restrictions, and grade levels. Some texts that are used and created in content-area classes are discipline based, like primary source documents, artifacts, or interviews with experts, while others are school based, such as textbooks or tests.

School-based content areas are modeled on the work of practitioners in the field. In the "real world," scientists, journalists, policy makers, and economists all use reading, writing, listening, speaking, and the language arts to do their work. But they use language in different ways. When doing the work of Earth science or global history, scientists and historians pose different kinds of questions and use different types of texts as well as real-world experiments and applications, to pursue their answers.

To demonstrate different approaches to texts found within different content areas, Mary Ann likes to have the teachers in her graduate content literacy course begin the class by looking at a rock. She asks them to pose questions about the rock from the perspective of the different disciplines. When she asks them to think like scientists when examining rocks, students ask questions like "Is it sedimentary, igneous, or metamorphic?" or "Where was it found?" When asked to think like a historian, they are initially stumped. But then they ask, "Who might have used the rock? For what purpose?" When asked to think like a poet, some students remember the Robert Frost poem "The Mending Wall," even quoting that "[g]ood fences make good neighbors" (Frost [1913] 1991). Others use the rock as a metaphor. This quick demonstration shows that something as obvious as a rock can be examined quite differently through the lens of each content area. When Mary Ann tells her students that the rock was used as a chimney brick for a house built in 1700 in New York's Hudson River Valley, an entirely new set of history-specific questions emerge.

When we ask our students to think like historians or scientists, we require them to use language in specific contexts; this allows them, over time, to internalize that specific learning contexts necessitate specific literacy tools. While we know we are only scratching the surface, we call this *content literacy*.

Unit Planning

Now that we have established an understanding of the centrality of content and content literacy, we begin unit planning with three important questions:

- Based on state and local curriculum standards, what content do all students need to know?

- Based on my personal knowledge, what content do I think all or some students need to know?

- Based on my knowledge of my students, what content will engage them?

Identify Standards

All unit planning starts with identifying the content knowledge that students need to learn. When designing a curriculum unit for a content area, whether it is science, social studies, language arts, or the arts, we suggest that you start with the content dictated by state and local standards. Scan the standards so that you have a sense of the range of content you are required to teach. Next, take a look at content standards for other areas that you are required to teach. How can your social studies standards be used as a tool for exploring your science standards? How can science standards be used to scaffold learning experiences in mathematics? How can the Common Core State Standards for language arts be used as a tool for planning an interdisciplinary unit of study? We like to start with one set of standards first as an anchor and expand outward from there.

So how did our potential unit on trees begin? It began with an examination of science content standards at the elementary levels and identification of the standards that could be considered for use in a unit centered on trees (page 37). Because we work in Massachusetts, we used the standards for that state. By scanning your own state and district content standards, you can follow the same process. We refer to specific standards here because we want to model how to teach with text sets from the ground up with actual standards.

Trees Text Set: Science Content Standards
Classify plants and animals according to the physical characteristics that they share
Identify the structures in plants (leaves, roots, flowers, stem, bark, wood) that are responsible for food production, support, water transport, reproduction, growth, and protection
Recognize that plants and animals go through predictable life cycles that include birth, growth, development, reproduction, and death
Differentiate between observed characteristics of plants and animals that are fully inherited (e.g., color of flower, shape of leaves, color of eyes, number of appendages) and characteristics that are affected by the climate or environment (e.g., browning of leaves from too much sun, language spoken)
Give examples of how changes in the environment (drought, cold) have caused some plants and animals to die or move to new locations (migration)
Recognize plant behaviors, such as the way seedlings' stems grow toward light and their roots grow downward in response to gravity; Recognize that many plants and animals can survive harsh environments because of seasonal behaviors (e.g., in winter, some trees shed leaves, some animals hibernate, and other animals migrate)
Give examples of how organisms can cause changes in their environment to ensure survival; Explain how some of these changes may affect the ecosystem
Describe how energy derived from the sun is used by plants to produce sugars (photosynthesis) and is transferred within a food chain from producers (plants) to consumers to decomposers

Some of the standards selected focus specifically on plants, while others focus on ecosystems. These standards confirmed for us that we could develop locally based explorations of seeds, plants, and trees while also looking at ecosystems around the world, combining hands on experiences with an examination of a variety of texts. Some of these standards can be explored with texts, while others can only be learned through direct observation and experiments.

Next, we took a look at the grade level social studies standards to consider which standards might help us study trees locally. We identified the standards below:

Trees Text Set: Social Studies Content Standards
Observe visual sources such as historic paintings, photographs, or illustrations that accompany historical narratives, and describe details such as clothing, setting, or action
Use cardinal directions, map scales, legends, and titles to locate places on contemporary maps of New England, Massachusetts, and the local community
Describe the difference between a contemporary map of their city or town and the map of their city or town in the 18th, 19th, or early 20th century
On a map of Massachusetts, locate the class's hometown or city and its local geographic features and landmarks

We were excited about the possibility of using the social studies standards to explore a local community, specifically as a way to locate trees throughout the community's history and consider the role they might have played in the regional economy. By comparing and contrasting maps from throughout a town's history and by exploring available photographs and paintings of a town from different time periods, changes over time became more concrete and less abstract to students with developing senses of time. We also wanted the students' exploration of trees to have a global range. This global range falls slightly outside the social studies standards for elementary school, but we felt it was important nevertheless.

At the onset of planning, we did not feel as if we had to use all of these standards. But we knew we could use some or many of them, depending on the direction of the unit. In the context of the school year, decisions about standards for one unit are always made in the context of the other standards and units so that you cover your required standards by the end of the year. As you may have experienced in your own school, teaching to the standards can often become a lockstep march, or a wild sprint, toward coverage. With so many standards to cover, particularly at the elementary level, we find it can be energizing and time-saving to go more deeply into a unit of study, using more standards from several content areas, than to spread ourselves too thin, attempting to cover them all separately.

Get Current

Before we begin mapping out our unit, we always consider what we ourselves know about the topic and what else we might need to know. This is the case for whatever the topic may be—the American Revolution, jazz music, the solar system. In our ever-expanding knowledge base, there are few topics studied in school that are not in constant flux. Even some of the "oldest" fields of study, like ancient civilizations or dinosaurs, are changing all the time because of new research driven by new technologies. Therefore, before beginning any new planning, consider what might have changed since the last time you taught this subject or studied it in school.

Conducting a search of digital databases available through the local library system is a good way to get started. You might be thinking that this is very time-consuming, but it does not have to be. If you are unfamiliar with the databases provided by your state or local library system, have your school or public librarian show you how to use them. Once you are up and running, you can create a file of short magazine and newspaper articles that provide you with a new and up-to-date context for exploring content. In Chapter Three, we will also discuss more specifically how to access digital databases. The new information you learn may contribute to how you want to structure your unit. It may be new content or a current event that you can make an important connection with to enhance student understanding. Often, while you are planning a unit, you will be more in tune to current events that relate to the content you are exploring. For example, while we were researching and writing this book, Wangari Maathai, the Nobel laureate and founder of The Green Belt Movement, died. News of her death and the obituaries that we read were catalysts for broadening our exploration of trees within this unit, shifting it from a purely local perspective to a global one. While we planned our unit of study on space with secondary students, as described in Chapter Seven, solar flares and NASA's announcement of Kepler-22—a Goldilocks Zone planet more earthlike than any other discovered so far—were the current events that were unfolding during the planning and delivery of the unit. Those events and the new reading we did on the current classification of celestial bodies in the solar system fed our understanding of the universe and greatly shaped how we approached an elementary-appropriate space unit.

Select Content and Establish Goals

Once you have familiarized yourself with new information or theories on the topic that you will be teaching, it is time to decide what content standards must be taught for mastery and what content is important to explore but falls outside the standards. Engagement is a very powerful tool for learning, so it is important to consider what content will best capture student interest. Curriculum has to meet the standards, but it also has to be interesting. It should provide teachers and students alike with the opportunity to explore the world, ponder important questions, and dig into the details.

In the case of our tree unit, we selected content standards from science, social studies, and the Common Core State Standards for English Language Arts. We did not use every standard that we originally identified; some could be studied outside of our tree unit with more specific focus. Particularly, the first science standard, which focuses on the characteristics of plants and animals, would be taught prior to the tree unit. The animal components of some of the science standards would also be explored in a separate unit; in essence, half of a standard would be taught to mastery and the other half completed in another unit.

We determined the Common Core State Standards that would best address the range of reading, writing, listening, speaking, and viewing experiences that we wanted students to have and that would help students best navigate the content. Not all the Common Core State Standards included are ones that would necessarily be taught to mastery. The beauty of the Common Core State Standards, from our perspective, is that you have an opportunity to layer the standards as processes throughout the school year so that you can return to them again and again.

At this level of planning, we do not try to address all of the hands-on activities and specific experiments that students will complete in the unit nor do we tackle the assessments. All of that comes later. At this point in the planning, we are affirming our decisions on state and local standards as well as the Common Core State Standards that will be addressed in the unit. We are clarifying our vision by establishing unit goals based on standards; our understanding of what content, classroom experiences, and assessments will engage students; and what we think our students need to work on at this particular moment in the school year regarding their disciplinary skills, reading and writing habits, and critical-thinking skills.

The Trees Unit Planning Chart on pages 42–43 serves as a model for how to map out student goals, identify content vocabulary, and commit to state and local content standards and the Common Core State Standards. A blank template is also provided on page 44.

Be Flexible

While we have a designated section on the Trees Unit Planning Chart (pages 42–43) for both content vocabulary and the Common Core State Standards, it may be premature to try to complete these sections at this stage. In your own planning, based on your reading of the state and local content standards, there may be certain vocabulary words that you know you will need to either pre-teach or teach explicitly at particular points in the unit. As an example, we have included some words from the science and social studies standards in the Trees Unit Planning Chart. However, additional words will certainly be identified as the texts are selected and read.

Additionally, we have identified Common Core State Standards that we plan on using, but we recognize that we have come up with a lot of them. It is a long and in-depth unit that fuses three different content areas, but we are confident that we can use all of these standards while not necessarily teaching to mastery. However, we think it is better to make a final decision on the Common Core State Standards after texts are selected and we are making decisions about what kinds of texts students will compose.

Determine a General Time Frame

As you complete your own Unit Planning Chart and organize your "big picture" thinking, you should consider the length of time needed to meet your goals. How long will it take you to accomplish your goals? How long can you realistically spend on this unit of study compared to the other content you need to cover within the school year? You may be able to accomplish more in a shorter period of time because you are *integrating* a content-area and language arts curriculum, or the reverse may be true. Your goals may be ideal, but the reality of your school calendar suggests that you cannot spend the time necessary to meet those goals, and so you have to revise them. Because curriculum planning is recursive, you may discover new texts and resources to use in the unit that necessitate that you rethink your goals and/or your timing. It may be that you want to devote more time than you originally planned to the unit because it will accomplish even more than you initially planned. Since this stage of planning is still so fluid, keep the time frame flexible and approximate.

Trees Unit Planning Chart

Unit Name: Going Out on a Limb: Trees in Our Community and Around the World

Unit Length: 6–8 weeks

Core Vocabulary

bark, cardinal directions, characteristics, consumer, decomposer, ecosystem, energy, environment, flowers, inherited, leaves, legend, map scale, organisms, photosynthesis, reproduction, roots, stem, wood

Guiding Questions
- How do trees grown and maintain life?
- What trees grow in our community?
- What changes have occurred for the trees in our community over time?
- What roles have trees played in our community? In other communities around the world?
- How can people make a difference within an ecosystem?

Unit Goals

The students will…
- Gain an understanding of the role of trees and the types of trees in the community (past, present, and future)
- Gain an understanding of a tree as an ecosystem in and of itself and as part of a larger ecosystem as well
- Understand the significance of one particular type of tree within an ecosystem and the reverse as well: what happens when that tree is removed from the ecosystem?
- Appreciate the beauty of different tree types
- Understand human beings as agents of change in an ecosystem, for better or worse

State Content Standards

Life Science: Identify the structures in plants (leaves, roots, flowers, stem, bark, wood) that are responsible for food production, support, water transport, reproduction, growth, and protection

Life Science: Recognize that plants and animals go through predictable life cycles that include birth, growth, development, reproduction, and death

Life Science: Differentiate between observed characteristics of plants and animals that are fully inherited (e.g., color of flower, shape of leaves, color of eyes, number of appendages) and characteristics that are affected by the climate or environment (e.g., browning of leaves from too much sun, language spoken)

Life Science: Give examples of how changes in the environment (drought, cold) have caused some plants and animals to die or move to new locations (migration)

Trees Unit Planning Chart *(cont.)*

State Content Standards *(cont.)*

Life Science: Recognize plant behaviors, such as the way seedlings' stems grow toward light and their roots grow downward in response to gravity. Recognize that many plants and animals can survive harsh environments because of seasonal behaviors (e.g., in winter, some trees shed leaves, some animals hibernate, and other animals migrate)

Life Science: Give examples of how organisms can cause changes in their environment to ensure survival; Explain how some of these changes may affect the ecosystem

Life Science: Describe how energy derived from the sun is used by plants to produce sugars (photosynthesis) and is transferred within a food chain from producers (plants) to consumers to decomposers

History and Geography: Observe visual sources such as historic paintings, photographs, or illustrations that accompany historical narratives and describe details such as clothing, setting, or action

History and Geography: Use cardinal directions, map scales, legends, and titles to locate places on contemporary maps of New England, Massachusetts, and the local community

History and Geography: Describe the difference between a contemporary map of their city or town and the map of their city or town in the 18th, 19th, or early 20th century

Cities and Towns: On a map of Massachusetts, locate the class's home town or city and its local geographic features and landmarks

Common Core State Standards

Reading Standards for Informational Text Grade 3 Key Ideas and Details 3

Reading Standards for Informational Text Grade 3 Craft and Structure 6

Reading Standards for Informational Text Grade 3 Integration of Knowledge and Ideas 9

Writing Standards Text Types and Purposes Grade 3

Writing Standards Production and Distribution of Writing 3.4

Writing Standards Production and Distribution of Writing 3.5

Writing Standards Production and Distribution of Writing 3.6

Writing Standards Research to Build and Present Knowledge 3.7

Writing Standards Research to Build and Present Knowledge 3.8

Speaking and Listening Standards Grade 3.1

Writing Standards Research to Build and Present Knowledge 3.7

Unit Planning Chart Template

Unit Name:	
Unit Length:	
Core Vocabulary	
Guiding Questions	
Unit Goals I want students to…	
State Content Standards	
Common Core State Standards	

Summary

This chapter used the Unit Planning Chart to focus on:

- The centrality of content in curriculum planning
- The balance between content standards and your original student goals
- The concurrent consideration of a broad range of content standards from several content areas

Reflection Questions

1. How do you define content literacy?

2. What currently guides your curriculum planning, and how does our emphasis on content shift or deepen what you think of as both literacy and content instruction?

3. What unit do you currently teach that you believe you could further integrate by drawing on content standards from different subject areas and the Common Core State Standards?

#50688: *Teaching with Text Sets*   ©*Shell Education*

Building a Text Set

So what exactly were those students reading in our tree exploration? They were reading books, magazines, and digital texts. How did we find those texts? This chapter will show you how. Now that we have established our goals for the tree unit as well as identified content and Common Core State Standards that we would like to build the unit around, it is time to begin looking for appropriate texts in a variety of genres and modalities. At this point in our planning process, we recognize that our unit goals and some of the standards that we are building the unit around might still change. Nothing is fixed. The texts that we unearth might suggest new goals or new content standards. But for now, we will use our established goals and standards as a compass to guide us through the thick forest of print and digital resources that awaits us.

Typically, we start our search with children's and young adult literature, because those texts are written with *your* students in mind. Whether you are supplementing a textbook or basal that you are required to use or designing a unit from scratch, well-written books for children and young adults should be a core component of teaching with text sets. We recommend the following order for your search, the same order used in this chapter:

Building a Text Set

Search for children's and young adult literature using:

- School and public librarians
- Searchable databases of book reviews
- Awards lists
- Professional blogs

Search for children's and young adult magazines and general periodicals using:

- Online databases provided to you by your school, public, or state library

Search for multimodal primary sources, including photographs of artifacts, objects, or data using:

- Established research institutions, museums, libraries, and other collections

Search for multimodal secondary sources using:

- Established research institutions, museums, libraries, and other collections
- Websites for educators
- Tablet app reviews

We want you to know right now that searching for these texts can be time-consuming, particularly at first when you are not used to using the strategies that we are about to share. It does take time to locate and read these texts, but we will teach you shortcuts. You don't have to read every text there is on your topic, just the ones that look most promising for your purposes.

Then, you can use the miracle of interlibrary loan to have the texts you are interested in delivered right to your local library. This will allow you to maximize the time that you have to read each text. While reading them, you may consider the relationship that each has to the other, or how they "speak" to one another, so that you can create curriculum that allows you to meet your goals. The more and more you incorporate our search strategies into your classroom planning, the easier and simpler it will become.

We think you will find, as we have, that the time spent searching for and evaluating texts is a worthwhile investment. No one knows your students and your school community like you do, and a teacher or team of teachers is best positioned to make the connection between content, curriculum standards, and materials like trade books and digital resources. Plus, it is interesting! To lose yourself in the topics that you teach is a pleasurable experience. It also gives the content time to percolate in your head.

Because of the time commitment, the most efficient way of teaching with text sets is by sharing the search for texts with a team of teachers at your grade level. You can divide up the search by genre or subtopic. Or, at the end of the school year, once you have initially established unit goals and content standards for key units of study, you could divide up who is responsible for identifying possible texts and use time over the summer to generate text charts (you will find our planning chart later in this chapter). As you get to know your students and coordinate your unit planning throughout the year, you can then choose the texts that best meet your students' needs and interests and the standards and goals for each unit established by the team.

What if you and your team members don't plan together? What if you work in a relatively small school as an intermediate or middle grade subject-specific teacher and are the only one teaching at your grade level? Never fear. Mary Ann spent most of her time in the classroom as the sole language arts teacher for a grade level. It is possible, and if you are able to coordinate some of your planning and instruction with other content-area teachers at your grade level, you can search for books while the other content teacher searches for multimodal resources. You can also manage this independently by starting small with one particular unit of study for which you would like to diversify the texts. We think the benefits of teaching with text sets far outweigh the time commitment in planning, and you will discover this, too, as you find texts to meet reading abilities, modality preferences, and topics and subtopics of interest to your students.

Even when you divide the planning among team members, as you may already do, we know that you are very, very busy. When you are constantly striving to keep up with the content you teach, the latest educational methods, the most cutting-edge technology, updated state and local curriculum standards, and the ins and outs of home/school communication, you may feel as if you do not have the time to locate and consider quality classroom materials. You may make decisions based on what you find quickly, rather than what is the best fit for curriculum goals. With over 17,000 children's and young adult books published each year and a burgeoning and ever-changing world of online resources, ebooks, and tablet apps, it is no wonder that you may feel overwhelmed.

In this chapter, we hope to alleviate some of those feelings (although admittedly, we often feel the same way!) by sharing the steps that we take and the resources that we use for building a text set. By doing so, we hope to illuminate pathways for planning instruction that make it easier for you to incorporate well-written and illustrated children's and young adult literature as well as a variety of text types and modalities into your curriculum. Once you are familiar with these pathways, you will find it easier to add new resources from year to year and build on the core set of texts in use for any one unit of study.

This diagram, which we also shared in Chapter One, is a helpful way to think about classifying the types of multimodal, multigenre texts that you will want to use in your classroom.

A Multimodal, Multigenre Text Set

Children's Literature:
realistic fiction, fantasy, historical fiction, mystery, science fiction, traditional literature, poetry, nonfiction

Primary Sources:
documents, photographs, artifacts, photographs of artifacts, historic homes, clothing, newspapers

Periodicals:
newspapers, magazines, magazines for children

Multimodal Digital Texts:
webcasts, podcasts, photographs, webcams, websites, online government reports, works of art, songs, interviews

As useful as these categories are to help you classify texts for classroom use, it is important to recognize that they can all overlap in a variety of ways. Many picture books and chapter books have been converted into picture book apps or ebooks. Audio books have grown more popular and versatile in the digital age, while the once-cumbersome cassette tapes and CDs are now confined to convenient MP3 files that can play on laptops and desktops, MP3 players, smartphones, and tablet computers, among other devices. Primary sources are more accessible than ever, as museums, government institutions, and libraries have digitized their collections. Even television networks have programming archived on their websites.

The Text Set Chart on page 51 can be used to keep track of the different types of texts that are located in a search. Throughout this chapter, this chart will be used to organize the different types of texts considered for the tree unit.

Text Set Chart

Text Set Chart for _____

Unit _____

Text Title	Key Content	Genre	Modality	Possibilities

Considering Text Complexity When Selecting Texts

Before we begin discussing how we locate, consider, and select multimodal, multigenre texts for curriculum purposes, we think it is important to discuss text complexity. For us, the starting point for considering text complexity is the role of the text in the curriculum and the tasks students are asked to complete.

The subject of text complexity has become a central discussion regarding the implementation of the Common Core State Standards. While you may not follow the Common Core State Standards in your school or district, there is something we can all learn from the complicated considerations of complexity made based on a variety of criteria taken together. In Appendix A of the Common Core State Standards, text complexity is represented as a triangle with three components: qualitative determinations, quantitative determinations, and the context, described as "reader and task" (Common Core Initiative 2010). There are many differing perspectives on how to balance quantitative and qualitative measurements of text complexity and the particular ways in which texts are measured quantitatively within the Common Core State Standards.

It makes sense to us that the reader and the task are the foundation of consideration, as we know that teachers make decisions on texts based on what role the text will play in the classroom. This has always been the driving force behind our initial consideration of text. What will we do with it? *Why?* A book can be used one year with a whole class, and the next year, it may be better used in a small-group setting, given the reading abilities, interests, and dynamics of a different collection of students. Within the context of how a text will be used, the Common Core State Standards ask you to consider the qualitative aspects of text complexity: levels of meaning or purpose, text structures, style, and knowledge demands (the prior knowledge required to read and understand the text). Knowing how you will use the text in your curriculum will determine how you weigh these four aspects of text complexity. These qualities of a text will be considered in a different way if it is an option for independent reading or small-group reading, or as a read-aloud as compared to a required independent read.

The Common Core State Standards also ask that teachers consider the quantitative analysis of text complexity, which is often based on vocabulary, syntax, and sentence length and usually results in a reading level score denoted by a number or a letter, depending on the analysis system being utilized. These quantitative measurements of texts are provided by research organizations and companies. Most likely, your school has a method of quantitative analysis for texts in place for balanced literacy instruction, or it is in the form of a basal reading program that has been adopted. You can incorporate quantitative analysis of texts from those programs and use them alongside your qualitative assessment of text complexity, the task, and the diverse readers in your classroom.

Text complexity can be considered differently depending upon the primary purpose for reading a text. If you are teaching with text sets for the sole purpose of acquiring information in science, social studies, or the arts, you may be more flexible with your considerations of text complexity, since the primary purpose of reading the text is to learn content. As such, the texts serve as scaffolds for one another to build content knowledge. With the content knowledge they learn, students are able to then tackle increasingly more-sophisticated texts within that topic. Rigidly adhering to a particular quantitative range of texts is not essential.

If you are teaching with text sets in a language arts or integrated curriculum unit, you will pay more attention to the intricacies of text complexity in order to further the individual reading abilities and stamina of all of your students. The texts will still serve as scaffolds for one another to build knowledge or understanding, but the layering of independent, small-group, and whole-class readings of texts may be organized more specifically around texts of different complexities.

Finding High Quality Children's and Young Adult Books

Frequently, teachers ask us how we are able to keep up with the field of children's and young adult literature. We don't! We can't! No one can. However, it is possible to search strategically and locate the books that are right for your classroom. Knowing what tools are available to you makes all the difference. You cannot walk into a bookstore, or even a single library, and see all the books that are in print on a topic. In this section, we will discuss some of the tools and resources that are useful in locating books for consideration for classroom use. When teaching with text sets, start by looking for the most carefully written and up-to-date children's and young adult books because you know that they are written with children's developing understanding of the world in mind.

School, Public Libraries, and Librarians

Those who do the very best job of keeping up with the latest books for children and young adults are often right under your nose—your school and public librarians. Neither of us can imagine our teaching careers without the supportive assistance of the librarians that we have worked with over the years. Neither of us has ever felt that we could not teach a unit of study because we did not have access to books. With the help of librarians, we made it happen. If you are lucky enough to have a certified library media and/or information specialist working at your school, we encourage you get to know him or her. This relationship can be one of the most important in your day-to-day teaching life.

School and public librarians read book reviews regularly. In the next section of this chapter, we share with you some of the resources for these reviews, and we advocate that you, too, become a consumer of book reviews and learn to read them strategically. However, librarians can devote much more time to reading reviews, and they possess an awareness of the new trends in the field, as well as knowledge of the veteran authors in specific genres who can be relied upon again and again. Most importantly, librarians read many of the new books that come into their libraries—more than you can possibly keep up with!

Over the years, it has been our experience that working with one librarian on one unit of study usually leads to ongoing collaborations. For instance, when Mary Ann began to work on a genre study of historical fiction with the Middle Ages as the focal point, her school librarian culled together books from the school library and was instrumental in locating other books for Mary Ann to use in her classroom. Knowing that this unit of study was an important part of the curriculum, the librarian also began to develop her collection in the school library to have even more books ready and available for that particular unit of study in future years. As you work with your librarian on a unit of study, you may find that he or she builds the collection with this and other units of study in mind, and knows that the books will be put to use by young patrons and their teachers. Usually, these books can be brought directly into your classroom for use. Additionally, in many states, countywide or statewide interlibrary loan networks afford you access to books that are not in your local library collection.

Who is responsible for purchasing books for classroom use at your school? Sometimes teachers confront administrators or school boards who confidently approve budgets for textbooks in social studies or science but will not do the same for trade book text sets, even though sets of trade books can often be purchased more cheaply than text books. This is another area where your relationship with the school librarian can be essential. Not only can your school librarian work with you to establish a great text set, but he or she can also equip you with book reviews, award descriptions, and professional blog entries about books that might educate the school leadership about the positive potential of trade books to teach content and differentiate instruction. Moreover, the school librarian can plan with grade level teams so that the school library and the team are both budgeting for certain texts to use in a multimodal, multigenre text set. When you are first doing a unit of study using a text set, the librarian can provide the resources through an interlibrary loan to ensure that it happens. Citing such instances as pilot studies provides further evidence to convince skeptical school leadership about the power of the text set.

Text sets work best if you have ongoing, dependable access to those books each year. That may mean that your team shares all of the same books and you have enough for each classroom to run the unit of study concurrently. In some schools, it means that one classroom at a time conducts a unit of study in order to optimize the use of a single text set. It all depends on the size of your school, district, and budget and the ways in which your grade level team operates. As we write this book, we know that many children's literature specialists, educators, and librarians are suggesting that more trade book nonfiction gets published in paperback and ebook format to help reduce the cost of using these books in curriculum units.

Book Reviews

So how do librarians do it? How do they find all of those great books? The fact is, you have access to many of the same resources that they do. Through a variety of digital resources, you can turn to what experts in the field have already vetted in order to locate engaging and well-written nonfiction texts on a particular topic from your grade level content standards.

School Library Journal and *The Horn Book Magazine* are journals that provide a good starting point for finding reviews. *The Horn Book* also publishes *The Horn Book Guide*, which is available digitally and in print and includes reviews of many more books than can be included in the bimonthly journal. Print copies can usually be found at your local library. As veteran review journals, each has a long history of reviewing children's and young adult literature, and each writes quality reviews that we have come to count on in an age when anyone and everyone can offer opinions on books through blogs, wikis, and personal websites. We believe that parents, teachers, and students have much to gain from sharing their reactions to books through digital means, and we welcome the larger conversation about children's literature that now exists online. However, as educators, we value the background knowledge that professional review journals possess. With a deep knowledge of the very broad field, each journal applies specific evaluation criteria to texts, mixed with an understanding of the developmental needs of target audience age spans. Both journals have free monthly eBulletins that also help teachers stay up-to-date. *The Horn Book* offers "Notes from the Horn Book" and *School Library Journal* provides "Curriculum Connections." You can visit their websites to learn how to subscribe.

We have also relied on Titlewave, the website of Follett Library Resources. As a collection development resource for school librarians and a pathway for purchasing books, Titlewave provides a free searchable database of book reviews. Using the advanced search feature, you can search for books on a topic by genre, interest level, the number of book reviews, and book award. When we examine a book on Titlewave, we are able to see multiple reviews from a variety of sources, including *The Horn Book* and *School Library Journal*. We can compare and contrast those reviews and decide whether the book makes sense for us to seek out, read, and consider.

Well-written reviews also shape our teaching. Sometimes a review points something out that we would not have thought of on our own; it might be an observation about the way point-of-view is used in a nonfiction text, or it might be a certain theme that surfaces in a subtle manner. Other times, the written reviews confirm what we each have observed in a text. Each of those observations becomes a useful tool in considering the different roles a book can play in a language arts or content curriculum.

For example, take a look at the following *School Library Journal* review for *The Mangrove Tree: Planting Trees to Feed Families* (Roth and Trumbore 2011), from May 1, 2011:

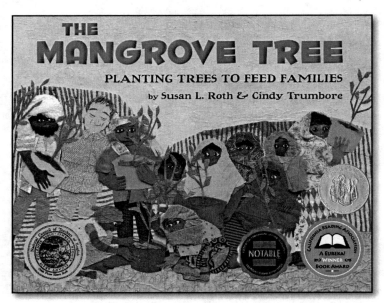

Grades 3–6: This is a true story set in a small village in Eritrea. "The families used to be hungry./Their animals were hungry too./But then things began to change…/all because of a tree." In poignant text that alternates between cumulative verse and prose, Roth and Trumbore describe how Dr. Gordon Sato, a Japanese-American cell biologist, helped to relieve poverty and famine by planting mangrove trees in saltwater. Tended mainly by

women, the trees flourished and multiplied, supplying food for animals and fish that, in turn, provided food for the people. Roth's large paper and fabric textured collages first reveal a barren village that is then gradually transformed as pots of mangrove seedlings are transplanted and become abundant mangrove forests. Depictions of women in colorfully patterned long dresses and head scarves, shepherds in capes and head coverings, and children playing outside houses "made of cloth, tin cans, and flattened iron" convey a sense of place and culture. The cumulative poem ends with an introduction to and picture of the smiling scientist himself: "This is Gordon,/Whose greatest wish/Is to help.../By planting trees,/Mangrove trees,/By the sea." A lengthy afterword contains additional information about Dr. Sato and photos of him working with the local people. Pair this inspiring story with Donna Napoli's *Mama Miti: Wangari Maathai and the Trees of Kenya* (S & S, 2010) to spark discussion about how one individual can improve the lives of others.

—Marianne Saccardi, formerly at Norwalk Community College, CT Copyright 2011.
Library Journals LLC, a wholly owned subsidiary of Media Source, Inc.

This review provided a great deal of information, not the least of which is that it mainly designates the book of interest for upper elementary students. It tells that the text structure is both a cumulative verse and nonfiction prose about Dr. Gordon Sato's work in Eritrea. We learn of Dr. Sato's credentials as a cell biologist. The reviewer shares the emphasis on a variety of life cycles, including human beings, that depend upon the mangrove tree, thus reinforcing the utility of this book in our own focus on shared ecosystems. We were intrigued by the mention of a "lengthy afterword," which we might be able to mine in the classroom for further information on the content of the book. We discovered this book after we learned of Wangari Maathai's death when our focus for the unit expanded to a global context. The fact that the reviewer refers to one of the four picture book biographies about Dr. Maathai was yet another sign that this book had the potential to be an excellent addition to our text set. We still had to read the book to know for sure, but the review helped to suggest the role it could play in our tree unit. If we did not already know about the Maathai books, this review would have been helpful in pointing the way to other books on the topic, another important aspect to why book reviews are so important.

These review journals are useful for staying apprised of new books as they are published; they also often have articles that talk about sets of books on a topic or specific genres of literature. However, when looking for books to use in a text set for a particular unit of study, it is easiest if you can search for multiple books concurrently. There are a variety of digital resources that you can turn to for award-winning books and lists of exemplary texts on particular topics.

Awards and "Best Of" Lists

There are many annual awards in the world of children's and young adult literature, and "best-of" lists can be very helpful when teaching with text sets. One helpful way to use these lists is at the end of the year when schools sometimes have surplus funds that must be spent, often very quickly, by the end of the fiscal year. School librarians can publish the latest versions of these lists in the faculty room or library and have teachers check off books they want that focus on topics frequently taught at particular grade spans. It is a simple way to make target decisions to buy well-written books on required content.

From the sources below, you can identify texts written on a particular topic that might be appropriate for your text set. As always, you have to read the texts to determine whether they are a good match for your students in terms of interest and readability, and whether they fit your content goals. This chart represents the most important awards in the world of children's and young adult literature.

Children's Book Awards

The Boston Globe-Horn Book Awards (picture book, fiction/poetry, nonfiction)

http://www.hbook.com/bghb/current.asp

Caldecott Medal (ALA)

http://www.ala.org/ala/mgrps/divs/alsc/awardsgrants/bookmedia
/caldecottmedal/caldecottmedal.cfm

Coretta Scott King Award (ALA)

http://www.ala.org/ala/mgrps/rts/emiert/cskbookawards/recipients.cfm

Newbery Medal (ALA)

http://www.ala.org/ala/mgrps/divs/alsc/awardsgrants/bookmedia/newberymedal
/newberymedal.cfm

Notable Books for a Global Society (IRA)

http://clrsig.org/nbgs_books.php

Notable Social Studies Trade Books for Young People (NCSS-CBC)

http://www.ncss.org/resources/notable/

Orbis Pictus Award for Nonfiction (NCTE)

http://www.ncte.org/awards/orbispictus

Outstanding Science Trade Books for Students K-12 (NSTA-CBC)

http://www.nsta.org/ostbc

Sibert Medal for Nonfiction (ALA)

http://www.ala.org/ala/mgrps/divs/alsc/awardsgrants/bookmedia/sibertmedal
/index.cfm

Blogs and Children's Literature Websites

Blogs play an increasingly important role in evaluating children's and young adult books. While awards are designated once a year and reviews are often published monthly or bimonthly, blogs provide more immediate access to reviews of new books.

Blogs are also written from a variety of perspectives. Some bloggers are teachers, some are parents, and some are librarians. These blogs allow for "cross-fertilization" and may give you interesting insight into books you are considering for classroom use. Bloggers who began writing about children's books a decade ago have now formalized themselves into a society called *The Kidlitosphere*.

We began blogging in November 2010 with our colleague Grace Enriquez from Lesley University. Each Monday during the school year, "The Classroom Bookshelf" posts a new entry. We review a new children's or young adult book, and then provide a variety of teaching ideas for different grade spans as well as an additional list of related titles and digital resources.

The blogs on the *School Library Journal* website are a wonderful set of resources. The site has become one of the most important traffic points for bloggers reviewing children's and young adult literature. Most of the bloggers on the site are practicing school or public librarians. There are blogs that review children's literature in general, and there are those that focus on specific content. We find ourselves reading the blogs on this page almost every day, as a quick and easy way to hear about new books or new trends. The threaded conversations that are an embedded part of the blogs often shed light on how other people consider using a particular book with children either in the classroom or in a library setting. Some bloggers post every day, others just a few times a week. The tags used by bloggers allow you to find books that share common content, genre, or characteristics.

There are many authors of children's and young adult literature who blog as a way to connect with teachers and students. Of particular note is a group of nonfiction writers who write for the blog *I.N.K.* (Interesting Nonfiction for Kids) and the website iNK THINK TANK. Both serve to educate teachers, parents, and students about the changing world of nonfiction literature for children and young adults.

Another repository of information on children's and young adult literature is the Cooperative Children's Book Center (CCBC) at the University of Wisconsin-Madison. Their website has a "Book of the Week" feature, lists of bibliographies that contain 40 books on a topic directed at specific age levels, and author and illustrator podcasts. There is also a page devoted to all of the major national and global book awards.

Finally, to support your English language learners in their native language, you can find free open-access electronic picture books in PDF format at the International Children's Digital Library, a project of the University of Maryland.

Blogs

The Classroom Bookshelf
http://www.classroombookshelf.blogspot.com

Cooperative Children's Book Center (CCBC)
http://www.education.wisc.edu/ccbc/

Cooperative Children's Book Center Bibliographies
http://www.education.wisc.edu/ccbc/books/bibBio.asp

iNK THINK THANK
http://www.inkthinktank.com/pages/accolades-and-support-materials.html

Interesting Nonfiction for Kids (INK)
http://inkrethink.blogspot.com/

International Children's Digital Library
http://en.childrenslibrary.org/

The Kidlitosophere
http://www.kidlitosphere.org/

School Library Journal Blogs
http://www.slj.com/slj-blog-network/

We found all of the books for the tree text set, depicted in the table on pages 61–63 by searching Titlewave, reading reviews, examining awards lists, and checking online bibliographies.

Trees Text Set: Books

Text Set Chart for _____ Books _____ Unit _____ Trees

Text Title	Key Content	Genre	Modality	Possibilities
Trees, Leaves, and Bark (Burns 1995)	leaves bark tree types	field guide reference	print	Large close-ups for students to examine leaves and bark against North America focus
Mama Miti: Wangari Maathai and the Trees of Kenya (Napoli 2010)	Wangari Maathai Green Belt movement Maathai's role as healer trees' role in ecosystems	picture book biography	print	Illustrations and text content can be used as comparison and context with other books on Maathai More of a folktale structure used Theme—how one individual can make a difference in his or her community Global focus
Planting the Trees of Kenya: The Story of Wangari Maathai (Nivola 2008)	Wangari Maathai Green Belt movement trees' role in ecosystems	picture book biography	print	Theme—how one individual can make a difference in his or her community Global focus
Wangari's Trees of Peace: A True Story of Africa (Winter 2008)	Wangari Maathai Green Belt movement trees' role in ecosystems	picture book biography	print	Winter's use of frames in her illustrations focuses content Theme—how one individual can make a difference in his or her community
Trout Are Made of Trees (Sayre 2008)	trees' role in ecosystems	nonfiction picture storybook	print	Great for examining interrelationships
Looking Closely through the Forest (Serafini 2008)	different parts of the forest focusing on small part of something, and then revealing the whole	nonfiction photo essay	print	Mentor text for students to create their own photo essays using local trees and tree parts Good for practicing prediction as a reading strategy through visual cues

Trees Text Set: Books (cont.)

Text Title	Key Content	Genre	Modality	Possibilities
Poetrees (Florian 2010)	different types of trees; different parts of trees	nonfiction poetry collection	print	Mentor text for both poetry and illustrations of trees; Local, national, global focus with tree examples
The Mangrove Tree: Planting Trees to Feed Families (Trumbore and Roth 2011)	Dr. Gordon Sato; planting mangrove trees in saltwater; trees' role in larger ecosystem; focus on single type of tree	nonfiction picture book	print	Global focus; Theme—how one individual can make a difference in his or her community; Cumulative verse parallel with prose
Giants in the Land (Appelbaum 1993)	King's Pine; White pines in New England; colonization; focus on single type of tree	nonfiction picture book	print	Impact of deforestation (disappearing tree species); Local connection for Massachusetts
Redwoods (Chin 2009)	Redwood trees; California forest ecosystem; focus on single type of tree	hybrid of nonfiction and fantasy picture book	print	National focus; "Informational fiction" focus of fantasy narrative
A Log's Life (Pfeffer 1997)	ecosystem within a tree; decomposition; life cycles	nonfiction picture book	print	Interrelationships; Collage art as mentor illustration style

Trees Text Set: Books *(cont.)*

Text Title	Key Content	Genre	Modality	Possibilities
Life in the Boreal Forest (Guiberson 2009)	boreal forest ecosystem	nonfiction picture book	print	Interrelationships
The Forest in the Clouds (Collard 2000)	cloud/rainforest ecosystem	nonfiction picture book	print	Interrelationships
Quest for the Tree Kangaroo (Montgomery 2006)	rain forest ecosystem	nonfiction chapter book photo essay	print	Interrelationships Endangered species and ecosystems explored concurrently. Challenging read for students
Garden of the Spirit Bear: Life in the Great Northern Forest (Patent 2004)	boreal forest ecosystem	nonfiction picture book	print	Interrelationships
The Wolves are Back (George 2008)	Yellowstone National Park	nonfiction picture book	print	Interrelationships Western forest and meadow ecosystems
Breakfast in the Rain Forest: A Visit with Mountain Gorillas (Sobol 2008)	rain forest ecosystem	nonfiction picture book photo essay	print	Interrelationships Endangered species and ecosystems explored concurrently
A Tree Is a Plant (Bulla 2001)	survey on tree parts	nonfiction picture book	print	Basic tree information
Tell Me Tree: All About Trees for Kids (Gibbons 2002)	survey of trees and tree parts	nonfiction picture book	print	Basic tree information

Note: Bibliographic information for titles listed in this chart can be found in the Trees Text Set in Appendix C.

Trade Books at Reduced Prices

The reality is that many teachers must purchase books for the classroom using their own funds. If you want to teach with text sets but must spend your own money, here are two pathways to trade books at a discount. We use these resources all the time, and so do many teachers with whom we work around the nation.

ABE Books Online: Your school may have restrictions on how you purchase trade books and from where. If you are not bound by a particular district-approved vendor or you are willing or required to spend your own money on trade books, we want you to know about the American Book Exchange (ABE) (http://www.abebooks.com). We have been using ABE since its early days as a pioneer in global online bookselling. ABE comprises used and private booksellers around the world. Sellers often have hardcover library discards of well-reviewed trade books on sale at drastically reduced prices. In 2008, ABE was bought by Amazon.

Locally Owned Independent Bookstores: If you have a locally owned independent bookstore, you might be able to buy books with a 10–20 percent discount, matching larger wholesale catalogue prices and avoiding shipping costs. When Mary Ann was teaching in public schools, she was able to transfer her school book orders to a locally owned independent bookstore. This kept dollars within the community and saved her school money.

Locating Magazine Articles

Children's and young adult magazines serve many roles in a text set because of their brevity, valuable content, and the different text structures and access features they model. There are a wide variety of children's and young adult magazines for teachers and librarians to choose from.

After searching for children's and young adult books with the content of the text set, we look for accompanying newspaper and magazine articles. For content-based curriculum units, we found it useful to buy targeted back issues of magazines. Many of the children's and young adult magazines published today are available for purchase without a traditional subscription as single back issues in multiple copies from the publisher's website. For example, if you are teaching about the Great Depression, you can order back issues of *Kids Discover* and *Cobblestone* magazines published by different companies to round out your text set. Such back issues often offer the opportunity for real differentiation, as you can order magazines written for different audiences at different levels. It also allows you to differentiate for content. Incorporating magazine and newspaper reading into the routine of classroom life is important for cultivating curiosity about current events and exposure to diverse nonfiction articles.

Many children's and young adult magazines are now available for free in digital form through subscription database services, such as EBSCO and Gale. State library systems often pay for a subscription to the database that is then made available through public schools, libraries, and universities. The EBSCO database allows you to tailor your searches by Lexile levels, which may be helpful for differentiating your instruction.

The best digital magazine articles are those that are available as PDF files. PDFs, also known as "portable document format," maintain all of the access features of hardcopy texts, such as columns, photographs, and captions. Some magazine articles are only available in hypertext markup language, or HTML format, which is less appealing to most readers and particularly to student readers, as it lacks all of the formatting, illustrations, and access features of a PDF version. The benefit of HTML files is that many include audio recordings of the article so that students can read and listen simultaneously.

We have printed out color copies of magazine articles for students to read individually or in small groups. We have also had students read the articles digitally; the short nature of children's and young adult magazine articles makes them wonderful tools for monitoring your students online and offline reading comprehension of informational texts. You can project magazine articles on a screen for whole-class reading or have literacy stations where students at each one are reading different articles on tablet computers. Be sure to work with your school librarian so that when you use magazine articles from databases, you are following the copyright laws of Title 17 of the U.S. Code.

Print and Online Magazine Resources

Publisher: Cobblestone/Carus
Cobblestone; Appleseeds; Dig; Calliope; Spider; Ladybug; Cricket; Click; Ask; Faces; Muse
> http://www.cobblestonepub.com/magazines.html

Publisher: Scholastic Super
Science; Science World; Scholastic News; Scholastic Art; Upfront
> http://classroommagazines.scholastic.com/

Publisher: Kids Discover
> http://www.kidsdiscover.com/

Publisher: National Geographic
National Geographic for Kids; National Geographic for Little Kids
> http://www.nationalgeographic.com/magazines/lp/kids-sem/?source=sem_g _ngkids_us

Publisher: Time for Kids
> http://www.timeforkids.com/

Publisher: National Wildlife Federation
Ranger Rick; My Big Backyard; Wild Animal Baby
> http://www.nwf.org/Kids.aspx

The chart below shows the variety of magazine articles that we discovered for the trees text set. While the articles are written for different grade spans, it is important to consider such a broad array at this point in order to help differentiate instruction and provide background information for readers at different reading levels.

Trees Text Set: Magazine Articles

Text Set Chart for _____ Magazine Articles _____ Unit _____ Trees _____

Text Title	Key Content	Genre	Modality	Possibilities
"Looking at Leaves" *Click*, September 2011	how leaves hold water	magazine article	digital	Shows an experiment students can do on how leaves hold water
"Whose Leaf?" *Click*, September 2011	parts of a leaf how to identify trees by their leaves	magazine article	digital	Portable and laminated printout to take on leaf/tree walks or use in the classroom
"Wangari Maathai: Trees for Peace" *Faces*, February 2011	Wangari Maathai	magazine article	digital	Theme: One individual can make a difference Interrelationships Global focus Can be used with books on Maathai Written before her death
"Working the Woods" *Faces*, September 2005	logging conservation	magazine article	digital	Local focus on New England logging/timber industry and conservation
"Amazing Trees" *Ranger Rick*, June 2004	how long trees can live trees are the oldest living things on Earth	magazine article	digital	Focus on how long trees can live can complement students' developing sense of time and history Examine trees that have been "witnesses" to change over decades or even centuries
"The Busy Life of a Rotting Log" *Ranger Rick*, July 1997	ecosystem of a tree decomposition	magazine article	digital	Could work well with *The Log's Life* picture book

Note: Bibliographic information for titles listed in this chart can be found in the Trees Text Set in Appendix C.

Locating Historical Primary Sources and Artifacts

When teaching with text sets, we constantly draw on primary source materials. Given the bounty of our digital age, it is difficult to imagine a time when teachers and students did not have access to primary source documents and artifacts unless they traveled to a museum or had a book in which those documents or artifacts were published. Now, the world is literally at our fingertips. We have access to an overwhelming load of information that grows by the day. So, how can you take advantage of all that is available to you online without getting lost in a universe of Internet searches?

It is important to note that the online world allows us to access all sorts of historical evidence and we are no longer confined to look solely at primary source documents. We can look at photographs of objects and artifacts to explore another time period, listen to music, watch television news footage of historic events, or sift through collections of clothing. In the context of history and social studies, the Library of Congress defines primary sources as "the raw materials of history—original documents and objects that were created at the time under study"(Library of Congress website, "Using Primary Sources"). Primary sources can be used as tools for student inquiry, prompts for writing, or as a means of building prior knowledge about a time period with students before they read a lengthier piece of writing on a topic. In Chapter Six, you will see examples of how an elementary-level team strategically used historic photographs of people, objects, Ellis Island, and an early film from 1904 in their study of immigration.

To find quality primary sources, go to the websites of history museums, historic sites, national parks, and government archives and collections. Nonprofit and governmental organizations are great resources, whether private museums or national and state sites, because the mission of the organization is more important than the financial bottom line. You may be able to visit local and state institutions near you that are logical starting places for primary source materials. You may also be surprised to find a great deal of local history available to you via larger national institutions like the Library of Congress or the National Archives.

For anyone working with primary source materials for the first time, start with the "Using Primary Sources" portion of the Library of Congress website. It provides helpful guidance on selecting and using primary source materials for your classroom and offers wonderfully rich examples. If you want to look for local, national, or international primary sources, you can use the list below or the resources listed in Appendix B, which are organized by subject. Or you can try searching, starting with an Internet search engine. It is important to be as precise as possible in searches for digital artifacts using such terms as "medieval cooking pots" or "medieval tapestries." If those terms do not provide good results, try reversing and revising the terms, such as "cooking pots Middle Ages" or "tapestries Middle Ages." The more you do these kinds of searches for primary source materials, the better you get at it. It can also be helpful to include the name of an organization in your search, such as "landscape paintings and the Los Angeles County Museum of Art" or "Greek vases and the British Museum."

Online Resources for Primary Sources

The Library of Congress
http://www.loc.gov

The Library of Congress American Memory
http://memory.loc.gov/ammem/index.html

The Library of Congress: Primary Sources
http://www.loc.gov/teachers/usingprimarysources/

The Library of Congress: Teachers
http://www.loc.gov/teachers/

The National History Education Clearinghouse
http://www.teachinghistory.org

What kinds of primary source materials did we find for our tree unit? The chart on the following page shows the variety of primary source materials that we could consider using in different towns and cities in Massachusetts, our home state. The primary sources range from the 1600s to 1984 and consist of maps, paintings, photographs, and sketches. We think this broad array of visual texts will engage students and make more concrete the shifting views of one place over time. Similar sources most likely exist for your local community.

Trees Text Set: Primary Sources and Artifacts

Text Set Chart for _____ Unit _____ Trees

Text Title	Key Content	Genre	Modality	Possibilities
		Primary Sources and Artifacts		
Massachusetts maps from the Massachusetts Historical Society	maps of towns, cities, and counties in Massachusetts from 1637–1809	maps	digital	Use the maps from different centuries to see how mapmaking has changed and how to read maps from different times with a different set of expectations
View from Mt. Holyoke landscape painting by Thomas Cole, 1836, from the Metropolitan Museum of Art	one specific scene in Massachusetts	landscape oil painting	digital	Find a landscape painting of their community via a local historical society or art collection Compare and contrast what this looks like now in terms of forest
Digital photographs of Cambridge from 1866–1984, from the Cambridge, Massachusetts Historical Society	views of different neighborhoods, streets, and buildings in Cambridge, MA	photographs	digital	Search through the database to find photographs of streets near the school (teacher should sift through, too)
Sketch of *The Village Smithy* by Henry Wadsworth Longfellow, 1840, from the Washington's Headquarters — Longfellow National Historic Site and Maine Memory Network	Chestnut tree on Brattle Street in Cambridge, MA, where a blacksmith shop was run	sketch	digital	Students could compare and contrast the spot over time using this sketch, historic photographs, and their own photographs

Note: Bibliographic information for websites listed in this chart can be found in the Trees Text Set in Appendix C.

Locating High Quality Digital Multimodal Texts

As mentioned earlier in this chapter, the four categories of texts (children's literature, magazines, primary sources, and multimodal texts) overlap a great deal. Most, if not all, of the primary sources that a teacher will use in the classroom will come via a digital portal. Magazine articles are also widely available in digital form. Therefore, many of the multimodal text types discussed in this section and found online or through tablet apps also have other labels like *primary* or *secondary sources, poems* or *paintings, documentaries* or *government studies.* Some are created specifically for contemporary children; others are products of another time and place.

Audio Files

Audio files are an exciting resource to use with students. Listening to audio files that are available for streaming online or as downloadable MP3 files makes the past immediate, brings the world into your classroom, and lets recordings come to life. Audio files are embedded in many different kinds of websites related to museums, research libraries, archives, universities, zoos, and government institutions.

Many lectures and short explanations of content, such as descriptions of objects in museums, are also available as audio files. Students studying the Great Depression can listen to one of Franklin Delano Roosevelt's fireside chats, courtesy of the American Presidency Project at the University of Santa Barbara (UCSB American Presidency Project website, Audio/Video, Franklin D. Roosevelt) or different recordings of "Brother, Can You Spare a Dime?" on the National Public Radio site (NPR Music website, A Depression Era Anthem for Our Times). If you are studying local wildlife, the Cornell University Ornithology Lab has North American bird information that includes audio files of birdcalls that you can bring into your classroom (Cornell Lab of Ornithology website, All About Birds).

Video Files

Videos or film clips are now a common component of classroom life. The treasure trove of online data allows you to share videos with your students in short segments in a variety of settings—whole class, small group, or individual—and through a variety of methods—on a computer with a projector, a television, or compactly on a tablet. With video files, you can bring Robert Frost's presence into your classroom as he reads "Stopping by Woods on a Snowy Evening" courtesy of the Poetry Foundation (Poetry Foundation website, video of Robert Frost).

Not only does the video file connect the written poem with the poet, but it also models one way of reading the poem aloud. You can share early film footage that Thomas Edison's company took of immigrants arriving at Ellis Island in July of 1904, courtesy of the Library of Congress (Library of Congress website, Original Format Motion Pictures, Edison Companies, Immigration) or watch the latest webcam views of Earth from the International Space Station, courtesy of NASA (NASA website, NASA TV).

General Web Resources

The websites below provide audio and video footage that can be useful in your curriculum planning. The websites included in the Primary Source section of this chapter also offer audio and video footage of or about historical events and people. Please be mindful that these categories overlap a great deal and that a resource in art or music might also serve as a resource for history, and vice versa. See Appendix B for lists of multimodal resources broken out by content area.

Web Resources

American Library Association Great Websites for Kids
http://gws.ala.org/

WGBH Teacher Domain
http://www.teachersdomain.org/

World Digital Library
http://www.wdl.org/en/

The chart on pages 73–74 shows the audio, video, and other multimodal resources used in the trees text set. There are a range of text types to support local, national, and international exploration of trees from fact sheets to interactive software, webcams, and town websites. At this point, the materials represent as broad a range of topics and modalities as possible.

Trees Text Set: Digital Multimodal Resources

Text Set Chart for   Multimodal Resources   Unit   Trees

Text Title	Key Content	Genre	Modality	Possibilities
Fact sheet from Massachusetts Department of Environmental Management	differences between a tree survey and tree inventory; poses important questions for communities to consider	government fact sheet	print or digital	Models the kinds of questions and thinking that students can pose about how they want to design their tree survey and what information they want to glean from it
Town of Lexington, MA, Tree Inventory 2004–2010	types of trees in town; health of trees; data over a period of six years	website: circle graphs, bar graphs	digital; visual texts	Used as a mentor text for formats to show information from the students' tree survey within several blocks of the school or on their own streets
MCTI—Mobile Community Tree Inventory	templates for tracking tree types and guidance for conducting tree inventories	Microsoft® Excel spreadsheet; PC software	digital or print	Used to create students' own original research on trees in their community, presented as a tree survey (rather than an inventory)
National Arbor Day Foundation Tree Identification Guide	Tree Identification Guide (divided up into Eastern and Central US and Western US)	field guide; reference	interactive digital	Scaffolds the process for children learning how to identify leaves

Trees Text Set: Digital Multimodal Resources (cont.)

Text Title	Key Content	Genre	Modality	Possibilities
Arbor Day Foundation Rain Forest Rescue Program	rainforest facts and statistics program to raise funds and save rainforests globally virtual tour of rainforest	website, interactive virtual tour	interactive digital	Act on the information learned in order to protect rain forests
U.S. Forest Service Ad Council: Discover the Forest	photographs facts and Information how-to for leaf rubbing searchable database of parks and forests throughout US	website	interactive digital	Spanish version of the site available
Junior Forester Program—City of Cambridge, Massachusetts	information on what junior forest rangers in Cambridge, MA, do	website with text and photographs	digital	Volunteer to become junior rangers
World Land Trust—Wildlife Webcams	South American rainforest	webcam streaming	digital	Complete real-time research on another continent, tracking data day-by-day

Note: Bibliographic information for websites listed in this chart can be found in the Trees Text Set in Appendix C.

Picture Book and Content Apps for Tablets

Before 2010, tablet computers did not exist and apps were something people used for entertainment on their smartphones. Today, these highly compact and portable computers offer limitless possibilities for classroom use. With the flick of a finger your students can touch virtual insects, explore space, watch videos, or create their own digital books.

However, finding quality apps, whether they show previously published picture books or new content constructed specifically for classroom use, can be difficult. Hundreds of new apps are made available each month. We have come to rely on several review sources for selecting tablet apps. Otherwise, we have to search in the iTunes® store, and it is difficult to find exactly what we need. Once we discover an app that we like, we often look to the developer of that app for other apps as well.

App Resources

Touch and Go Column, School Library Journal
http://www.slj.com/

Kirkus Reviews: iPad Apps
http://www.kirkusreviews.com/book-reviews/ipad/

Teachers with Apps
http://teacherswithapps.com/

Commonsense Media App Reviews
http://www.commonsensemedia.org/app-reviews

Moms with Apps
http://momswithapps.com/

110 Amazing Apps for Education
Shell Education, 2012

For our tree text set, we found three apps that were particularly useful for finding and identifying locations of trees as well as identifying trees based on the physical leaves that students find.

Trees Text Set: Tablet Apps

Text Set Chart for	Tablet Apps		Unit	Trees
Text Title	**Key Content**	**Genre**	**Modality**	**Possibilities**
NatureFind (Moonshadow eCommerce)	parks and forests based on your location	tablet app	digital	Tablet computers are portable and can be taken out of classroom
Leafsnap App (Columbia University, University of Maryland, and Smithsonian Institution)	explore and identify leaves found locally	tablet app	digital	Take pictures of leaves and identify the trees from which they came Tablet computers are portable and can be taken out of classroom
Audubon Society: Field Guide to North American Trees (Green Mountain Digital)	tree identification	tablet app/ field guide	digital	Research trees found locally Tablet computers are portable and can be taken out of classroom

Note: Bibliographic information for titles listed in this chart can be found in the Trees Text Set in Appendix C.

Balancing Modalities Within a Text Set

When selecting texts for a unit of study, provide students with as much balance as possible among the different modalities so that they can read across diverse text types. Using a variety of texts of different genres and modalities allows your students to explore multiple perspectives, consider primary versus secondary sources, and use their own abilities to synthesize information gleaned from different modalities.

Utilizing different modalities not only allows you to differentiate instruction based on students' individual learning styles but it also allows you to carefully scaffold instruction. For example, some students might simply prefer hearing information as opposed to reading it, and an audio file provides a hook for engagement. Other students who struggle with reading comprehension can use knowledge gained from an audio text as a tool for comprehending a more complex written text they may not be able to access otherwise.

You may wonder, "When do I stop gathering? When do I have 'enough' resources across the different modalities?" The answer, of course, differs for every teacher, every unit, and every group of students. It is not an exact science. But here are some guiding principles:

- In addition to the children's and young adult books you identify, strive to include at least one audio and video text and at least one shorter print text, such as a children's magazine article, in your text set.

- If you are teaching a very complex concept, strive to have a wider range of text types so that students have multiple opportunities to read, listen, and view information related to that concept.

- If you are unable to find quality resources in all the modalities, don't force it. A few good resources that are well matched to your content and your student population are more powerful than a greater number of mixed-quality resources.

- If you are unable to find children's or young adult books to serve as the core of your text set, it is important to find more digital resources.

How you organize and use the texts in your text set is more important than just having a lot of them. Chapter Four will introduce a variety of models for organizing all of these texts for instruction.

A full tree text set appears in Appendix C so that you can see the full range of resources that we consider as we plan the unit of study more specifically in Chapters Four and Five. You can also use the resources from the text set to create your own multimodal, multigenre tree study for any elementary or secondary classroom.

Summary

This chapter, we:

- Modeled the various tools that we use to locate children's and young adult books, magazines, and digital multimodal resources, including primary sources and audio and video files

- Demonstrated how to use the modality chart as a helpful way to keep track of the different text types and modalities that you are considering for a unit of study, which helps you to document some initial thinking that emerges on how the texts can work in relationship with one another

The next step in teaching with text sets is to identify ways to strategically organize the broad array of texts that you have located for use in your curriculum unit. Chapter Four will demonstrate how to carefully organize and arrange a multimodal, multigenre text set to achieve your unit goals.

Reflection Questions

1. With what resources in this chapter were you familiar? Which new ones are you interested in exploring?

2. What unit do you currently teach that you believe you could enhance with the use of digital texts?

3. How could adding a greater variety of genres and modalities to the texts that you currently use enhance the learning of your culturally and linguistically diverse students?

Organizing Texts

You are probably now wondering what we plan to do with all of the multimodal, multigenre tree-related texts that we discovered in the previous chapter. There are a lot of them, and that is why it is so important to consider how to strategically arrange them. Organizing texts for instruction is the *heart* of teaching with text sets, the most essential step in layering and scaffolding access to content.

This is the step at which the planning really starts to get fun. We love considering the ways in which the different texts "talk" to each other, how they challenge our assumptions about content, and make us think about the same fact or theory from different perspectives. You have already seen some of our thinking in the modality chart that we shared in different parts of Chapter Three. We can't help but begin to think about the teaching possibilities in texts as we read through them initially.

In this chapter, we will discuss various instructional practices to support student understanding, and we will propose some organizing models for teaching with text sets that will guide you. We recommend the following process for organizing texts for instruction:

Organizing Texts for Instruction
Organize Content • How does the content suggest a way to organize the unit? • How do the multimodal, multigenre texts that you have gathered suggest an organization?
Select Text Models • Duet • Tree Ring • Mountain • Sunburst • Solar System
Combine Text Models • Will just one text model suffice? • What different combinations of text models allow you to organize a unit?

Our models for organizing texts all have different purposes, and you can match those purposes to your unit goals, the content standards you want your students to learn, and the ways in which the Common Core State Standards suggest the production of particular student-created texts. Bibliographic information for the titles and websites mentioned in this chapter can be found in the Trees Text Set in Appendix C.

Organizing Content

In Chapter Two, we talked about how you might go about identifying the most important understandings you want students to take away from a unit of study and how to think about opportunities for students' inquiry within the unit of study. Now that you know which texts are available to you, it is time to fine-tune the organization of your content so that you can then make decisions about how to use the texts you have identified.

As you read through the texts that you have identified, you will begin to recognize different perspectives on the content in the texts. These differences in perspective can help you to make organizational choices. For example, if you are studying the colonial period of American history, you might want to organize small groups by geographic region within colonial America and the multiple perspectives within those regions. Or, you might want to take advantage of the conflict between the British colonists in Colonial America and the British citizens in England, and split the class in half. Or, you might explore the period specifically through the lens of religion and the different religious groups that settled in the different regions, including the "melting pot" of some of the mid-Atlantic colonies such as New York. You could also easily explore that same time period and regions through the lens of commerce and the natural resources that were the catalysts for settlement and trade. Finally, you could consider the gender roles in different classes (free, indentured, and enslaved) as a way to explore colonial society and the political, social, and economic tensions that led to both the settlement of the colonies and ultimately the American Revolution.

Studying the Colonial Period of American History

Option 1: Perspectives of various geographic regions

Option 2: Perspectives of the colonists versus the perspectives of British citizens in England

Option 3: Religious groups in geographic regions

Option 4: Commerce and natural resources in geographic regions

Option 5: Gender roles

Science content similarly drives classroom structures. For example, if your class is studying ecosystems, you could examine a variety of ecosystems concurrently, exploring each through the lens of the problems they face as the focal point for small-group work. One group could study honeybees, the ecosystems of which they are a part, and the different theories regarding Colony Collapse Disorder and the disappearance of bees starting in 2006. Another group could study the polar bear, its role in its ecosystem, and the different theories as to why its livelihood is jeopardized due to the melting of polar ice. Another group could study the codfish or salmon, its role in the Atlantic or Pacific oceans, and why stock is becoming depleted. Yet another group could explore the reduction in numbers of the kakapo parrot of New Zealand due to the introduction of nonnative animal and plant species to the area.

Studying Ecosystems
Group 1: Honeybees
Group 2: Polar bears
Group 3: Codfish or salmon
Group 4: Kakapo parrot

Even the content of language arts can shape the organizing structures. For example, if you are studying the genre of biography, there are several different ways to organize content by small-group explorations. One method is based on form. Each group could read a different kind of subgenre within the biography genre: cradle-to-grave biographies, collected biographies, partial biographies, and autobiographies. Or, you could focus on the content, not the form, and each group could explore the representation of a single individual, reading multiple biographies of different lengths and text types, from partial picture book biographies to full-length chapter book explorations. Or, you might study the genre based on form in the first half of the year and return to it the second half of the year and focus on content, embedding the exploration of individuals within a particular unit in social studies or science.

Studying Biography
Option 1: Different subgenres of biography
Option 2: Multiple biographies and subgenres of biography of a single individual
Option 3: Different subgenres of biography, and multiple biographies and subgenres of biography of a single individual at different times of the academic year

When you read through the resources that you have gathered, you will begin to identify multiple perspectives and different ways of framing the content. As you flesh out the questions and possible tensions within the content, certain connections may emerge for you. It may also become clear how you can connect the content to the everyday lives of the students in your class, making the content more relevant and thus increasing student engagement.

When designing the tree unit, we gathered the range of children's texts shared in Chapter Three and read through them. As we read through the texts, we began to group them in a variety of ways that suggested how to organize the content we could explore in the classroom. For instance, two nonfiction picture books that focused on the life cycle of trees, April Pulley Sayre's *Trout Are Made of Trees* and Wendy Pfeffer's *A Log's Life,* were a logical grouping for exploring the ecosystem within a tree as well as the role of trees within a larger ecosystem. Several nonfiction survey books focused on specific types of forests around the world, and we grouped those together, too. Four picture book biographies of Nobel Prize winner Wangari Maathai were also a logical grouping for exploring how one person can impact an ecosystem. Still other survey books, such as *Poetrees* by Florian, *A Tree Is a Plant* by Bulla, *Tell Me Tree: All About Trees for Kids* by Gibbons, and *Trees, Leaves, and Bark* by Burns, could provide basic information about trees and support tree identification in the classroom. Through this process of grouping books, the following categories of content emerged:

- tree life cycles and ecosystems

- different types of forests

- the different ways in which individuals can make a difference in their community by planting trees

After establishing these groupings of books, we then began to consider how to organize them for instruction and make use of the multimodal texts as well, and seek out new multimodal resources to complement the subtopics we were exploring.

Models for Organizing Texts

As we have used text sets in our classrooms in our work with both students and teachers, we have noticed that certain models frequently emerge in our arrangement of texts. We offer these models to you to simplify your planning process. Rather than starting with a massive collection of texts and trying to figure out an arrangement from scratch, consider these different models of text use as you search for, think about, and select texts to use with your own students.

It is easier for students to understand your expectations for how they are to read across texts if they understand the arrangement of them. Using the names of these models with students will help them become more metacognitive. As they understand your purpose for reading particular texts, they begin to associate different ways of thinking about content, theme, or genre with different text models. If text sets are used as tools across the grade spans, students will be able to do so with ever-increasing sophistication.

These text models can be used separately or in combination with one another, depending on your instructional goals, the nature of the texts, and how much time you have to spend on the unit as a whole. We first describe how we could use each model separately in our tree exploration and then describe how to use them in combination with one another for a more concentrated unit of study.

Duet

The Duet Model is a simple pairing of two texts to initiate your students in the process of comparing and contrasting two books of the same genre or that share the same content. What is exciting about this pairing is the opportunity to consider text structure, organization, perspective, and point of view. If you are comparing and contrasting two nonfiction picture books on the same topic, you can purposefully select books that share the same content but have very different organizational structures. Or, you can select two fictional books on the same topic that represent the content from very different perspectives. Or, you can pair fiction and nonfiction and explore the content from both complementary and opposing perspectives.

Duet Model

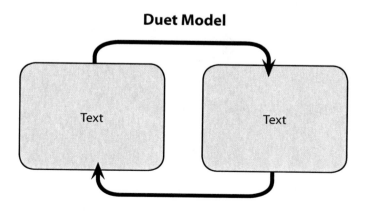

Choose the Duet Model when you:

- Want to introduce a focused comparison and contrast of content and/or genre

- Find two texts that are ideally matched for comparison and/or contrast

- Want to model writing decisions authors make regarding genre and structures

In our tree study, we could use April Pulley Sayre's *Trout Are Made of Trees* and Wendy Pfeffer's *A Log's Life* to compare the ways in which decomposition is an important contribution of trees to their ecosystems. Both are illustrated nonfiction picture book. In *Trout Are Made of Trees*, the title itself invites the reader to consider the ways in which trees and trout may be interconnected. In *A Log's Life*, the tree, throughout its lifecycle, plays a central role in supporting the animals, plants, and organisms of the forest ecosystem.

Trees Unit Duet Model

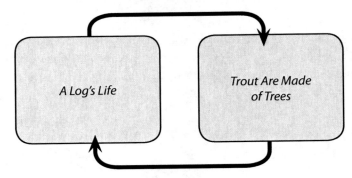

Sunburst

The Sunburst Model is the model that you might employ most frequently in your instruction. It provides the opportunity to model some of the thinking *across* texts that you will be scaffolding into your curriculum throughout the school year. In the Sunburst Model, you have a core text that serves as a touchstone for your exploration of content, theme, or genre. In language arts, it may more often be a work of fiction that serves as the core text. In social studies or science, it may be a textbook chapter or workbook. In music or art, it could be a particular composition, like a painting or a song. The additional texts, periodicals, websites, audio files, poems, and videos are carefully arranged around the core text to expand its content and offer varying perspectives on it. The "rays" are always in service of the core text at the center of the unit of study.

Sunburst Model

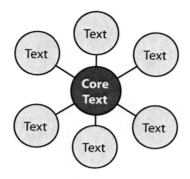

Choose the Sunburst Model when you:

- Want to model and practice the process of reading across multimodal, multigenre texts

- Have a required text that you must teach

- Want to extend a core text with other texts of varying complexity and perspective

In our exploration of trees, we could select Douglas Florian's *Poetrees* as our core text. As a compilation of poems, it provides a survey of trees from around the world as well as a snapshot of different tree parts. There are a variety of multimodal, multigenre texts that we could use to extend the information introduced in the core text. For example, students could read all or some of the articles in the September 2011 issue of *Click* magazine, which was devoted to trees. These articles could be read in print by ordering back issues from the publisher, or digitally, courtesy of a library database. The target audience for *Click* is students ages 5–7; thus, elementary students could read the articles for information with confidence and extract important details to apply to the information they were gathering from *Poetrees*. Students could then use the *Audubon Field Guide to North American Trees* app to identify leaves they had brought in to the classroom. Additionally, students could examine the tree life cycle on the interactive "Life of a Tree" page on the Arbor Day Foundation's website.

Trees Unit Sunburst Model

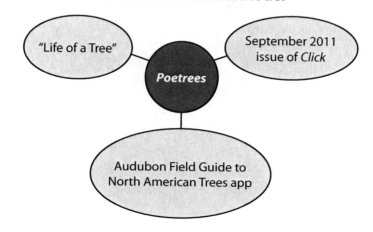

Tree Ring

The Tree Ring Model can be used to conduct an in-depth exploration of any core text. What differentiates this exploration is that students complete the text and then explore the sources the author used to write or create it. Like the Sunburst Model, the Tree Ring Model begins with a core text that all students read. From there, the focus expands as the rings move outward from the text to its back matter, the bibliography, source notes, and further resources. Even young readers can engage in this process now that authors of nonfiction picture books often introduce their research process in the text itself, the source notes, or author's notes.

By reading and observing some of the sources used by the author to write the book or create the text, students develop an understanding of how writers make choices about content. They also begin to see the book as one representation of content, not the final word on the content. Hopefully, this leads students to question sources and compare and contrast information. More and more authors are complementing their books with research stories on their websites. For example, zoologist and photographer Nic Bishop provides extensive information on his research process for each book on his website (http://www.nicbishop.com), as does biologist Loree Griffin Burns (http://www.loreeburns.com/). Authors Marc Aronson and Marina Buddhos created a blog site to extend their nonfiction chapter book, *Sugar Changed the World*, because they wanted to provide their readers with the opportunity to hear and see their research: the music and dance first created by the enslaved men and women working on Caribbean sugar plantations in the 18th and 19th centuries (http://sugarchangedtheworld.com/).

Finally, after reading excerpts of the author's source material, students will read "across texts," reading other texts on the topic to compare and contrast the information in the core book with other texts written for their age or grade span. There may be times where information conflicts between one book and another, and there, too, is a rich opportunity to explore the author's different sources.

Tree Ring Model

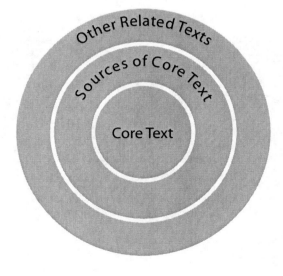

Choose the Tree Ring Model when you have a text that:

- Is a clear match to the content you want or need to cover
- Has depth of coverage and content
- Has rich resources in the front or back matter (author's note, bibliography, source notes)
- Prompts inquiry and further exploration
- Can be used to model authors' processes within a focused genre study

In our exploration of trees, we could select *The Mangrove Tree: Planting Trees to Feed Families* for in-depth exploration using the Tree Ring Model. In addition to the rich information found within the book, the authors provide a list of websites to explore in addition to their own sources of research, a combination of newspaper and magazine articles and webpages. Students can learn additional information by exploring these resources and could see what the authors included and excluded. Additionally, they could consider what information made it into the two running verse narratives in the story and what made it into the Afterword. As result, students can question the rationale for this and consider other ways of presenting the information.

Finally, reaching the outer ring, we could explore the mangrove tree's role in ecosystems around the world as we consider the books and resources about the Manzanar Mangrove Initiative in Eritrea in a global context. Students can gain a broader understanding of the role of mangroves on other continents, including North America, the role of mangrove trees within their ecosystems, and an understanding of the ways in which mangrove forests are threatened by natural and human forces. Additional texts that students could explore include the following:

- Lynn Cherry's picture book *The Sea, the Storm, and the Mangrove Tangle*
- National Public Radio's story on the impact of climate change on mangrove trees in Fiji (2007)
- the Oceans for Youth Foundation's informational video on mangroves
- maps of mangrove forests worldwide, created by NASA satellite imaging

Trees Unit Tree Ring Model

Solar System

In the Solar System Model, the content, theme, or genre to be examined is at the center, rather than a core text, as was the case with the Sunburst Model and Tree Ring Model. Each "planet" in the Solar System Model represents a text. Like the Duet Model, in which two texts are explored in the context of each other, the Solar System Model asks students to examine three or more core texts simultaneously in relation to one another. By comparing and contrasting texts, students gain a larger sense of content knowledge, theme, or genre. In its broadest sense, the Solar System Model can encompass the entire unit. However, it can also be more focused on a particular subtopic.

One of the benefits of the Solar System Model is that it asks students to bear more responsibility in the construction of knowledge. By using more than one core text, students are exposed to both a breadth and depth of content not normally achieved with a single text at the core. Additionally, it provides some flexibility in exploring content by offering different subtopics or perspectives and organizing your unit based on content, not texts.

Solar System Model

Choose the Solar System Model when you:

- Seek breadth and depth in your content coverage
- Are looking for the greatest flexibility in text complexity and instructional grouping
- Can devote time to a longer unit of study

Within our tree unit, we want to focus on the challenges experienced by ecosystems around the world and the impact of deforestation in addition to a local, hands-on exploration of trees in the community. There are two ways we employed the Solar System Model in order to do this. One way is a focused examination of one individual's role in tree conservation and forestation. The other is an examination of different forest regions around the globe.

To explore an individual's role in conservation, we focus on Wangari Maathai, who won the Nobel Peace Prize in 2004 for founding the Green Belt Movement and planting over 30 million trees in Kenya. There are four excellent picture book biographies about Maathai, each offering a different perspective on both her life story and her impact on the land and people of Kenya: *Planting the Trees of Kenya: The Story of Wangari Maathai, Mama Miti: Wangari Maathai and the Trees of Kenya, Wangari's Trees of Peace: A True Story of Africa*, and *Seeds of Change: Planting a Path to Peace*. These books were complemented by the articles "Wangari Maathai: Trees for Peace" from the February 2011 issue of *Faces* magazine and "Growing Trees for Kenya," in the March 2009 issue of *Highlights for Children*; Maathai's Nobel Acceptance speech; various obituaries and online slideshows reporting her death in September 2011; the Greenbelt Movement website; and interviews with Maathai on National Public Radio.

Trees Unit Solar System Model 1

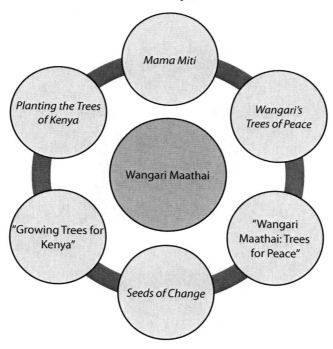

To examine the challenges to forest ecosystems, we explored the three types of forest biomes—boreal, temperate, and tropical—and the animal and plant life within. To accomplish this, students read *Life in the Boreal Forest* by Guiberson, *The Forest in the Clouds* by Collard, *Quest for the Tree Kangaroo* by Montgomery, *Garden of the Spirit Bear: Life in the Great Northern Forest* by Patent, *The Wolves Are Back* by George, and *Breakfast in the Rain Forest: A Visit with Mountain Gorillas* by Sobol. For each of these forest types, students also explore a variety of multimodal, multigenre texts, ranging from newspaper and magazine articles to government reports and audio and video recordings. For the temperate forest, students can draw on their previous readings and experiences studying trees locally. Students can also write and draw daily observations of South American rain forests provided by World Land Trust webcams.

Trees Unit Solar System Model 2

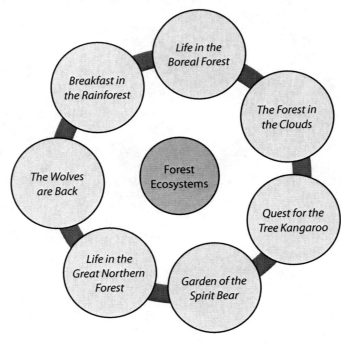

Mountain

The Mountain Model is deceptive. It looks like a simple triangle, and yet it is the model that puts the most responsibility for learning on individual students. The Mountain Model works best for research on a single topic or larger subject area; individualized, multigenre research on self-selected topics; and genre study. The Mountain Model is best employed during the second half of the school year when expectations, habits, and routines about using text sets have been established.

At the foundation of the Mountain Model is the content or genre to be studied at its broadest. At the peak is the content or genre to be explored in its most precise and compact form. The narrowing of the "mountain" serves as an important visual reminder to students that as they conduct individual research, their focus narrows. If conducting content research, research questions and subtopics grow narrower. If exploring genre, each student will seek out increasingly specific examples of variations within the genre; for example, students may move from examining various poetry forms to looking at free-verse poems to looking at free-verse poems with nature as their subject. Depending on the age of your students, you may be asking them to share at least some of the responsibility of finding and locating the variety of texts that they will be using for their research. You might have some texts assembled for class use, but you can also use this model as an opportunity to further refine and deepen students' ability to find multimodal, multigenre texts.

What does this look like for different kinds of studies? If a class is doing individual research on a single topic, students might start off reading a variety of survey texts on the topic. For instance, if the topic is mammals and students must select individual mammals to research, you might start off by having them read several books or articles or listen to podcasts on mammals. As students select mammals to research individually, they will develop research questions and use texts selectively to answer questions on their particular mammal. The focus of the texts and their research will increasingly narrow. From using general texts on mammals, students will move to more precise texts on their particular mammal, the regions in which it lives, etc.

If you are using the Mountain Model to do an individualized genre study, the process looks a little different. For instance, if you are studying science fiction, students might start by reading novels individually or in small groups. Because the emphasis is on individual instruction and not small groups, and because the emphasis is on the genre and not the content, you can be highly flexible with students' reading choices. As students read their science fiction novels, they can develop research questions about a contemporary scientific issue. They can then begin to grow their own fictional stories and develop the research questions that will allow them to learn what they need in order to write fiction. Each student's story and research will require a narrowing of their topic as they seek out precise information. They are learning scientific content and research strategies while further exploring a literary genre.

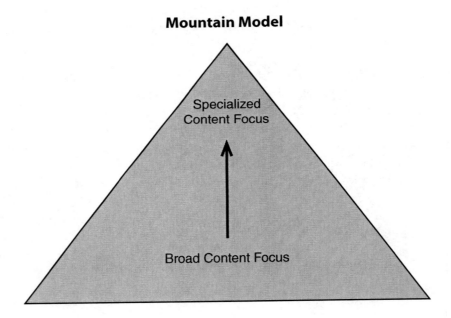

Mountain Model

Specialized
Content Focus

Broad Content Focus

Choose the Mountain Model when you want:

- To give students the responsibility of individual, paired, or small group content research

- To give students the responsibility of individual, paired, or small group genre exploration

In our exploration of trees, the Mountain Model could be used as an opportunity for students to explore individual research questions about trees. To start the research, the class explores several survey books on trees. This exposes students to general content knowledge and gives them an opportunity to develop research questions. The books *A Tree Is a Plant* by Bulla, *Tell Me Tree: All About Trees for Kids* by Gibbons, and *Trees, Leaves, and Bark* by Burns can be used for this purpose. With that foundation, students then establish their own research questions. They read magazine articles and nonfiction picture books and chapter books. They also research websites from national organizations, listen to audio files from National Public Radio programs such as "Living on Earth," and interview local tree and forest experts and conservation professionals in person or via Internet video conference.

Trees Unit Mountain Model

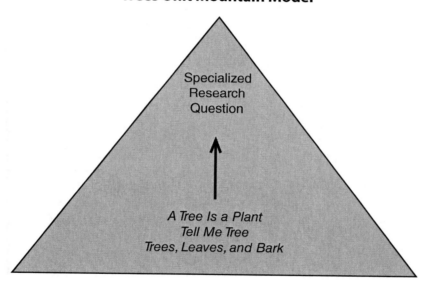

Combining Text Models

Text models can be used independently as the focal point of a unit of study or in combination with one another as progressions of exploration within a unit of study. It all depends on the depth and length of your unit and how much time you have to spend on the topic. How might this work?

In our tree unit, we could launch the unit with the Duet Model, reading *Trout Are Made of Trees* and *A Log's Life*. Students would compare and contrast the life cycle of a tree, its connection to its ecosystem, and the ways in which each individual tree is an ecosystem on its own for insects and microorganisms.

Next, we transition into the Sunburst Model, reading *Poetrees*. This model allows us to explore a variety of trees around the world as well as the different parts of the tree, through print and digital texts, photographs, and video. Students will locate and identify trees in their community.

Using the Tree Ring Model, the class could explore *The Mangrove Tree: Planting Trees To Feed Families*, and in conjunction with the information presented in its back matter, explore the significance of one kind of tree within an ecosystem.

With the Solar System Model, we could explore one individual's role in tree conservation by examining the four picture book biographies of Wangari Maathai along with periodicals and supporting websites for conservation organizations such as the Green Belt Movement. We could also extend that into an even deeper immersion experience through an exploration of the three types of forest biomes around the world.

Finally, the unit concludes with the Mountain Model as students establish individual research questions and explore multimodal, multigenre texts in pursuit of answers. In our experience, the content that drove the organization of the unit moves from specific to general, then back to specific, and then outward again in different directions, as shown in the table below.

Text Set Models Employed in the Tree Unit

Content Focus	Model Employed
The life cycle of the tree within an ecosystem	Duet Model
Different trees in different ecosystems	Sunburst Model
Deep exploration of one type of tree's role in the ecosystem	Tree Ring Model
Challenges to the ecosystems: Wangari Maathai and Kenya	Solar System Model
Different forest regions of the world	Solar System Model
Individual research on trees	Mountain Model

The instructional options for a text set are multifold and complex, but we encourage you to experiment with these models as you engage in curriculum design. Start slowly, using one of our models, and work up to using the models in combination with one another.

What the Texts Offer for Content Inquiry and Instruction

When selecting texts for use in a text set, it is important to recognize that no one text is going to stand on its own to represent a topic or a theme. Rather, each text is read, viewed, or listened to in relationship to other texts. However, in the relationships between texts, different texts play very specific roles.

Sometimes you will rely heavily on certain texts as you begin your unit because these texts are well served to introduce necessary background information about the topic. Other texts may stand out as texts that will be central, or core, to your unit of study because they are rich sources of information that you have determined that all of your students need to know, or because they are excellent points of departure for inquiry that will take students in different directions, building knowledge toward a jointly constructed overview of the topic of study. Still other texts will be best suited for reading in small groups or by individuals who will contribute their understandings gleaned from these texts through small group or individual presentations. In addition to making these kinds of decisions about the texts you have gathered, you will also be considering the diverse academic needs of your class as you review them. You will think about how the multimodal, multigenre texts are matched to the reading practices of your students and identify the texts that will provide the greatest amount of support for your English language learners.

Scaffold

Sometimes a text is a scaffold and is used to generate some interest or inquiry on a topic or to connect to students' previous knowledge. Often, but not exclusively, short texts serve best as scaffolds. Audio, video, or artifacts are ideal, as they provide the greatest access to the broadest audience. The ideal scaffold texts are not too precise or too large or too dense. Sometimes texts used as scaffolds are referred to again and again throughout the unit of study for the concise theme or concept they introduced. Scaffold texts are often successful as read-alouds as they cultivate interest, prompt inquiry, and build students' knowledge. The text may also be particularly compelling due to the writing style, the organization, the vocabulary it introduces, or the effectiveness of its visual features.

In the tree unit, a pair of texts serve as a scaffold. *A Log's Life* and *Trout Are Made of Trees* in the Duet Model prompt students to consider the roles that trees play within ecosystems and as ecosystems. The content of these nonfiction picture books is used to develop shared understandings about the importance of the tree within an environment and serves as inspiration to further inquiry.

Immersion

Some texts are best for more in-depth exploration, as they provide important information or a particular perspective on a topic that students can mine as they read, question, and reread. We use these texts for *immersion into the content* where students are diving into the deep waters of content, theme, or genre.

In immersion, you might have students reading core texts as a whole class or in small groups. You may divide your class into small groups that focus on teacher-generated explorations of texts or literature circles (Daniels 2002) that are student-led and centered on students' personal responses to a text. Each small group could be reading the same text, or, alternatively, each group could be reading a different but complementary or opposing text. You may choose to have different groups reading different texts if you have several texts that can be positioned in conversation with each other, but usually time does not allow all students to read all the texts. In these instances, each group becomes responsible for sharing the meaning they have constructed from the texts they have read.

When teaching with text sets in the literacy block, immersion texts may also be used for guided reading (Fountas and Pinnell 1996). This often occurs when you have a clear goal in mind for the reading experience and will be engaging in direct instruction of a reading strategy for learning content or for engaging in inquiry. In selecting a text from the text set for guided reading, you are often selecting texts that contain more complex concepts, employ text structures that may be less familiar to students and therefore require greater teacher support, and/or clearly lend themselves to practice with a particular reading or inquiry strategy.

There is always room for independent reading when teaching with text sets. Independent reading allows students to personalize their exploration of content. While engaged in content study with a text set, students may read independently as part of their immersion experience to deepen their understanding of the content area and to pursue a particular area of interest or inquiry related to the topic. When engaged in a genre study with a text set, students spend time reading independently to immerse themselves in the genre with a text of their own choice. Independent reading as immersion allows students to develop greater fluency when reading in the content area, expand their vocabulary, and satisfy personal motivations.

In the trees text set, Douglas Florian's *Poetrees* is read and reread in combination with other books, articles, and websites to explore a wide range of subtopics related to trees. *The Mangrove Tree: Planting Trees to Feed Families* offers students an in-depth look at a particular type of tree and serves as a model for the whole class to explore before launching individual research. The biographies of Wangari Maathai offer differing perspectives on the life of a tree conservationist and can be read using the Solar System Model as a whole class. Similarly, the six titles described in the Solar System Model focus on challenges to forest ecosystems around the globe and could be assigned to small groups of students.

Extensions

Extension texts serve to deepen students' understanding. Extension texts are frequently shorter texts and are used in order to allow students to apply their newly found knowledge in particular ways. Extension texts can be primary source materials that require a certain level of prior knowledge gleaned from immersion texts before being rendered accessible by young readers. Extension texts may also be controversial, articulating opposing viewpoints and beliefs that challenge students to sift through the information learned in immersion texts and take a stand or take action in the community. As such, extension texts are often wonderful vehicles for exploring multiple perspectives.

Extension texts can also be an opportunity to differentiate instruction further for individual students. Individual research or paired research on subtopics related to the content explored by the whole class allows students to extend their knowledge in personally meaningful ways. This allows you to leverage their engagement into more specific and sophisticated reading and writing practices.

Finally, independent reading is another form of extension, which allows students to extend what they have learned in the whole-class exploration and apply it to texts of their own choice that they would not have been able to read or understand with the same level of understanding prior to the immersion reading.

You can think about extension texts either as single texts or texts within one of the text set models. In the tree unit, students working with the Mountain Model would use extension texts to pursue individual or small-group inquiry.

Summary

This chapter:

- Introduced specific models as strategies for organizing texts

- Explained how each model provides a different way to synthesize and critique various perspectives on topics

- Demonstrated how different texts play different roles to scaffold, immerse, and extend student learning

The final step in teaching with text sets is to consider how students will respond to the texts within the text set and how they will demonstrate their evolving understandings of content or genre. Chapter Five will map out how to conceptualize and carry out the text production process.

Reflection Questions

1. Which text model most mirrors how you currently use texts? Which text model represents the most significant restructuring of how you use texts?

2. How could the various text models help you to address the varied needs of the students in your class, particularly the culturally and linguistically diverse students?

3. Think about a current unit of study. In what ways are you already using different texts as scaffolds, immersions, and extensions?

Creating and Responding to Texts

Let us return to our vision of elementary students studying trees. In the opening pages of this book, we described a classroom in which students were doing thoughtful and purposeful work that brought their community into the classroom and the classroom into the community. Students were creating digital nonfiction books, community field guides, and poetry collections. They were painting murals in public places. They were documenting the changing trees around them for data collection. When we teach with text sets, we strive to create a classroom environment in which students are not only immersed in reading print and digital texts but authoring original texts of their own as well.

In our own classrooms over the years, we have always felt most comfortable when the room hummed with activity, much like a beehive. You know that feeling from your own classroom when students throw themselves into projects and their individual engagement with the material and text production propels the class as a whole. It is thrilling to see what happens when young creative minds are given the opportunity to synthesize and apply their content learning in products, presentations, and performances.

So how do you channel excitement about learning into student production of new multimodal, multigenre texts that can be shared with a variety of audiences? In this chapter, we will present many options available for students to explore and share their learning from text sets and ways to assess both literacy learning and content learning. We recommend using the following outline to guide your process:

Creating and Assessing Student Responses

Explore the Content: Note-Making

- What kinds of note-making formats will you provide your students?
- What balance of teacher-created note-making forms and student-created note-making forms will you have, and why?

Design Authentic Assessments

- Will your assessment be content driven?
- Will your assessment be genre driven?
- Will your assessment focus on the integration of content and genre?

Evaluate According to the Assessment Planning Model

- Revisit your unit goals and the content standards you have identified in your Unit Planning Chart.
- Consider the content literacies that you hope students will acquire. Revisit the standards that you identified in your Unit Planning Chart (page 44).
- Think about authentic products that are logically connected with the area of content study.
- Think about the balance you want to strike within the unit between how many assessments you will use that demonstrate formative and summative collective understanding of content and how many assessments you will use that demonstrate individual understanding of content or genre.
- Finalize the list of assessments you want to include in the unit.

Assess Student-Created Texts

- What formative assessments will be used?
- What summative assessments will be used?
- Will you create rubrics that assess content standards, language arts standards, or both?

We'll start with a discussion of note-making—how students record and consider the new information they are learning—and move into a discussion of the different ways that students can demonstrate and present their learning.

Exploring the Content: Note-Making

As students work with text sets, you will initially want to help them to find a way to capture their evolving thinking about the content, ideas, and perspectives of the multimodal, multigenre texts. We like to introduce students to a range of note-making tools and strategies so that they have a way to record their in-process thinking. These tools range from sticky notes and chart paper—staples of classroom life—to reading journals and teacher-created graphic organizers. The kinds of tools that are used for any particular reading is dependent upon the purpose of that reading.

In whole-group or small-group content-specific explorations, it is helpful to use teacher-created graphic organizers on chart-sized paper that include questions that prompt consideration of the content to which we want students to pay particular attention. Often, this content is connected to content standards students need to learn. For example, as you will read in Chapter Seven, when we launched our study of space with a read-aloud of Kathleen Kudlinksi's *Boy, Were We Wrong About the Solar System*, we wanted to highlight the changes in thinking about the solar system that have occurred since humans first began observing the sky. To direct students' attention to these shifts in thinking, we divided the class into groups, assigned each group a time period, and asked them to complete a teacher-created graphic organizer with the prompts: "During our time period, they thought…." And "Boy, were they wrong! They realized…." Each group shared their organizers with the rest of the class, creating a time line of changing thinking across the centuries. We often use this kind of directed note-making when we want to make sure that all students have exposure to the same content.

However, there are times when we want thinking to emerge from the students. Instead of guiding them through a text with teacher-created graphic organizers or questions, we ask them to read and mark up the text with sticky notes. This can be done individually, in pairs, or in small groups. When we come together as a class, the sticky note becomes a very portable way of sharing captured thoughts and organizing what students think is important about what they read, viewed, or heard. They can use the sticky notes to create charts or put the sticky notes directly onto charts for the whole class to examine. Sticky notes can be used to identify questions that students have and to flag important points about content. Sticky notes can also be used in genre study to identify important features, such as the use of similes and metaphors or to track a particular kind of text structure or motif.

When students work on individual research projects, we want them to use a range of strategies to help them track their progress and thinking. Early on in the year, we teach them to use sticky notes to mark spots of interest in the texts that they are reading. We coach them to record connections, questions, and contradictions that they note while they are reading. Depending on the content and goals of their research, we may then also provide students with organizers to help them to keep track of the information they are learning. We teach them to transfer information, ideas, and questions written on the sticky notes into a graphic organizer, which helps them to make connections across texts and categories of information or ideas. Over time, we hope that students will rely less on organizers that we have created for them because they will have learned their own useful note-making strategies.

One method of note-making for individual research is color-coding the note-making forms based on the type of texts the students are researching. Mary Ann began doing this with her colleagues a number of years ago. Note-making graphic organizers were created that helped students identify and organize all of the required information needed for a bibliography. Students entered the appropriate data in the template and thus had an example of what it would look like in their bibliography. The organizer for each type of text was photocopied on different color paper. Students could look in their research folders and see whether they had a wide range of source materials. If everything was the same color or just one or two, they did not. However, if they had yellow forms for books, pink for newspaper articles, blue for websites, etc., then they knew they had an appropriate range of source materials. It is helpful for students to have concrete supports when doing the complex task of research. If they have exposure to these note-making forms throughout the first half of the school year and work with them text type by text type, then they will have the skills and confidence to use them more independently during the second half of the school year.

You will see a variety of specific note-making forms in Chapters Six and Seven in the studies of immigration and the solar system. When you view them, you will see that note-making forms are a support for reading to help guide students through a text. But you will also see how they can be used as an informal assessment that demonstrates what students understand as they read the text. This can be a helpful way to monitor understanding and adjust instruction within a unit.

Let's consider our tree unit and how we could shape a specific note-making form to use with two of our texts in the Duet Model. One way to take notes with the Duet Model is to have the students pose their own questions about trees and then you as the teacher help organize those questions into categories with the students before they read. Students could also pose and organize their questions individually or in small groups, and the results can be shared together and compared and contrasted with one another. There are times, however, when you want to direct students' thinking more expeditiously and ask specific questions that direct the thinking to the content standards. By posing the same standards-based questions for more than one text, students have the chance to use the standard as a lens for inquiry within each text and between texts. For example, the sample on the next page shows a note-making form that could be used with the Duet Model for the tree unit, exploring April Pulley Sayre's *Trout Are Made of Trees* and Wendy Pfeffer's *A Log's Life*. The graphic organizer focuses on a single content standard: Recognize that plants and animals go through predictable life cycles that include birth, growth, development, reproduction, and death. This graphic organizer could be given to individual students, small groups, or even to the whole class to serve as a series of charts that are filled out by everyone.

Sample Note-Making Form for Students: Trees Duet Model

Questions	A Log's Life	Trout Are Made of Trees
What insects, fish, and/or animals live in the ecosystem depicted in each book? Make a list in each box.	Within the log:	Within the stream:
How do the insects, fish, and/or animals listed above help the leaves and/or tree decompose? List all the things they do in the box.	Within the log:	Within the stream:

Map out the cycle of life within the tree in *A Log's Life*:

Sample Note-Making Form for Students: Trees Duet Model (cont.)

Map out the cycle of life within the stream in *Trout Are Made of Trees:*

_____   _____

_____   _____

_____

Similarities Between Cycles	Differences Between Cycles

Within this note-making form, you will see that we move from parallel explorations of the content to a synthesis of the content between the two texts, helping to direct students' thinking more specifically towards the cycles of life that plants and animals experience.

Designing Authentic Assessments

When students have completed a portion of a unit, you will want to assess what they have learned. The purpose of your unit will guide the kinds of texts you ask your students to create. Balancing the types of assessments you offer and providing students with choices often leads to stronger evidence of student learning. Sometimes you will be assessing for content and language arts standards. Sometimes your assessments will focus more on the content being learned. Still other times, you will be focusing your assessment on the genre from which students are constructing new texts. We present three scenarios for you to consider:

- Content-driven assessments
- Genre study
- Integrated content and genre study

Content-Driven Assessment

Often the main focus in a unit is on the content that students need to learn to meet curriculum standards. When units of study are organized around content, the products or performances that demonstrate student learning can vary greatly by genre or can be multigenre in nature.

During an interdisciplinary study of World War II and the Holocaust in secondary social studies and language arts, Mary Ann's students were reading and viewing a variety of primary source materials, including photographs, newspapers, newsreels, and radio shows. Holocaust survivors came to speak to classes. Students read historical novels and memoirs set during that time period from different points of view. They viewed a documentary on Anne Frank and researched selected aspects of the global conflict individually and in small groups. Students had the choice of creating a variety of texts individually, in pairs, or in small groups to demonstrate what they learned. Some of their choices included historical fiction; paintings or other visual art forms; an original monument design; narratives based on their interviews with Holocaust survivors, veterans of World War II, and people who lived through the war on the home front; and fictional videotaped newsreels.

Genre Study

At times, it is the genre itself that serves as the focus of a unit of study. If you are a language arts teacher or an elementary school teacher responsible for teaching all the subject areas, it is likely that you have received a list of genres that you are expected to teach the students in your classroom. Even if you do not have such specific expectations, many of us must now consider the genres required by the Common Core State Standards. We believe that students learn to write well in a genre when they have had extensive exposure to quality texts that are examples of that genre and its variations. These texts then become mentor texts that students read closely to learn about authors' choices and techniques when writing in this genre.

In Erika's experience, even the youngest writers can engage in genre study. When Erika was working as a literacy supervisor in an urban setting, she worked with teachers on a summer program designed to support readers who were not reaching grade level expectations. The focus of the program was on engaging students entering lower and upper elementary grade levels with the reading and writing of nonfiction texts in a variety of genres, including procedural texts, personal narratives, and sequential texts. Students first read many texts that were examples of the genre, discussed with their teachers the characteristics of the genre and stylistic choices made by the authors, and then worked through the writing processes of planning, drafting, revising, and editing to publish finished pieces of writing in the focus genre on a subject of their own choosing. All the participants in the program—students, teachers, and administrators—were amazed at the quality of writing these students were able to produce. Erika and the teachers she worked with learned that when students engage with interesting texts, have the opportunity to study those texts as mentor texts, and are then able write on topics directly related to their own interests, they are far more capable of exceeding all performance expectations.

Integrated Content and Genre Study

Sometimes, the texts that you gather may fortuitously suggest the incorporation of genre study as a literacy focus within your content-focused unit. This may allow you to meet the expectations of your language arts curriculum through your content-area study. We know that teachers often face enormous time challenges and expectations to cover a wide array of curriculum topics over the course of the school year. We encourage you to seek out connections between the content and genres that you teach. Selected texts in the text set then serve as "mentor texts" or model texts for student writing.

When studying historical fiction with students in her language arts course concurrent with the students' study of the Middle Ages in social studies, Mary Ann had each student read a self-selected historical novel set during the Middle Ages. Using a field trip to local museums with medieval artifacts as the basis for brainstorming, Mary Ann had students begin to compose their own original historical stories using their self-selected novels as mentor texts. In class, they established research questions and researched a specific time and place during the Middle Ages, and in some cases, specific events such as battles, buildings, or historical figures. Each student used his or her research to write and publish short historical fiction books. Very specific genre-based feedback forms were created to help students respond to one another's work, and Mary Ann used the same format for her responses. Students were evaluated using a genre-based rubric.

Whether your focus is content, genre, or both, you have many choices when making decisions about how students will demonstrate their learning. While the process of designing assessments will be distinctive to your particular teaching context and students, we will share some guiding principles and questions in the sections that follow to support your design process. In Chapters Six and Seven, you will find specific examples of student-created products that provided us with evidence of student learning in units of content study incorporating text sets.

Assessing Student Learning

As students read across the texts that comprise a text set, they encounter a wide array of information and a range of perspectives. We want to know whether our students are able to synthesize this information and apply it to answer their own questions and share their learning with others. To find this out, we ask students to demonstrate their learning in written or multimedia products or through presentations or performances. We evaluate student work products to assess both their learning of key content in the unit and their ability to use language arts to express their learning.

As we consider how our students will demonstrate their new content knowledge, literacy skills, and strategies, we are guided by the following principles:

- Student responses should reflect how they are grappling with the diversity of perspectives in the text set and how they are synthesizing information across texts.

- Student responses should allow us to see their increasingly sophisticated use of content literacies.

- Student products should be multigenre and multimodal whenever possible, reflecting the variety in the text set with which they have been working.

- Students should have authentic audiences instead of limiting responses to a private set of comments between teacher and student.

- Students' options for assessment should be varied. Sometimes students are all writing in the same genre, sometimes they have a limited number of choices to choose from to show what they know, and sometimes they are the sole designers of the assessment products.

Assessment Planning Model

When we design student assessments, we consider our unit goals, the texts available in our text sets, and our knowledge of our students. We suggest the following steps to scaffold your planning:

1. **Revisit the unit goals and content standards you have identified in your Unit Planning Chart.**

   - What content standards need to be included within the assessment?

   - How can you balance student interests and questions with the content standards?

2. **Consider the content literacies you hope students will acquire. Revisit the standards that you identified in your Unit Planning Chart.**

   - What Common Core State Standards need to be a part of ongoing work for the unit and the assessments?

   - What kinds of specific reading and writing experiences do you want the students to have?

   - How is disciplinary literacy an important component of the reading, writing, speaking, and listening that students could do around the text models?

3. **Think about authentic student products that are logically connected with the area of content study.**

   - What kinds of reading experiences are students having in the text model and how do those experiences suggest certain kinds of assessments?

   - Does the unit suggest a genre study?

   - Are there particular standout texts within your text model(s) that you want to use as mentor texts for student writing, visual art, or media production?

   - Do the texts suggest that students should work in a variety of genres and/or modalities on several smaller projects or one in-depth project?

   - How do you want to balance paired and small-group text production with individual text production?

   - How much choice do you want to allow your students?

4. **Think about what balance you want to strike** within the unit between how many assessments demonstrate formative and summative *collective* understanding of content or genre and how many assessments you will use that demonstrate *individual* understanding of content or genre.

- How many formative and summative small-group and whole-class projects are desirable?

- What kinds of individual summative assessments will you use?

- To what extent can pieces of collective and individual work be used in portfolios of student work as a summative assessment?

5. **Finalize the list of assessments you want to include in the unit.**

- Recognize that you and your students may have new ideas for student-created products as you use the text set in your unit of study.

- Be open to revising the list of assessments as you move through your unit, recognizing that some may end up being more appropriate or useful than others.

Student Responses to Texts

One of the most exciting aspects of teaching with text sets is that the engaging range of multimodal, multigenre texts in the text sets invites a similar range of student-created texts. On the following page, you will find a list of types of texts your students can produce to show their learning. This list will be useful to you in your own planning. When students have the opportunity to create these varied types of texts, it is important to emphasize that the process is as important as the final product. Students should also share their thinking about both the process and the final product in either written or spoken form so that classmates, the teacher, and other members of the school and local community can best understand what each student learned. Sometimes this means having a "museum card" next to objects or visual artwork, like the rectangular identification cards that hang in museums next to artwork, or on the wall that introduces an exhibit. Sometimes this means carving out time for formal student presentations, or this can be "farmers' market" or "science fair" approaches to sharing information on a more informal basis. It is important for students to know that there is a public audience for their work. These speaking and listening opportunities are also vital components of the Common Core State Standards.

In Mary Ann's experiences at the secondary level, she felt that it was always important to provide students with a balance of teacher-created assessments and ones in which students could make their own choices. For every assignment that provided students with teacher-suggested choices, there was always the option of creating a project proposal. Mary Ann kept blank copies of project proposal forms available at all times. Each assignment always included a date by which a proposal would have to be submitted for approval. Students had to demonstrate what they would be learning and why it would help them learn the content, genre, or process in a way that the teacher-created options did not, and how they should be evaluated.

The list below provides ideas for student-created texts and can be seen as a menu of possibilities for student products.

Student-Created Texts

- advertisements
- audio or video documentaries
- biographies and autobiographies
- book reviews
- budget documents for a local government or proposed business
- charcoal sketches
- charts and graphs
- class magazine
- classroom, hallway, or community murals
- comic books and graphic novels
- costume design/historic clothing
- crime files/reports for real or imaginary unsolved crime cases
- debates
- governmental bill proposals
- informational blogs
- lab reports for experiments

- land use studies for imaginary land or real land
- letters to the editor
- literary criticism articles
- maps and globes
- memoirs
- newspaper stories
- oral histories
- paintings
- photograph collections or photo essays (online or in print)
- picture books of any genre
- podcasts for the school or community
- poetry collections
- posters
- public service announcements
- quilts
- reference books
- scenes, one-act plays, puppet shows
- scrapbooks

- sculpture
- short stories of any genre
- speeches
- student-created experiments
- student-created surveys
- student-made objects or models
- tableaux
- traditional compositions and essays
- traditional research papers

Assessing Student-Created Texts

Teaching with text sets affords us many opportunities to assess student learning both formatively and summatively. Because students are reading across multiple texts to compare, contrast, and synthesize information, we have a prime opportunity to evaluate their comprehension of texts and their ability to apply their content literacy and content learning in original texts that they compose.

Formative assessment allows you to see the evolution of students' understandings and abilities to express these understandings. This type of assessment is ongoing throughout a unit of study. Knowing how students understand the content allows you to make adjustments to your instruction, slowing down the pace when needed and/or bringing in additional text resources to support the understanding of specific concepts, or extending the content for students who are eager and ready for more. The note-making strategies that we have discussed in this chapter will allow you to engage in formative assessment of students' comprehension of the texts they are reading. Additionally, students are sometimes creating short texts as part of classwork and discussion, and those texts are not assessed formally but serve as formative assessments that provide important information on what students understand. Sometimes students are spending a class period or two creating a text, and you provide a checklist for how they will be assessed.

It is always important to provide students with clear expectations of what you want them to learn and how they will be assessed. Depending on the role the particular assignment plays in a unit and the time involved, the ways in which you formally assess how students have met the content and standards of a unit will vary. For summative assessments at the end of one section of a unit or the end of unit, rubrics are very helpful tools. Constructing rubrics for an assignment with student input is ideal, as the very process of constructing the rubric can be another type of formative assessment; you will gain insight as to what students think is important in their final products. This takes time, however, and it may not always be possible to engage in the process of co-constructing rubrics with students. Regardless, students should always have the rubric available as they work on their compositions.

Students are able to use the criteria outlined on the rubric as they complete their assignment, gaining practice with self-evaluation. You will see samples of rubrics that we used in our upper elementary study of the solar system in Chapter Seven. The rubrics include attention to students' content literacies and the important content goals of the unit.

When teaching with text sets, you can use any and all of the types of formative and summative assessments that you currently use in your classroom. Teaching with text sets allows for such flexibility so you can use the kinds of assessment measures that you prefer to work with, such as teacher- and/or student-created rubrics or checklists for written or constructed texts. You can even create tests and quizzes if your school demands them. When teaching with text sets as part of language arts, you can even use all of the literacy assessments that you have previously relied on to measure individual student reading.

To further explore the possibilities of student-created texts inspired by text sets, let's return to our tree unit. The charts on the following pages show texts selected for our tree exploration and the student-created product options for each subtopic or genre explored.

Trees Text Set: Student Responses to Texts

Subtopics and Genres	Mentor Texts	Student-Created Texts
Subtopic: History of Trees/ Lumber in Your Community	*Giants in the Land* (Appelbaum 1993)	Create a class history of trees in your area Create a tree mural at school or in the community showing the impact of trees over the years on the local economy and the environment
Standards Assessed		
Observe visual sources such as historic paintings, photographs, or illustrations that accompany historical narratives, and describe details such as clothing, setting, or action Describe the difference between a contemporary map of their city or town and the map of their city or town in the 18th, 19th, or early 20th century Give examples of how changes in the environment (drought, cold) have caused some plants and animals to die or move to new locations Write informative/explanatory texts to examine a topic and convey ideas and information clearly		

Trees Text Set: Student Responses to Texts (cont.)

Subtopics and Genres	Mentor Texts	Student-Created Texts
Subtopic: Trees and People as Agents of Local Change	*Mama Miti: Wangari Maathai and the Trees of Kenya* (Napoli 2010) *Planting the Trees of Kenya: The Story of Wangari Maathai* (Nivola 2008) *The Mangrove Tree: Planting Trees to Feed Families* (Roth and Trumbore 2011)	Write and illustrate picture book biographies of people active in preserving the environment in your local community Write a class newspaper on different environmental issues connected to trees and forests in your community, whether you live in a city, suburb, or rural area Write articles about the food webs or food chains in your local community and the ways in which trees are and are not a part of those webs Write public service announcements (e.g., podcasts) to raise both awareness and funds for the initiatives depicted in these books

Standards Assessed

Give examples of how changes in the environment (drought, cold) have caused some plants and animals to die or move to new locations

Give examples of how organisms can cause changes in their environment to ensure survival. Explain how some of these changes may affect the ecosystem

Recognize that plants and animals go through predictable life cycles that include birth, growth, development, reproduction, and death

Describe how energy derived from the sun is used by plants to produce sugars (photosynthesis) and is transferred within a food chain from producers (plants) to consumers to decomposers

Write informative/explanatory texts to examine a topic and convey ideas and information clearly

Write opinion pieces on topics or texts, supporting a point of view with reasons

Describe the relationship between a series of historical events, scientific ideas or concepts, or steps in technical procedures in a text, using language that pertains to time, sequence, and cause/effect

Compare and contrast the most important points and key details presented in two texts on the same topic

Recall information from experiences or gather information from print and digital sources; take brief notes on sources and sort evidence into provided categories

Trees Text Set: Student Responses to Texts *(cont.)*

Subtopics and Genres	Mentor Texts	Student-Created Texts
Subtopic: Different Types of Trees	*Poetrees* (Florian 2010) Audubon Society's *Field Guide to North American Trees* App *Trees, Leaves, and Bark* (Burns 1995) *Tell Me Tree: All About Trees for Kids* (Gibbons 2002)	Create a tree identification guide for your community Create a class book of original tree poems

Standards Assessed

Classify plants and animals according to the physical characteristics that they share

Identify the structures in plants (leaves, roots, flowers, stem, bark, wood) that are responsible for food production, support, water transport, reproduction, growth, and protection

Recognize that plants and animals go through predictable life cycles that include birth, growth, development, reproduction, and death

Differentiate between observed characteristics of plants and animals that are fully inherited (e.g., color of flower, shape of leaves, color of eyes, number of appendages) and characteristics that are affected by the climate or environment (e.g., browning of leaves from too much sun, language spoken)

Write informative/explanatory texts to examine a topic and convey ideas and information clearly

Recall information from experiences or gather information from print and digital sources; take brief notes on sources and sort evidence into provided categories

Trees Text Set: Student Responses to Texts *(cont.)*

Subtopics and Genres	Mentor Texts	Student-Created Texts
Subtopic: Trees Around the World	*Life in the Boreal Forest* (Guiberson 2009) *The Forest in the Clouds* (Collard 2000) *Quest for the Tree Kangaroo* (Montgomery 2006) *Garden of the Spirit Bear: Life in the Great Northern Forest* (Patent 2004) *The Wolves Are Back* (George 2008) *Breakfast in the Rain Forest: A Visit with Mountain Gorillas* (Sobol 2008)	Create 3-D maps of trees on the continents, with the different types of trees on each map projected in a 3-D format and share maps with younger students Create a class survey book on different forest types in different parts of the world Build a class website on different forests in different parts of the world

Standards Assessed

Give examples of how changes in the environment (drought, cold) have caused some plants and animals to die or move to new locations (migration)

Give examples of how organisms can cause changes in their environment to ensure survival. Explain how some of these changes may affect the ecosystem

Describe how energy derived from the sun is used by plants to produce sugars (photosynthesis) and is transferred within a food chain from producers (plants) to consumers to decomposers

Classify plants and animals according to the physical characteristics that they share

Identify the structures in plants (leaves, roots, flowers, stem, bark, wood) that are responsible for food production, support, water transport, reproduction, growth, and protection

Recognize that plants and animals go through predictable life cycles that include birth, growth, development, reproduction, and death

Write informative/explanatory texts to examine a topic and convey ideas and information clearly

With guidance and support from adults, use technology to produce and publish writing (using keyboarding skills) as well as interact and collaborate with others

Trees Text Set: Student Responses to Texts (cont.)

Subtopics and Genres	Mentor Texts	Student-Created Texts
Subtopic: Fictional Neighborhood Trees	*One Day and One Amazing Morning on Orange Street* (Rocklin 2011) *"Three Skinny Trees"* from *The House on Mango Street* (Cisneros 1991)	Create fictional vignettes using trees as metaphors Write memoirs about special places in your own neighborhood or community
Standards Assessed		
Give examples of how organisms can cause changes in their environment to ensure survival. Explain how some of these changes may affect the ecosystem On a map of Massachusetts, locate the class's home town or city and its local geographic features and landmarks		

Subtopics and Genres	Mentor Texts	Student-Created Texts
Genre: Figurative Language in Nonfiction	*Trout Are Made of Trees* (Sayre 2008)	Make life cycle books that use similes, alliteration, rhythm, and rhyme to convey meaning, just as Sayre does in *Trout Are Made of Trees*.
Standards Assessed		
Classify plants and animals according to the physical characteristics that they share Identify the structures in plants (leaves, roots, flowers, stem, bark, wood) that are responsible for food production, support, water transport, reproduction, growth, and protection Recognize that plants and animals go through predictable life cycles that include birth, growth, development, reproduction, and death Write informative/explanatory texts to examine a topic and convey ideas and information clearly		

Trees Text Set: Student Responses to Texts *(cont.)*

Subtopics and Genres	Mentor Texts	Student-Created Texts
Genre: Photo Essays	*Looking Closely Through the Forest* (Serafini 2008) *Quest for the Tree Kangaroo: An Expedition to the Cloud Forest of New Guinea* (Montgomery 2006)	Using digital cameras, create a class book or individual volumes of photo essays on trees, forests, parks, and green spaces in your area (The essay could include the history of those areas and threats to open space in your area. Or, they could be more exploratory in nature, prompting inquiry, such as the Serafini book.) Using digital cameras, create concept books on leaves and trees for a local preschool

Standards Assessed

Classify plants and animals according to the physical characteristics that they share

Identify the structures in plants (leaves, roots, flowers, stem, bark, wood) that are responsible for food production, support, water transport, reproduction, growth, and protection

Recognize that plants and animals go through predictable life cycles that include birth, growth, development, reproduction, and death

Observe visual sources such as historic paintings, photographs, or illustrations that accompany historical narratives, and describe details such as clothing, setting, or action

Describe the difference between a contemporary map of their city or town and the map of their city or town in the 18th, 19th, or early 20th century

Give examples of how changes in the environment (drought, cold) have caused some plants and animals to die or move to new locations

Recall information from experiences or gather information from print and digital sources; take brief notes on sources and sort evidence into provided categories

Summary

This chapter focused on:

- Different ways that students respond to text sets and create new texts
- Note-making strategies that help students access and process information across text sets
- Guiding principles and key questions to guide your assessment design
- The range of possibilities for student-created multimodal, multigenre texts

In Part II of this book, you will have the opportunity to see how all of the steps that we have presented to you in Chapter One through Chapter Five fit together in an actual classroom. First, you will read about elementary classes exploring immigration. Next, you will read about an integrated secondary science and language arts unit.

Reflection Questions

1. How do your students currently demonstrate their understanding of text content? How does note-making allow you to see students' evolving understanding of content?

2. How can the standards be used as tools for creating opportunities for students to express their learning in original multimodal, multigenre texts?

3. How does offering a variety of genres and modalities as assessment options provide your culturally and linguistically diverse students with greater opportunities to demonstrate their content learning?

Part II
Text Sets in Action

Exploring Immigration in Elementary Social Studies

Case Study Background Information

For many years, the focus of the elementary social studies curriculum at the Lance School (a pseudonym) for the first half of the year has been "Coming to America." Typically the unit starts with a study of the seven continents. The team of teachers use the exploration of the continents and the teaching of specific geography skills as tools for studying migrations of prehistoric peoples. This leads into a study of American Indian migrations, specifically the Wampanoag of Massachusetts. After studying the Wampanoag, the students examine the first encounter experience at Plimouth Plantation, which culminates in an annual field trip to the site for the students. The team has been satisfied each year with the students' experiences and feels that they have sufficient texts for the study of the continents, early migrations, and the Wampanoag-Pilgrim encounter.

For the next portion of the "Coming to America" curriculum, the team was seeking out new texts and new ways of exploring the topic in developmentally appropriate ways for young students. In the past, the team jumped from the early colonial period to the intensive period of immigration during the late 19th and early 20th centuries, with a particular focus on immigrants' experiences going through Ellis Island. The immigration portion consisted of a sequence of activities leading up to a simulation experience. Each year, the students listened to the book *Molly's Pilgrim*, watched a video of the book, and made an ancestor doll. At the heart of their immigration study was the students' own ancestry. Often, a parent who was an immigrant came to speak, and the team wanted to keep that important connection to community. The school subscribes to Culture Grams (http://www.culturegrams.com/), a database of print and visual resources on countries, which became the centerpiece of student research. After completing their research, students created posters to teach one another about their cultural heritage. Most of the research was done at school, while the posters were completed at home. Finally, the students also learned a great deal from an Ellis Island simulation in which they were placed in family groups and took on the identities of actual people who went through Ellis Island.

Before we joined them, the team had been wrestling with identifying the primary goals for the unit. Was it to learn about the historic period of immigration in the late 19th and early 20th centuries? Was it to have students connect with their cultural heritage? They had a rich history of instructional activities to draw from and a large span of history to consider. The team wanted to use more nonfiction throughout the school year and saw an expanded use of nonfiction within this unit as a catalyst. Because the grade level has social studies three times a week for 30 minutes, the scope of the immigration unit was typically 10 to 12 lessons over a six- to eight-week period. However, to incorporate new material into the unit, they decided to use other parts of their schedule, including morning meetings and an hour on Thursdays immediately following social studies.

At the start of our mutual planning, the team felt committed to keeping some of those successful activities and was ready to consider changing other content and projects of the unit. They felt that they had many books that worked well as read-alouds for the students but not as many that students could read independently. Virtually all of these books focused on European immigration and the Ellis Island experience. They liked the idea of seeking more texts to expand the unit. Our initial brainstorming sessions also included discussion of student products that would reflect learning from the unit. The poster project had a long history at the school. The team was concerned about changing it since families had grown to expect it as their children moved through the school. But because it was dependent on a great deal of work being done at home, it was more difficult to assess student learning. The team was open to a classroom-based research exploration that could achieve some of the same goals as the poster project.

Starting with Content

Following our initial conversations about the ways the unit has been taught in the past and the possible areas to focus on as we reworked the unit, we focused our conversations on the content of the unit. We realized from the start how very big the topic of immigration is and the many ways in which we could explore it. In the past, during the second half of the year, the team had followed a chronological sequence that began briefly with slavery, transitioned to historic immigration and Ellis Island, and then touched upon contemporary immigration.

Each year, the team wrestled with how to present an immigration narrative to the students that was inclusive of all kinds of immigration, both willing and forced, that occurred in the United States in order to touch upon enslaved people and refugees. In the past, the team had used a Scholastic website to introduce slavery as a forced migration, as they felt an obligation to address it, even though students study it in depth at the secondary level. Yet another possibility was to make the 19th century global slave trade a part of the study of immigration. How to do this in a developmentally appropriate way clearly posed a challenge.

Each year, the teachers also wrestled with how to discuss contemporary immigration, in the context of their focus on the period of tremendous immigration at the turn of the last century, and the Ellis Island experience. In their classes, they often have a combination of students whose families are recent immigrants, students who are adopted from other countries and raised in the United States, students who are first-generation Americans, and some students whose families have lived in New England since the colonial period. No one wanted to give one experience importance over another. Moreover, the team felt that it was problematic to try to link the Ellis Island simulation with every family's history, since not everyone is connected with a country that historically had people traveling through Ellis Island.

Initially, the team considered if it might be important to allow students to choose whether to research a country or their family's immigration experience. This cut into the heart of the content "up for consideration." Should this become a unit in which students learn more about immigration from a country on one of the seven continents that they started the year studying? This would allow the students to extend their understanding of geography, which had been a main emphasis in the social studies curriculum in the first half of the year. Alternatively, if the focus remained more generally on immigration, it became clear that it might be helpful to frame a unit that focused more equally on contemporary and historic immigration than had past iterations of the unit. This would help to reinforce the concept of immigration as ongoing over time and as a current rather than a historical phenomenon.

One way that we considered shaping the content was by focusing on family history. The students could pretend to be someone from their family's past and start individual research into their family's background at the beginning of the unit of study. Students would be placed in continent or regional groups, exploring in general the countries and cultures their ancestors came from. Incorporated into this study would be research on the Ellis Island and Angel Island immigration stations of the 19th and early 20th centuries. Again, the question surfaced: How much should Ellis Island be at the core of the focus? Another question repeated itself: What outcome could be a summative assessment? Is one single summative assessment needed? Rather than the poster project that they have focused on for years, what other kind of assessment could be used to capture the goals of the unit? In organizing the instruction by continent and geography, the following unit questions emerged:

- What do I know about the countries my family came from?

- How did my family get to America?

- Who came and when?

- Where did they go?

- How does this connect to my life now?

This would provide fewer opportunities to focus as a class on contemporary immigration issues, but it would allow the whole unit to focus concurrently on the past and the present and would provide the family connection to which the team felt committed to retaining.

Another way the team considered framing the content was by focusing on different groups of people who came to the United States through force or by choice, and how these groups influenced regional cultures. Students' family histories could be incorporated into this focus, and it would parallel the migration strand that the unit started with in September. The key question that would guide instruction is "Who are we?" We discussed defining who an American is or who a citizen is as a bridge from the Pilgrim unit to the immigration unit. We also considered these questions:

- Why do people leave a country?

- What do immigrants bring with them?

- What of your culture do you keep when you immigrate?

- How do you integrate into American society?

- What do you bring with you into the future?

From this discussion, an overarching question emerged from one of the team members: "How is our classroom like America?" From that question, we refined our guiding questions. After much discussion, the following questions emerged as our finalized guiding questions for the unit:

- Who came to America? When? Why?

- What did people bring to America?

- What is cultural heritage? How do you and how can you connect with your ancestors?

Since students had focused on geography earlier in the year, we tentatively decided to try to organize students' study of these questions with a heavy emphasis on immigration from various parts of the globe. We also reminded ourselves that one pitfall we wanted to avoid was students completing the unit thinking that America is the only place with an integration of cultures when in fact many countries are like this. Keeping all this is mind, we then revisited the state standards to confirm a match between our approach to the content and our state curriculum frameworks for social studies. We also reviewed the Common Core State Standards to identify the standards that we thought the unit could meet. The chart on the following page is the Unit Planning Chart for the unit.

After making these decisions as a team, we agreed to come back with a variety of multimodal, multigenre texts for the team to consider and explore. We had already begun our search for immigration-related texts appropriate for elementary students as read-alouds and independent reads. Our task was to locate as many as possible and provide the team with different text models to consider based on the guiding unit questions. We recognized that the organization of the unit's content would be partially dependent upon the kinds of texts that were available and how well they fit within the guiding questions.

Unit Planning Chart: Coming to America

Unit Name: Coming to America

Unit Length: Eight weeks (social studies lessons three times a week; plus extra time once a week and morning meeting)

Core Vocabulary

immigrate/emigrate, immigrant, Ellis Island, Angel Island, refugee, ancestor, custom, tradition, culture, heritage

Guiding Questions
- Who came to America? When? Why?
- What did people bring to America?
- What is cultural heritage? How do you and how can you connect with your ancestors?

Unit Goals

The students will…
- Understand immigration patterns by making connections to the geography of the continents
- Understand that immigrants have come to the United States in the past and do so in the present for both similar and very different reasons
- Recognize that their own cultural heritage and traditions can originate from many different sources, including the countries where they or members of their family were once born
- Become more fluent in reading, comprehending, and using informational texts for research

State Content Standards

On a map of the world, locate the continent, regions, or countries from which students, their parents, guardians, grandparents, or other relatives or ancestors came; With the help of family members and the school librarian, describe traditional food, customs, sports and games, and music of the place they came from

With the help of the school librarian, give examples of traditions or customs from other countries that can be found in America today

Common Core State Standards

Reading Standards for Literature, PreK–5, Key Ideas and Details, 2.1

Reading Standards for Literature, PreK–5, Integration of Knowledge & Ideas, 2.7

Reading Standards for Informational Text PreK–5, Key Ideas and Details, 2.3

Reading Standards for Informational Text, PreK–5, Integration of Knowledge & Ideas, 2.9

Writing Standards PreK–5, Research to Build and Present Knowledge, 2.7

Writing Standards PreK–5, Research to Build and Present Knowledge, 2.8

Locating Multimodal, Multigenre Resources

Bearing in mind the elementary level reader and thought process, we began a broad search for texts that deal with contemporary as well as historic periods of immigration, using the resources that we identified in Chapter Three.

Books

Many of the fiction and nonfiction picture books that we found were too long for read-alouds and too complex for small-group readings in elementary school. Moreover, we were searching for texts, thinking about the initial learning the elementary students had done on the continents, and trying to find texts that reflected immigration from many continents, not just Europe and Asia. We also knew the team had previously used *Molly's Pilgrim* and *Coming to America: The Story of Immigration*, which could ideally be incorporated into the text set. (*Note:* Bibliographic information for titles mentioned in this chapter can be found in Chapter Nine.)

As we searched, using reviews, the major award lists, and notable trade book lists, two recently published books emerged that seemed particularly ripe for elementary exploration: *All the Way to America* by Yaccarino and *Emma's Poem: The Voice of the Statue of Liberty* by Glaser. *All the Way to America* shares the author's family history, starting with his great-grandfather who emigrated from Italy to New York City and concluding with the author's own family. *Emma's Poem: The Voice of the Statue of Liberty* focuses on Emma Lazarus's work with the immigrant poor of New York in the late 19th century and how her poem, "The Great Colossus," inscribed on the pedestal of the Statue of Liberty, helped turn the statue into a symbol of immigration rather than independence, as originally planned. We thought that *A Picnic in October* by Bunting, about a New York family's annual multigenerational pilgrimage to celebrate the Statue of Liberty's birthday, could be paired with *Emma's Poem: The Voice of the Statue of Liberty* to show how the Statue has been viewed by immigrants over time.

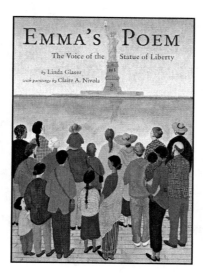

Locating picture books about immigration that focused on Africa, South America, and Asia proved more difficult for us, particularly during our search for titles that elementary students could read independently. Laurence Yep's *The Dragon's Child*, a short historical novel based on the life of the author's grandfather and great-grandfather and their immigration to America at the turn of the 20th century, would work best as a whole class read-aloud, which would not allow time for another read-aloud from another time period or continent. As an alternative, Allen Say's *Grandfather's Journey*, a nonfiction picture book about the author's grandfather's and father's travels to America from Japan, could represent a parallel cycle of immigration and return that Yep wrote of, but in a more compact book that elementary students could read independently. One of the team members suggested *Four Feet, Two Sandals*, a fictional story by Karen Lynn Williams and Khadra Mohammed about refugees in camps on the Afghan-Pakistani border.

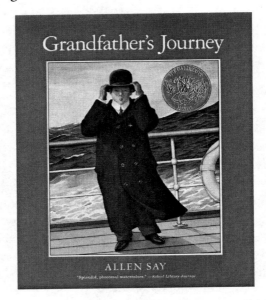

We struggled to find any texts about the forced immigration of Africans during the 18th and 19th century and of the Middle Passage experience. Most nonfiction and historical fiction picture books published in the United States focus on the Underground Railroad and the escape from enslavement. Few tell of the capture and Middle Passage, and none felt appropriate for this grade level. While we were researching, Patricia McKissack's *Never Forgotten* was released. It focuses on the family members that remained in Africa and not those who experienced the forced immigration, and the length and complexity of the language made it more appropriate for the intermediate grades. Books about contemporary immigration, particularly refugee crises, were also hard to find for this audience.

We also did not find any books about historic or contemporary immigration from South America that were appropriate for elementary students. However, Eve Bunting's *How Many Days to America?* provides a general sense of what it could be like for immigrants trying to enter the United States from one of the island nations in the Caribbean.

Digital Texts

To incorporate digital texts into the unit, we again sought texts appropriate for elementary students. Our search through immigration-related websites yielded useful multimodal content. Scholastic's website, *Immigration, Stories of Yesterday and Today*, includes narratives of a Polish immigrant who arrived at Ellis Island as a child in 1920; three contemporary children from Kenya, India, and Vietnam; and a Chinese immigrant who was seven when her family entered America through Angel Island. Additionally, the site includes charts, graphs, and maps that illuminate the story of past and present immigration to America. We were particularly impressed with the rich potential of the interactive tour of Ellis Island included in the site. The tour includes archival audio, videos, and photographs and highlights the various locations and rooms involved in the processes of entry to the United States at this immigration station.

As we looked for resources on contemporary immigration, we were excited to find an online resource that would also serve our content focus on what immigrants bring to America. In 2007, the *Weekend America* series on National Public Radio featured a series of stories titled *Immigration: One Thing* that focused on recent refugee immigrants talking about an object that "they brought with them from their old home to their new." We thought students would be engaged by the podcasts and photographs that accompany these stories. Knowing that we would need to think about how to use this website with our elementary audience, we added it to our list of possibilities.

Organizing Texts for Instruction

With a few books and digital texts identified as good potential material, it was time to start talking about how to use these texts to help students explore the guiding questions. With our geographical focus in mind, we considered the first guiding question: "Who came to America? When? Why?" We also knew that we wanted to keep the third question, "What is cultural heritage? How do you and how can you connect with your ancestors?," as a connecting thread throughout the unit.

Who Came to America? When? Why?

To launch the unit, the teachers chose to retain the use of a text that they had used in the past, *Molly's Pilgrim*. In this historical fiction picture book, Molly's class is making pilgrim dolls at Thanksgiving time. Molly's mother makes her one that looks like her and the class discusses the fact that Molly is a pilgrim because her family immigrated to America for religious freedom. The teachers liked the link that this book provides with their visit to Plimouth Plantation and the celebration of Thanksgiving. Traditionally, teachers had read the book aloud and had students watch a video interpretation of the book. To further expand the conversation around immigration and the significance of immigration in the history of the United States, we suggested pairing this with a more recently published text, *Emma's Poem: The Voice of the Statue of Liberty* using the Duet Model, which asks students to compare and contrast two books with related content. This biography of Emma Lazarus describes the writer's sympathy for the plight of the immigrants that she witnessed pouring into New York City in the late 19th century. The teachers intended to use this pairing of fiction and nonfiction to discuss reasons why people might choose to come to America.

Duet Model: Who Came to America? When? Why?

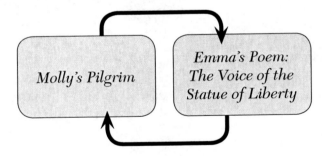

Following this introduction, during weeks two and three of the unit, we expanded our discussion of the question of who, why, and when, by employing a Solar System Model of four core texts with related content, all of which were read aloud initially by the teachers. The four texts were representative of immigration from four different geographical regions. *All the Way to America* by Yaccarino focuses on the experiences of a family whose ancestors emigrated from Europe in the early 20th century. *Grandfather's Journey* by Say tells the story of an immigrant from Asia in the early 20th century. The other two texts focused on more recent immigration. *Four Feet, Two Sandals* by Williams tells the contemporary story of life in an Afghani refugee camp, as a mother and daughter await immigration to America. With this title, we hoped to launch a discussion of why people might choose to leave their country to come to America. For a focus on the Caribbean island nations, we included *How Many Days to America* by Bunting to provide students with a general sense of why and how people might choose to come to America from this region during the 1980s; the book itself never names the country from which the family flees.

Solar System Model: Who Came to America? When? Why?

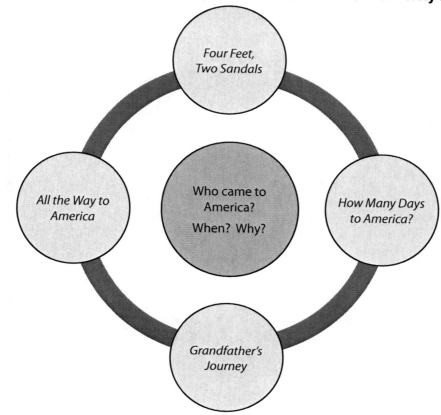

To further extend the focus on immigration to America from different regions of the globe, we felt at this point a need to seek out additional texts that could be used by the students in small-group work. The model that we used then became a Solar System Model with Duet Model pairings. The purpose was to engage students in a deeper look at why people came from different places by comparing the information found in two books. Students would reread and revisit the books that had been read aloud by the teachers and would read together a second geographically related title.

While this made great sense in theory, we discovered that by having such a specific focus on geography, we created a major challenge in locating age-appropriate texts. A search for four more texts, print or digital, that could be read independently by elementary students yielded books about Asia and Europe but left us empty-handed for the Caribbean and the Middle East. We had to take a different path. We instead chose books that focused on those regions that highlighted reasons why people might choose to leave those locations. To pair with *Four Feet, Two Sandals*, we identified *Nasreen's Secret School* by Winter, a nonfiction title that describes life in Afghanistan under Taliban rule through the story of Nasreen, a young girl whose parents have been taken away by the Taliban. To pair with *How Many Days to America* we identified the title *Josias, Hold the Book* by Elvgren, a fictional title emphasizing the hardships of life in Haiti. To pair with the two titles focusing on historical immigration from Europe and Asia—*All the Way to America* and *Grandfather's Journey*—we selected two nonfiction series titles written by Lori Mortensen, *Ellis Island* and *Angel Island*, that focus on those respective immigration stations. These survey texts included lists of countries from which people arrived at the immigration centers and reasons that they might have left their native countries.

Solar System Model with Duet Pairings

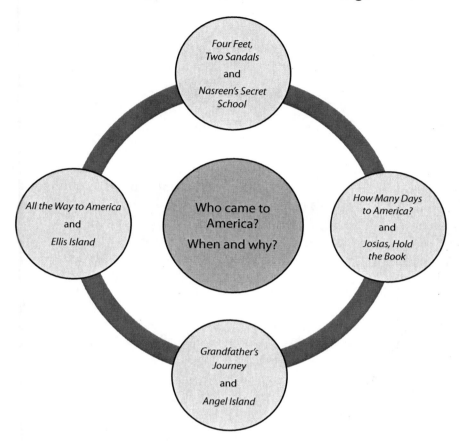

What Did People Bring to America?

In weeks four and five of the unit, we focused on the next guiding question: "What did people bring to America?" To accomplish this, we once again decided to employ the Solar System Model. At this point, we went back to the list of immigration resources that we were developing and selected titles that included discussion of a special object that traveled with an immigrant on the journey to America. In this instance, we looked for titles that would work well as whole class read-alouds in order to foster whole-class discussion.

The team began this phase of the unit by revisiting the titles previously read to identify items brought to America. The teachers then read aloud three new books, each highlighting the literal and figurative significance of an artifact brought to America. In *Annushka's Voyage* by Tarbescu, the Sabbath candlesticks given to her by her grandmother help Annushka and her sister to find each other when they are separated in the crowds at Ellis Island. Grisha, whose story is featured in *The Memory Coat* by Woodruff, refuses to leave behind a tattered coat that is lined with a woolen coat that had belonged to his mother. In *When Jesse Came Across the Sea* by Hest, the object of significance is a wedding ring that belonged to Jesse's mother.

In this Solar System Model, we also chose to incorporate the digital texts that we had identified. To complement the historical titles with a contemporary perspective, we decided to use the digital texts found in *Immigration: One Thing*, the National Public Radio series described previously that featured interviews with refugees and highlighted "one thing" they brought with them to America. To make this content most accessible for elementary students, we decided to use only the photographs and to create paragraph-long summaries describing the objects brought by featured families and individuals. The team made laminated cards of the photos and descriptions and shared them with the students in this format.

As a link to the upcoming Ellis Island simulation that had traditionally been part of the elementary unit, we also included Scholastic's website, *Immigration, Stories of Yesterday and Today*, specifically the Ellis Island interactive tour described previously. The tour allowed students to walk virtually through the sections of the station, reading and hearing about all of the different stops. Additionally, students watched the videos incorporated into the tour. Here, they studied how people were dressed and what they carried, and through this examination they were able to get a sense of the crowds and chaos. This multimedia exploration would serve to scaffold the living text experience of the simulation.

Solar System Model: What Did People Bring to America?

The final week of the unit focused on the Ellis Island simulation, student production of texts, and a cultural heritage celebration to which families were invited. In the next section, we will discuss how students responded to the texts they read and the texts that students created throughout the unit.

Student Responses to Texts

The question of what kinds of texts students would produce to demonstrate their understandings in relation to the guiding questions of the unit dominated our early planning discussions. In the past, students had produced posters that presented a country of origin in their own family history. As the questions of the unit evolved, however, the teachers decided to change the final product that students would produce.

Because the unit would have a dual focus, with students learning about the history of immigration to the United States and about their own family backgrounds, the teachers decided to have students create an America Trunk that would serve as a learning portfolio for the unit. The trunk would be a physical repository for all the written products that students would produce during the unit and would be shared with families at the Cultural Heritage Festival, traditionally a culminating activity for the unit of study that takes place during the last day of school before the December break. Students had the opportunity to select the boxes that would become their America Trunk and decorate them so that they looked like traveling cases. As students finished pieces of work, they placed them in the trunks so that by the end of the six-week unit, they were full of the thinking, writing, and art that students had done in response to their listening, watching, and reading.

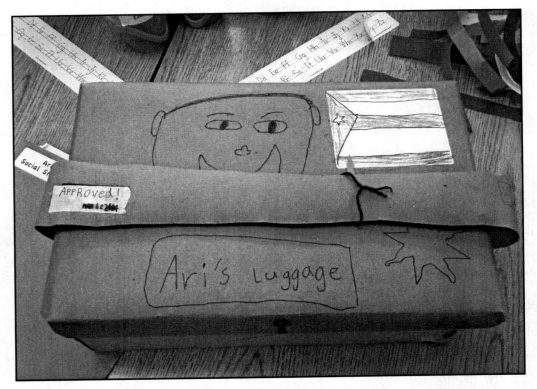

Many student trunks featured the flag of their country of ancestry

In response to the paired reading of *Molly's Pilgrim* and *Emma's Poem* with which teachers had begun the unit, student discussions and written responses focused generally on what it means to be an immigrant and why people might choose to come to the United States. Teachers recorded students' responses to these books on large chart paper, in some cases using Venn diagrams to compare and contrast the texts. Students were also encouraged to make personal connections to the texts.

Weeks One through Three: Who Came to America? When? Why?

During these introductory weeks, students also began the process of learning more about their own families' histories with immigration. Teachers sent home a "Cultural Heritage Questionnaire" that asked:

1. Does your family know where some or all of your relatives/ancestors came from? (Please list known relations and their countries of origin below.)

2. When did these relatives/ancestors come to America? (Exact years, time spans, or educated guesses are all encouraged.)

3. What is one interesting thing you could share with the class about your family that you learned from talking to your parents?

Students had the opportunity to share with their classmates the conversation that they had with their parents. Together, the class worked to make a composite map of the countries of origin represented in their family stories. In each classroom, a large world map was posted on a bulletin board. Students illustrated index cards that featured the names of their relatives/ancestors, and these cards were placed on or next to the countries of origin.

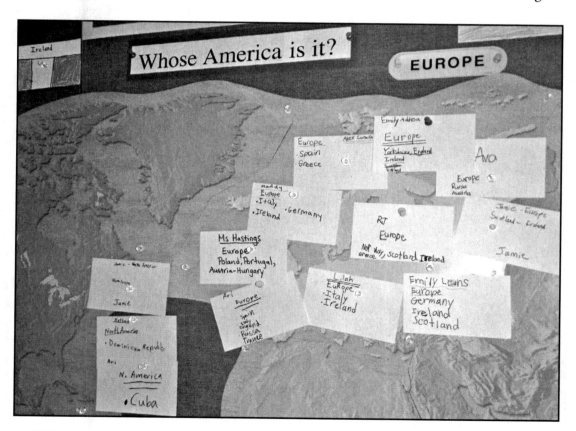

This map provided a great visual model of some of the many countries and cultural backgrounds represented in the class

Focusing on the questions "Who came to America? When? Why?," students worked with the Solar System Model with Duet Pairings of texts that focused on different geographical regions (see page 133). During the initial teacher read-alouds, the teachers guided students to think about who emigrated, from what country, and why, and recorded this information on chart paper. Following this, students worked in small groups; each group was responsible for a geographical pairing. As they read and reread the titles together, the groups worked to record information on two graphic organizers. The groups were asked to use the information from the two books along with some additional online research to create a written product to share with their classmates. The product would be in the form of a poster, a short picture book, or a newspaper that would convey information about immigration to the United States from that region, focusing on reasons why people might have chosen to come to America from that area during particular time periods. The students completed the Coming to America Notes (pages 139–142) for each book they read and the Coming to America Project Planner (page 143) to help them plan their presentations.

Coming to America Student Work Samples

Coming to America: Who Came and Why?
Book One

Names _____

Continent of investigation: __Asia__

Book being used for investigation: __Four Feet two Sandals__

In the book you are reading:

Who immigrates? __Lina, Najiib, Ismatu, and Lina's mom__

From **what country** are they emigrating? __Afghanistan__

Why are they immigrating? List some reasons below and the evidence from the book.

Why?	Evidence from Book (words or pictures)
for a betr life.	they were poor and needed clothes
girls need to go to school.	there was only enough room for the boys.
There was a war in Afghanistan.	It said sc.

11/16/11 MAC

When did they immigrate? Examine the illustrations. List some things you notice (*food, clothing, vehicles, buildings, toys*) that might tell you something about **when** the immigrants were leaving their country.

What We Noticed	Does it look like that now?
C 2007 There was 2000	This hap'n 4 years ago refugees worldwide

What's new? List **new vocabulary** words you noticed in the book. What might they mean?

Word	Possible Meaning
Kind	because they shared the sandles
Poor	they didn't have any more

11/16/11 MAC

Date _____

Coming to America Notes

Group Names: _____

_____

Continent of investigation: _____

Books being used for investigation: _____

_____

_____

_____

In the book you are reading:

Who immigrates? _____

_____

From **what country** are they emigrating? _____

_____

Coming to America Notes (cont.)

Why are they immigrating? List some reasons below and the evidence from the book.

Why?	Evidence from Book (words or pictures)

Coming to America Notes *(cont.)*

When did they immigrate? Examine the illustrations. List some things you notice (food, clothing, vehicles, buildings, toys) that might tell you something about when the immigrants were leaving their country.

What We Noticed	Does it look like that now?

Coming to America Notes (cont.)

What's new? List **new vocabulary** words you noticed in the book. What might they mean?

Word	Possible Meaning

Name_____ Date _____

Coming to America Project Planner

Goal: Your group needs to decide on a project that will show the rest of the class what you have learned about some of the people who immigrated to the United States from the country you are investigating.

Please create one of the following:

- newspaper page
- short picture book
- poster

Directions:

1. As a group, decide what you will create.

2. Read your notes from the two books you read. What is the most important information to share?

   Make sure to include the following information:

   - What continent and country are people emigrating from?
   - Why might they be leaving? What is the evidence?
   - What time period might it be, based on the things you noticed in the illustrations?

3. Remember that your newspaper, picture book, or poster should have words and pictures. You may also want to include a map.

Most groups opted to produce a poster demonstrating what they had learned about the project. The posters included graphics such as charts and maps, illustrations, and blocks of text.

This poster focuses on immigration from Caribbean nations

As a way to consider some of the questions that would be explored during the next portion of the unit, which focused on the question "What did people bring to America?," we designed a series of questions for students to ask relatives attending the school's pre-Thanksgiving Visiting Day. The timing of the Thanksgiving holiday and the school's tradition of Visiting Day provided an opportunity for students to share their exploration in the first part of the unit and transition into the second part, and a consideration of some of the ways in which artifacts or traditions from their families' countries of origin might continue to shape how they eat, celebrate, and share time with family and friends. Special family artifacts may only be used for religious holidays or special meals, and these artifacts might also reveal important stories about recent or ancestral immigration. In their interviews, students asked their relatives the following questions:

- What is your favorite family tradition? When did it start? Do you know how it started?

- What is your favorite family food? When did your family start making it? Is it only served on holidays and special occasions? Why or why not?

- Is there something special in your house that came from one of your ancestors? What is it? Why do you have it now? Where did it come from?

Weeks Four and Five: What Did People Bring to America?

During the next two weeks, the teachers and students focused on the question of what immigrants brought to America and began preparing for the Ellis Island simulation. Since all of the texts in the Solar System Models (see page 133 and page 135) featured objects of significance brought from one country to another, the teachers created a Book Comparison Chart (page 146) for students to complete as they read aloud each text.

We wondered if students would be able to discuss both the concrete and abstract significance of the objects identified in these stories, and their conversations revealed that, in fact, they could.

The student-created texts in this portion of the unit involved personal reflections. Students were asked to consider what they would bring with them if they were immigrating to a new country. As a homework assignment, students selected an item that they would bring with them and completed a note-making form that asked them to identify their item and their reasons for selecting it. Students were asked to bring either the actual item or something representing the item, like a photograph, to school to present to their classmates. Students clearly enjoyed the opportunity to share their artifact with their classmates. Their oral presentations explaining their rationale were thoughtful, revealing that they truly understood the significance of taking a piece of an old home along with them to a new one. Following their oral presentations, students drew a picture of their item and wrote a long narrative describing the item and their rationale for taking it to their new country. Teachers took a photo of each student with his or her artifact, and these were placed in the America Trunk along with their descriptions.

Name _____

Date _____

Book Comparison Chart

Directions: Record information from the books that you read in the chart below.

Book Title	Who came to America?	When did they come?	Why did they come?	What did they bring?

 #50688: *Teaching with Text Sets*

Some students brought in personal items such as stuffed animals or toys. Others brought items given to them by other members of the family. One student brought a ring that belonged to his great-grandfather in Pakistan; another brought in Chinese money, a souvenir from a family trip to China, his family's country of origin. Another student brought in baby shoes from Spain, which three generations of her family have worn in their infancy. Several students wrote about baptismal gowns, and one wrote about a military uniform. Another student wrote about his grandfather's clam chowder and the secret ingredient that makes it so good (he only uses clams he has dug up himself!). The students' oral presentations of these precious items expressed great family pride.

One student begins to write about his grandfather's World War II navy jacket

At the end of the fifth week of the unit, students participated in the Ellis Island simulation. Their reading of the online texts in the interactive tour of Ellis Island had prepared them to be part of family groups moving through Ellis Island and experience each step of the process. Students came dressed in costumes and were expected to remain in the role of their family member throughout their medical examinations, entrance interview, a lesson in the Pledge of Allegiance, money exchange, and consumption of sustenance before the next leg of their journey. Teachers, administrators, and staff members who were also in character helped make the experience a living interactive text for the students.

Following the immersion, students were asked to write from the perspective of the family member that they had been assigned. Their narratives indicated that the simulation allowed the students to empathize with the emotions that immigrants arriving at Ellis Island may have experienced. Here are a few of their stories. *Note:* The narratives have been edited to reflect conventional spelling, but the content is original.

> *My name is Liza von Allsburg and I am 10 years old. The trickiest part was your check-up for your health. My whole family was worried….The things in the places were a check-up on your health and the Pledge of Allegiance. There was also a place where you get a snack. When I went through the progress (sic) I was worried because me and the rest of my family did not want to go back to Austria because there was a war. And people were dying.*

> *My name is Sylvia. I am 54 years old. The year when I went through Ellis Island was in the 1900s. I was scared because I was leaving home for the first time. When I saw the Statue of Liberty I knew we were almost there. I lived in Turkey. When I saw a banana I did not now what it was. I liked snack because it was free and yummy. When I went into the medical room I was scared because I did not know if I would pass. My dad was there for me so I do not get lost.*

> *August 26, 1900. We just got through Ellis Island. My name is Petra Steffansan. I am 28 years old. It was scary 'cause I almost got sent back with my husband. But he did not get sent back and I didn't get sent back either. The doctor put an L on my back and an E on my husband's back. At the next station there were two Guys they asked our family lots of questions. Then we got to the last station there were two Girls and they gave us our money for America then the next girl gave us our ticket for the ferry ride."*

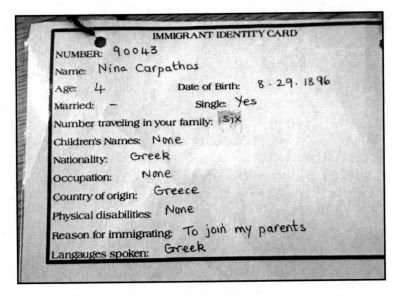

Each participant had an identity card for the simulation

The America Trunk Student Work Sample

The America Trunk

I brought a book with three pictures, my brother, sister and me. It reminds me of them, when I look at it.

Week Six: What Is Cultural Heritage? How Do You and How Can You Connect with Your Ancestors?

During the final week of the unit, students spent time making sure they had completed the items to be placed in their America Trunk so that they could be shared with their guests at the Cultural Heritage Festival. The written products that they created throughout the unit were carefully placed in the decorated trunks. The texts that they read throughout the unit were easily accessible on book display shelves or propped on the shelves along the perimeter of the room ready for families to peruse. Students and their families selected and prepared a food dish of personal significance to share with their classmates and their families on Cultural Heritage Day.

Review of Student-Created Texts

Throughout our planning process for student responses to text and student construction of texts, we were mindful of our initial Unit Planning Chart that outlined the social studies standards and Common Core State Standards that we were hoping to meet. This chart summarizes the unit.

Immigration Text Set: Student Responses to Texts

Guiding Questions	Model and Texts	Responses to Texts	Student-Created Texts
Who came to America? When? Why?	Duet Model: *Molly's Pilgrim* (Cohen 1983) *Emma's Poem* (Glaser 2010)	Charts and Venn diagrams comparing the texts	Map representing students' families' countries of origin
Standards			
On a map of the world, locate the continent, regions, or countries from which students, their parents, guardians, grandparents, or other relatives or ancestors came; With the help of family members and the school librarian, describe traditional food, customs, sports and games, and music of the place they came from Reading Standards for Literature, PreK–5, Key Ideas and Details, 2.1 (CCSS) Reading Standards for Literature, PreK–5, Integration of Knowledge & Ideas, 2.7 (CCSS) Reading Standards for Informational Text, PreK–5, Integration of Knowledge & Ideas, 2.9 (CCSS) Writing Standards PreK–5, Research to Build and Present Knowledge, 2.8 (CCSS)			

Immigration Text Set: Student Responses to Texts *(cont.)*

Guiding Questions	Model and Texts	Responses to Texts	Student-Created Texts
Who came to America? When? Why?	Solar System Model: *All the Way to America* (Yaccarino 2011) *Four Feet, Two Sandals* (Williams 2007) *How Many Days to America?* (Bunting 1998) *Grandfather's Journey* (Say 1993) Respective Duet Pairings: *Ellis Island* (Mortensen 2009) *Nasreen's Secret School* (Winter 2009) *Josias, Hold the Book* (Elvgren 2006) *Angel Island* (Mortensen 2009)*	Note-making form for each text	Poster, book, or newspaper describing immigration from a particular geographic region
Standards			

Reading Standards for Literature, PreK–5, Key Ideas and Details, 2.1 (CCSS)

Reading Standards for Literature, PreK–5, Integration of Knowledge & Ideas, 2.7 (CCSS)

Reading Standards for Informational Text PreK–5, Key Ideas and Details, 2.3 (CCSS)

Reading Standards for Informational Text, PreK–5, Integration of Knowledge & Ideas, 2.9 (CCSS)

Writing Standards PreK–5, Research to Build and Present Knowledge, 2.7 (CCSS)

Guiding Questions	Model and Texts	Responses to Texts	Student-Created Texts
What did people bring to America? What is cultural heritage? How do you and how can you connect with your ancestors?	Family conversations	Family questionnaire	America trunks Visiting Day interviews
Standards			

On a map of the world, locate the continent, regions, or countries from which students, their parents, guardians, grandparents, or other relatives or ancestors came. With the help of family members and the school librarian, describe traditional food, customs, sports and games, and music of the place they came from

With the help of the school librarian, give examples of traditions or customs from other countries that can be found in America today

Writing Standards PreK–5, Research to Build and Present Knowledge, 2.8 (CCSS)

Immigration Text Set: Student Responses to Texts *(cont.)*

Guiding Questions	Model and Texts	Responses to Texts	Student-Created Texts
What did people bring to America?	Solar System Model: *The Memory Coat* (Woodruff 1999) *Annushka's Voyage* (Tarbescu 1998) *When Jesse Came Across the Sea* (Hest 1997) *Immigration: Stories of Yesterday and Today* (Scholastic website) *Immigration: One Thing* (audio from NPR website)	Note-making form: Comparison chart	Artifact presentation and writing describing what they would bring with them if they were immigrating to another country

Standards
Reading Standards for Literature, PreK–5, Key Ideas and Details, 2.1 (CCSS)
Reading Standards for Literature, PreK–5, Integration of Knowledge & Ideas, 2.7 (CCSS)
Reading Standards for Informational Text PreK–5, Key Ideas and Details, 2.3 (CCSS)
Reading Standards for Informational Text, PreK–5, Integration of Knowledge & Ideas, 2.9 (CCSS)
Writing Standards PreK–5, Research to Build and Present Knowledge, 2.8 (CCSS)

Note: Bibliographic information for titles and websites listed in this chart can be found in the Immigration Text Set in Chapter Nine.

Teacher Reflections on Teaching with Text Sets

Once the unit was finished, we asked the team their thoughts on teaching a revised version of the immigration unit using text sets as a primary tool for learning. One teacher responded that the ongoing and recursive reading, writing, speaking, listening, and viewing put students into the position of "owning the information" in a way that she had not witnessed before. Because students had to grapple with making connections across texts, time periods, and cultures, they were invested in their learning. This led to what another teacher described as a "connection-rich" experience in which students were moving fluidly between their own lives and experiences and the lives of others as well as monitoring their own thinking on the subject of immigration as they explored different texts and text types. The team emphasized the strength of the multigenre focus and how reading and rereading fiction and nonfiction throughout the unit allowed for deeper engagement with and understanding of the texts and the content they conveyed.

Additionally, the team saw that the use of multimodal texts led to yet another level of engagement and inquiry. The Ellis Island simulation was successful because students could draw on what they saw and heard in the Scholastic virtual tour they took in a whole class session as well as at listening centers. Additionally, the examination of photographs allowed students to consider contemporary and historic immigration more closely.

There is still more work to be done in revising the unit for the future. The question of how to address forced immigration within the unit still remains, particularly in the context of 19th century African enslavement and the Middle Passage. We still have not found the ideal developmentally appropriate text. Perhaps it is a book that has yet to be written, or an article in a children's magazine we have yet to find in the digital databases. It remains our collective goal. During the first part of the unit, we all noticed that students struggled to extract the information from *Josias, Hold the Book* and *Nasreen's Secret School* in order to compare and contrast it to the information in *How Many Days to America?* and *Four Feet, Two Sandals*. While both books offer important information on why someone would want to leave a country, there was not a direct connection for the students, as neither one involved immigration. Revising the graphic organizer or creating a separate organizer for these two books would make sense in the future. We also are aware that few books are published about immigrants from South America; we will continue to look for books that could expand the geographical focus of the immigration exploration.

Creating the America Trunks, sharing the items and work that students put into them throughout the unit, celebrating the trunks on Cultural Heritage Day, and then displaying them in the school library allowed for students' private thinking throughout the unit to be made public in concrete ways. One team member suggested that the America Trunks and all they contained revealed a "less polished, but more kid-friendly" version of the unit; another believed "they will remember so much more" from it because the kids made so many decisions themselves. Finally, one team member shared that a former student passed the display in the school library, and instead of asking where the traditional family history posters were, asked, "Hey, how come we didn't get to do that?"

Our Reflections on the Unit

We are always working to refine our ideas about teaching with text sets. Working with the teachers and students in these elementary classrooms provided us with an opportunity to deeply consider not only the depth of content that students at that age can grapple with, but also the difficulty in finding texts that meet content goals and that newly independent readers can access without adult support that meet content goals.

At the time, we felt surprised by how long it took us to arrive at a shared vision of the content of the unit. In retrospect, this is not at all surprising. As curriculum designers, we have a wide array of choices in front of us. A rich content focus naturally contains many options for focusing and organizing a unit of study. We needed to engage fully in the process of considering all of the content permutations with the team members so that we could carefully consider the benefits and limitations of alternative approaches. We do this all the time as teachers, making decisions about what content to include, what to leave out, and how best to teach and assess the content we identify as our focus. Considering all of our options allows us to make the best choices for our students. While it may seem more expedient to do unit planning independently, a clear benefit of team planning is the opportunity it affords for multiple perspectives on how to organize and teach content. In other words, even though it was hard, it was worth it! If you are not able to work with a grade level team, we highly recommend that you seek out a curriculum design buddy at your school or through connections that you make through involvement with a local professional organization.

We were also forced to think more deeply about the relationship between content focus and available resources. We did not find "perfect texts" that focus on slavery at the elementary level and provide a geographical look at immigration across history. Our inability to locate these resources highlights a tension in teaching with text sets. Although we recommend thorough content planning before you seek out multimodal, multigenre texts to expand or create your unit, you need to be prepared to make adjustments if you cannot find a "just right" text for your purposes. Sometimes, it might mean seeking out a digital text instead of a children's book, but other times, even a review of the digital resources leaves you empty handed. You may need to rethink your content organization. We made it work for these teachers by including books that were tangentially related to the content focus, but it might have made more sense to take another approach. Moving forward, the team remains "on the lookout" for new fiction and nonfiction that can fill in those gaps. This is a reminder that teaching with text sets is always a work in progress. The continual process of learning by doing and refining our ideas after we try them out is one of the things we love most about teaching.

In Chapter Seven, we will give you a second example of text sets in action as we describe a unit of study on the solar system in an urban secondary classroom.

Reflection Questions

1. How does reading about a specific elementary experience of teaching with text sets provide you with a deeper understanding of the benefits of teaching with text sets?

2. What new ideas did you generate in relation to your own teaching practices while reading this chapter?

3. After reading about this unit of study, what do you see as some of the challenges and opportunities of teaching with text sets?

#50688: Teaching with Text Sets

Exploring the Solar System in Middle School

One thing is for certain, the more profoundly baffled you have been in your life, the more open your mind becomes to new ideas.

—deGrasse Tyson (2007, 305)

How do you look at the world? How does the world look through your lens? If you are scientifically literate, the world looks very different to you…. If you are not scientifically literate, you are in a way disenfranchising yourself from the democratic process and you don't even know it.

—deGrasse Tyson (2009b)

Case Study Background Information

When given the opportunity to help a teacher named Catherine in an urban district to plan a new unit on the solar system, we jumped at the chance to assist in planning curriculum grounded in the notion of scientific literacy and poised to take advantage of the ever-expanding body of research. While undergoing the initial planning stages of the unit, knowledge seemed to grow day by day. Discoveries related to the solar system and the universe continued to appear in newspapers, on television, and on the radio. New companies promoting space tourism were discussed; there were ongoing solar flares and solar tornadoes. On December 5, 2011, NASA announced the discovery of Kepler-22b, the most Earth-like planet to date, located within a "habitable" zone near a star like our sun.

Kepler-22b falls within a "Goldilocks Zone," a term scientists apply to areas of the universe that are not too hot, not too cold, but "just right" for life as we know and understand it. On the CBS *Early Show* on December 6, 2011, astrophysicist Neil deGrasse Tyson, Director of the Hayden Planetarium of the American Museum of Natural History, not only distinguished why the discovery was important but also he used it to frame the research strategy moving forward, suggesting that scientists would "build the catalogue of these planets that could have life," and use that data to "have a second round of observations to try to see if the atmosphere has bio-markers for thriving life on its surface." Tyson suggested, "If you ever have the chance to go somewhere or to target telescopes to listen for intelligent life, those will be at the top of the list" (Tyson 2011).

Neil deGrasse Tyson is one of the most visible faces of science in popular culture. As the host of the PBS show *Nova scienceNOW* as well as a frequent guest on news programs and talk shows, he captures complex thinking in ways that the general public can understand. In these appearances, Tyson models scientific literacy by posing questions, establishing categories of information, framing research strategies, and making connections between prior knowledge and new knowledge. We agree with Tyson that "[i]f you are scientifically literate, the world looks very different to you" (Tyson 2009a). Students need to understand how to *do* science, how to ask questions, consider theories, and be consumers and producers of research through their own experiments. They should not be simply memorizing facts for the purpose of standardized tests because those facts are changing all the time. Being scientifically literate does not mean you merely read science competently. It may include reading, but it is also involves knowing how to talk about science, how to ask and answer questions, and knowing enough of the vocabulary to participate in the conversation. In assisting in planning the upper elementary solar system curriculum, we wanted to bolster students' ability to be scientifically literate and pose and answer questions about our solar system. We recognized that a student-centered study might cause the students to be "profoundly baffled" at times. However, like Tyson, we agree that, "the more profoundly baffled you have been in your life, the more open your mind becomes to new ideas" (Tyson 2007, 305). We want to give students more opportunities to be baffled!

Starting with Content

Given all that was unfolding around us in the news, we started planning our unit with a keen awareness of the changing nature of knowledge about the universe and the solar system. It was Catherine's first year teaching the solar system, and she was awaiting word from her district on the exact state standards that she would be expected to address. As the first year in a new sequence for the science curriculum, much was in flux. We decided to frame our exploration of the topic widely at first in order to narrow it down as the district standards were selected. From there, our strategy was to use the new content information each of us had learned to frame a study that included, but perhaps went beyond, the content required. Catherine welcomed the opportunity to fuse the science unit with language arts and create an extended unit of study that would encompass the reading, writing, and science portions of her curriculum, including her weekly poetry workshop on Fridays. Concurrent with her space unit, the district expected that students would be writing feature articles for writing workshop. It was an ideal fusion of curriculum because students could learn specific information and theories in small groups while studying the solar system collectively and then use what they learned for more specialized individual research in order to write their feature articles.

In addition to regularly reading newspapers and listening to television and radio news about space exploration, we needed to read more about current ideas and research on the solar system beyond what we might find in children's and young adult nonfiction. In addition to reading online newspaper articles, websites such as the American Museum of Natural History's Rose Center (http://www.ny.com/museums/rosecenter.html) and the Hayden Planetarium (http://www.haydenplanetarium.org), and tablet apps, such as NASA's, we read Neil deGrasse Tyson's *The Pluto Files: The Rise and Fall of America's Favorite Planet* (2009). (It was an easy read where complex science was broken down and translated for the general public.) Developing our background knowledge was absolutely critical, as it shaped and developed our approach to the unit of study. Prior to this, each of us considered Pluto's "demotion" as a planet to be synonymous with "Pluto is not a planet." However, this is not the case, according to current scientific thinking. Pluto very much is a planet; it is a dwarf planet, a different category of planet from the eight current classical planets. We also learned the ways in which the scientific community admits that it has not yet captured a full definition of what constitutes a planet, that scientists classify the solar system by regions, and that each region has particular attributes.

We remember memorizing the planets in order of their distance from the sun in our elementary classes in the 1970s. We didn't want to replicate that planet-by-planet study of the solar system. Instead, we wanted to use the content literacy of the field, which frames the discussion in terms of planetary neighborhoods. Mercury, Venus, Earth, and Mars are all considered terrestrial planets because they all share similar rocky features. The next neighborhood in the solar system is the asteroid belt, composed of chunks of matter that were not formed into planets. Within the asteroid belt is Ceres, which was named a planet in 1801, deemed an asteroid in the mid-19th century, and, like Pluto, assigned dwarf planet status in 2006. Next come the gas giants, Jupiter, Saturn, Uranus, and Neptune, so called because they are comprised of gases; like the sun, there is no solid surface to them. Finally, we have the Kuiper Belt. Within the Kuiper Belt are a number of dwarf planets, including our old friend Pluto. Without this research, we might have replicated the old conversation about the planets—that there were nine and now there are eight—rather than the more important conversation, which is that each region of the solar system has particular qualities that scientists are learning more about all the time.

Ultimately, Catherine was given a few key state science standards to focus on in the space unit, all of which are limited to studying the solar system:

- Recognize that Earth is part of a system called the solar system, which includes the sun (a star), planets, and many moons; Earth is the third planet from the sun in our solar system

- Recognize that Earth revolves around (orbits) the sun in a year's time and that Earth rotates on its axis once approximately every 24 hours; Make connections between the rotation of Earth and day/night, and the apparent movement of the sun, moon, and stars across the sky

- Describe the changes that occur in the observable shape of the moon over the course of a month

Specifically, the district selected three guiding questions to consider:

1. What are the relationships between objects in our solar system?

2. How do these relationships impact our experiences on Earth?

3. How does the moon appear to change shape in the sky?

We considered these standards and guiding questions to be broad enough to give us some latitude with our exploration but precise enough that they could guide specific portions of the unit. In this case, since we were already doing a great deal of reading about the solar system while we waited for district guidance on the content, our knowledge of the available texts greatly influenced our content planning. We met with Catherine to outline several directions for the unit. We discussed the following options for content-focused progressions:

- Start locally with Earth, move to the moon, and then out into the solar system.

- Start globally with the solar system and work our way down to Earth and its moon.

- Start with the moon and what students can observe, use those observations/changes to consider Earth's role in the solar system (day and night, months, and seasons), and then expand the exploration further to other parts of the solar system.

- Start with the moon and what students can observe, and use that to explore how people have explained moon-related phenomenon over time. This would start with myths, legends, *porquoi* tales, and creation tales. It would then move into what scientists have thought about the universe over time, eventually focusing the discussion on the details of the solar system. This approach would incorporate a more detailed look at how new theories and new technologies are changing the way we view and define the solar system.

Catherine felt that starting with a global focus on the solar system followed by a look at Earth's place in the solar system was most logical for her students. With this broad structure chosen, we moved into a conversation about the district requirements and our desire to extend these standards by emphasizing current scientific inquiry in the field. Catherine shared with us sample questions from past state science tests, and we were confident that students would be able to answer similar questions while simultaneously gaining a broad perspective on how the field changes over time as new discoveries are made. We also knew that we wanted to integrate the language arts curriculum requirement of writing feature articles into the unit. Catherine values student choice in writing projects and wanted her students to be able to choose any solar system related topic that interested them as the subject for their feature articles. We considered which content students needed to know to meet the given standards and how to move into individualized student research in connection with feature article writing.

With all this in mind, we decided on three components for the unit:

1. **Whole-group knowledge-building**

   • Whole-group experiences focusing on the state science content standards

2. **Expert group work**

   • Small-group work extending students' knowledge of topics introduced in whole-group experiences

   • Small groups presenting expert group work to classmates

3. **Writing feature articles**

   • Studying the qualities of good nonfiction writing in mentor texts

   • Reading feature articles as mentor texts

   • Writing their own feature articles

Additionally, to help us to keep track of our expanded unit goals and the content standards that we wanted to meet, we constructed the Unit Planning Chart shown on page 163.

Unit Planning Chart: Exploring the Solar System

Unit Name: Exploring the Solar System

Unit Length: 6 weeks

Core Vocabulary: (giant brainstorm of words from readings; to be narrowed down)

asteroid, atmosphere, axis, comet, day, density, dwarf planets, full moon, galaxy, gas giants, geocentric, gibbous moon, gravity, heliocentric, meteorite, nebula, new moon, orbit, poles, Prime Meridian, quarter moon, revolve/revolution, rotate/rotation, solar system, star, terrestrial planets, universe, vapor (gas), waning moon, waxing moon, year

Guiding Questions

- What are the relationships between objects in our solar system?
- How do these relationships impact our experiences on Earth?
- How and why does the moon appear to change shape in the sky?

Unit Goals

The students will...

- Understand what are the celestial objects that compose the solar system
- Understand how and why Earth orbits around the sun and rotates on its axis and the result of those movements in terms of day/night, seasons, and location of the sun/moon in the sky
- Record and identify the moon's phases and talk about them
- Describe how our knowledge of the solar system is constantly changing from new discoveries/technologies by exploring previously held theories
- Become experts on some aspect of the solar system and share that knowledge with classmates in order to construct a deeper understanding
- Become more capable writers of informational text, using the various texts they read as mentor texts for their own writing, culminating in feature articles and other associated texts and presentations

State Content Standards

Recognize that Earth is part of a system called the solar system, which includes the sun (a star), planets, and many moons and Earth is the third planet from the sun in our solar system

Recognize that Earth revolves around (orbits) the sun in a year's time and that Earth rotates on its axis once approximately every 24 hours

Make connections between the rotation of Earth and day/night, and the apparent movement of the sun, moon, and stars across the sky

Describe changes that occur in the observable shape of the moon over a month

Common Core State Standards

Reading Informational Text PreK–5, Key Ideas and Details 5.1 and 5.3

Reading Informational Text PreK–5, Craft and Structure 5.6

Reading Informational Text Grade 5, Integration of Knowledge and Ideas 5.7 and 5.9

Writing Standards PreK–5, Text Types and Purpose 5.2

Writing Standards PreK–5, Research to Build & Present Knowledge 5.7 and 5.8

Locating Multimodal, Multigenre Resources

While we were exploring new content about the universe and the solar system, we were concurrently searching for children's and young adult books of all genres that could be used in a secondary classroom to teach the specific science content standards and beyond. Because of the emphasis on feature article writing, we also knew that sample feature articles would be an important component of the text set as mentor texts for writing. Recognizing that students would conduct individual research meant that it was also important for us to locate general space books and online digital resources that could be mined as research sites for a variety of topics.

Books

Initially, we gathered together the space-related books we use in the children's and young adult literature courses that we teach at Lesley University. Because this unit of study was new to Catherine, she did not have texts that she had used in prior years to consider. We then began to search in our usual sources (described in Chapter Three), scanning major awards lists and paying particular attention to the National Science Teachers Association Outstanding Trade Book lists from the past few years. Additionally, Titlewave searches provided us with lists of well-reviewed books of all genres, particularly nonfiction picture books and chapter books. From there, we headed to our local libraries, where we found the books, sometimes using interlibrary loan, and began to read. Initially, we had many, many books to choose from in a variety of categories. There were many moon books, some of which were devoted to the manned missions to the moon in the 1960s and 1970s, specifically to the first lunar landing in July of 1969. There were books on each and every planet, with many books on Mars specifically. Space technology was a whole other subset of books, with books on the Space Shuttle, the Hubble Space Telescope, the Mars Rovers, the International Space Station, etc. We took some of these books out of the library to preview it, some we left on the shelves, knowing we would go back to them when seeking material for individual student research. Primarily, we focused on contemporary books about the solar system as a whole, as they would include the content we needed to cover in the curriculum, particularly those that utilized the regional classifications used by scientists. (*Note:* Bibliographic information for titles and websites listed in this chapter can be found in the Space Text Set in Chapter Ten.)

With that purpose in mind, three books rose to the surface immediately: Elaine Scott's chapter-length *When Is a Planet Not a Planet?*, David Aguilar's picture book *13 Planets: The Latest View of the Solar System*, and Kathleen Kudlinksi's *Boy, Were We Wrong About the Solar System!* Each book presents our knowledge of the solar system as a shifting landscape that changes all the time. In fact, David Aguilar previously published *11 Planets: A New View of the Solar System*, only to revise and republish the book three years later with a different title. Both Scott and Kudlinski are well known authors for the quality of their science writing for children, and David Aguilar works at the Harvard-Smithsonian Astrophysics Lab in Cambridge, MA. As we discussed these books, we saw *Boy, Were We Wrong About the Solar System!* as a great introductory text to be read aloud to the whole class. *When Is a Planet Not a Planet?* would be a difficult read for students; Catherine knew that some students could handle it while others could not. All three of us felt confident that students could read *13 Planets: The Latest View of the Solar System*. In addition, we saw *Next Stop Neptune*, the collaboration between author-illustrator Steve Jenkins and his father, retired physicist Alvin Jenkins, as ripe for student exploration. However, we knew that since it was published *before* Pluto was named a dwarf planet in 2006, it could be confusing for students. However, there was such great content about the other classifications of the solar system (terrestrial and gas planets, the asteroid and Kuiper Belt) that we felt we might be able to use it as a "teachable moment" as well as for the non-Pluto-related information that it offered.

We also did a search for books on Earth's rotation, which causes day and night, as well as a search for books on Earth's tilt on its axis and orbit around the sun, which causes seasonal changes in the Northern and Southern Hemispheres at different times. There were a few books, particularly from the *Let's-Read-and-Find-Out* series published by HarperCollins that were useful (see the full text set bibliography in Chapter Nine for these titles), but for the most part, we felt that they were for more appropriate for a younger audience. G. Brian Karas's *On Earth* and Gail Gibbons's *The Reasons for Seasons* were good possibilities for scaffold texts; while also written for a younger audience, they had broader appeal and could serve as read-alouds to set the stage for exploring Earth's orbit and rotation. We also determined that *Sun Up, Sun Down: The Story of Day and Night* from the *Science Works* series, which is geared to the intermediate grades, captured Earth's rotation at a level that would satisfy the students. Additionally, four texts by Wendy Pfeffer could be used to explore Earth's position in relation to the sun and seasonal changes: *The Shortest Day: Celebrating the Winter Solstice, A New Beginning: Celebrating the Spring Equinox, The Longest Day: Celebrating the Summer Solstice,* and *We Gather Together: Celebrating the Harvest Season.*

Finally, we did a search for books that focused specifically on phases of the moon. There were parts of books that focused on this, but few books that did so in their entirety. Most seemed written for a younger audience. However, one text surfaced that we felt was appropriate for the students: Melissa Stewart's *Why Does the Moon Change Shape?* from the *Tell Me Why, Tell Me How* series—another series written for the intermediate grades.

As we searched for books, we also viewed them with an eye for multicultural representation, particularly the picture books and photo essays. This classroom was culturally and linguistically diverse, and we wanted the students to be able to identify with the scientists and the individuals represented in the texts.

Magazine Articles and Digital Encyclopedia Entries

In addition to searching for books, we did a search through InfoTrak and EBSCO for children's magazine articles on space in general. We knew that having as many articles as possible available to us in advance of planning the feature article writing workshop would be to our advantage. Through this search we were excited to discover that this body of texts gave a great deal of attention to the dwarf planets and the Kuiper Belt. You can find the list of articles that we located in Chapter Ten.

Digital Texts

We recognized that in teaching Earth's rotation and orbit and the phases of the moon, we might rely more on digital texts, including photographs and videos, rather than books, given the movement and change inherent to the concepts involved. For the unit as a whole, we discovered several superb websites for information on the universe, space exploration, and the solar system, as well as some powerful tablet apps on moon phases, orbits, and exoplanets. During this phase of the search process, we were particularly excited to find a trove of kid-friendly audio and video files produced by Hayden Planetarium Astrophysicist Neil deGrasse Tyson. We hoped that many of the students would readily identify with this dynamic New York City raised African American scientist. These digital resources are also listed in the space text set included in Chapter Ten. What was most frustrating for us in this part of the process was the quest for the right digital text to demonstrate how Earth's tilt impacts our seasons as it orbits the sun. There were plenty of pictures to demonstrate this process, but we wanted a more sophisticated set of short videos than what we were able to find.

Organizing Texts for Instruction

Catherine decided that her students would best understand the content by starting with the solar system and then moving into a closer analysis of Earth's orbit and rotation, day and night, the seasons, and finally, the phases of the moon. As such, we had four sequential phases of content and instruction around which to organize texts: (1) Exploring the Solar System, (2) Exploring Earth's Orbit and Rotation: Day and Night and the Seasons, (3) Exploring Phases of the Moon, and (4) Writing Feature Articles.

Exploring the Solar System

The first weeks of the unit focused specifically on exploring the solar system. As our initial thinking suggested, Kathleen Kudlinksi's *Boy, Were We Wrong About the Solar System!* was an ideal read-aloud to scaffold students' thinking about what we know about the solar system. Students heard the book first as a read-aloud but then read it again in small groups to revisit the information.

We organized the texts using, ironically or maybe naturally, our Solar System Model, focusing on the types of planets found in different regions (or neighborhoods, as we called them) of the solar system. This text model is illustrated below. Students were placed in four heterogeneous solar system neighborhood groups; each group researched its particular solar system neighborhood using the same core texts: *When Is a Planet Not a Planet?*, *13 Planets: The Latest View of the Solar System*, and *Next Stop Neptune*. This allowed students access to the same common knowledge of the solar system, while using a more specific lens, in order to become experts on a particular region of the solar system. Because they were in heterogeneously mixed groups, they could collectively handle the varying text complexities and reading demands of the texts.

Solar System Model: Exploring the Solar System

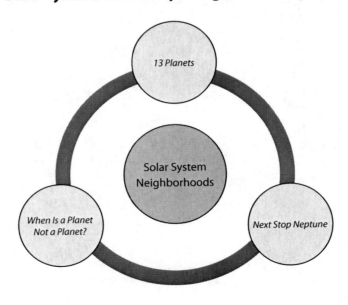

Exploring Earth's Orbit and Rotation: Day and Night and the Seasons

For the second portion of the unit, which focused on developing an understanding of how Earth's rotation and orbit causes day and night and seasonal changes, we organized the texts into two distinct models: the Duet Model and the Solar System Model. The Duet Model shown below was used in exploring Earth's rotation and the reasons for day and night. The simplicity and clarity of *On Earth* provided an overview of Earth's rotation and orbit, while *Sun Up, Sun Down* extended the overview and provided a more in-depth exploration and explanation of why and how we experience day and night.

Duet Model: Exploring Earth's Orbit and Rotation

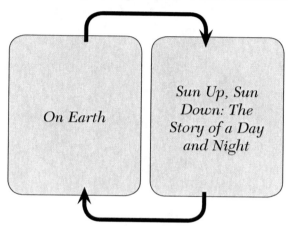

To explain the seasons as a direct result of Earth's tilt and its orbit around the sun, we used the Solar System Model shown on the next page. Here, we used a combination of books and digital texts. Gail Gibbons's *The Reasons for Seasons* served as an overview text. We also sought out digital animations that would physically illustrate rotation and orbit. While we struggled to find an animation that combined clear graphics with a clear explanation, we were able to locate several different options, hoping that students could integrate the information and images to arrive at a solid conceptual understanding. Additionally, we used four books written by Wendy Pfeffer that examine four key moments in Earth's orbit around the sun: *The Shortest Day: Celebrating the Winter Solstice, A New Beginning: Celebrating the Spring Equinox, The Longest Day: Celebrating the Summer Solstice,* and *We Gather Together: Celebrating the Harvest Season.*

By blending digital texts and nonfiction picture books, we provided the students with a combination of simple and complex texts. Between Gibbons's written text and illustrations and the visual animations provided by the digital texts, students had an opportunity to observe the movement of Earth's revolution and its rotation around the sun and to consider the different ways to capture that visually. From a literacy standpoint, neither the Gibbons text nor the Pfeffer texts were technically considered challenging reads for a diverse upper elementary classroom. But from a content standpoint, each served to provide additional background information and context for complex concepts.

Solar System Model: Seasons and the Earth's Rotation

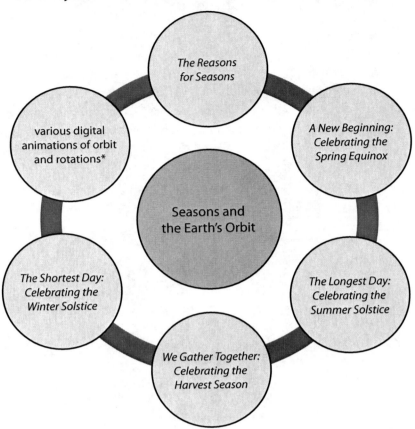

*Digital animations of orbit and rotation:

Prisms: Earth's Yearly Revolution Around the Sun
     http://prisms.mmsa.org/review.php?rid=353

Russell Knightley Media: Video Animation of Earth Moving Around the Sun Showing the Seasons
     http://www.rkm.com.au/animations/animation-seasons.html

YouTube: Mechanism of the Seasons
     http://www.youtube.com

Adler Planetarium: Astronomy Connections: Earth in Motion
     http://www.adlerplanetarium.org/documents/curriculum-resources/seasons3.9.swf

Exploring the Phases of the Moon

The phases of the moon is another concept that seems as if it should be simple, but it is rather complex for students to visualize beyond what they see in the night sky. To see what is not seen can be very difficult! For this portion of the unit, we relied again on a Solar System Model, shown below. Within the Solar System Model, we have student-constructed texts playing an equal role alongside texts created by science professionals. Students used their moon journals, which they had kept for five weeks prior to starting an "official" exploration of moon phases, as original data sources. Additionally, the text set includes two videos of students asking or answering questions and demonstrating the moon phases as well as a tablet app and a photographic animation of the moon's phases over one month. These multimodal texts, combined with student-created texts and expert science writer Melissa Stewart's book *Why Does the Moon Change Shape?*, provided students with a strong foundation for understanding why the moon's appearance changes in our night sky.

Solar System Model: Exploring Phases of the Moon

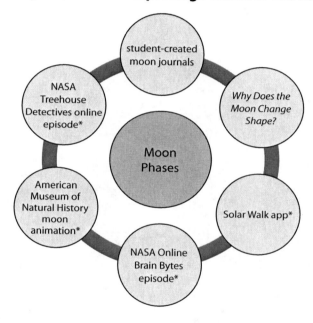

*Digital texts:

Moon Phase Animation: American Museum of Natural History in NYC
   http://www.haydenplanetarium.org/resources/ava/solarsystem/P0409moonphas

NASA Education, "Treehouse Detectives" show
   http://video.google.com/videoplay?docid=-4476254314239718422

NASA Brain Bites: "Why do we only see one side of the Moon?" video
   http://brainbites.nasa.gov/moonrotation.html#/one-side-of-moon

Solar Walk App: Vitotechnology Website
   http://vitotechnology.com/solar-walk.html

Writing Feature Articles

For writing workshop, the Mountain Model was used. The teacher provided students with a broad sampling of feature articles on many different space-related topics. The core texts from their neighborhood solar system exploration were used in writing workshop as a source of foundational knowledge about the solar system. Catherine then provided a more specific sampling of space-related feature articles from children's and young adult magazines as mentor texts for students to read. Finally, the students began their own individual research based on research questions developed during the unit of study as a class. Students working individually with Catherine and the school librarian, researched their topics. Catherine had space books from the school library available in her classroom, and students had access to a laptop cart to search subscription databases and recommended websites for additional information.

Mountain Model: Feature Articles for Writing Workshop

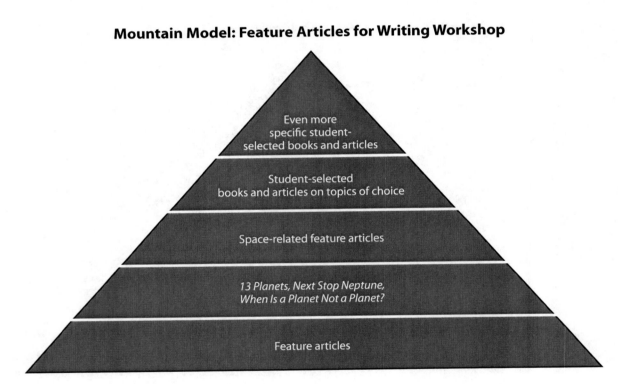

Student Responses to Texts

Since this was a new unit of study for Catherine and her students, we had broad license in shaping students' responses to the texts they were reading. We wanted students' work to demonstrate their understanding of the content in state science standards, and we hoped to design student projects and products that would allow them to demonstrate their achievement of the Common Core State Standards that we had identified as a possible match for the unit (see the Unit Planning Chart on page 163). Additionally, we were committed to encouraging multigenre, multimodal responses and offering an element of student choice in the assessment processes. In the sections that follow, we'll describe the students' note-making and creation of texts for each of the content phases of the unit.

Exploring the Solar System

Solar System Maps and Timelines of Changing Thinking

To begin the unit, Catherine had students first work individually and then in small groups to construct maps of the solar system. We decided that this would be an effective way to have individual students demonstrate their prior knowledge and would also be a platform for the collaborative talking, thinking, and negotiating that is an important component of scientific literacy. Why did one student put a planet in one location instead of another? How big is Jupiter compared to Earth? Why is it important? After comparing and contrasting initial individual sketches, each group created a single map of the solar system that represented its best thinking about where celestial bodies are in the solar system and the distances between them. These maps served as important "before" and "after" texts for both the teacher and the students to make sense of their knowledge. The students used the Solar System Maps Planning Sheet (page 174) for this planning. Sample student-created solar system maps are found on page 175.

Name_____ Date _____

Solar System Maps Planning Sheet

What is in the solar system?

What do you and your group members know about the solar system? This activity is designed to make you think about what you know about the solar sytem, what your classmates know about the solar system, and identify questions you have about the solar system.

Directions:

1. On a separate sheet of paper, draw what you think the solar system looks like. Make sure you include the different objects you think belong in the solar system as well as how far apart they are from each other. Don't let your group members see your drawing.

2. Compare and contrast your drawings with your group members. Use the chart below to write the similarities and differences between the solar system maps.

Similarities	Differences

3. Using a large sheet of paper, create a map of the solar system that you can agree on as a group. Remember to:
   - Label and identify all of the celestial bodies (objects) that you think are in the solar system.
   - Show how far apart they may be from each other.

Sample Solar System Maps

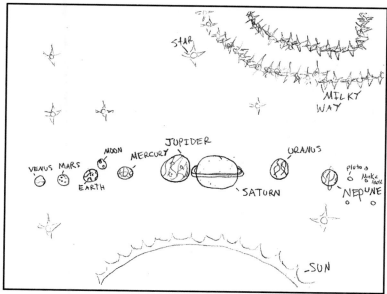

One student's initial brainstorm of what the solar
system looks like

A small group works to construct a group vision of the
solar system before any reading occurs

The next student-created texts were time lines of the changing knowledge of the solar system, as presented in *Boy, Were We Wrong About the Solar System!* This text traces the history of scientific thinking about space. After the teacher read the book aloud, students were put into small groups to reread the text the next day, exploring discoveries made during an assigned range of time. In response to this close rereading, students created posters in small groups that highlighted the big shifts in theories or knowledge about space and used the posters to create a complete time line that could hang on the wall for reference for the duration of the unit. The students used the Solar System Time Line Planning Sheet (pages 176–177) for planning. A sample student-created time line is found on page 178.

Name _____ Date _____

Solar System Time Line Planning Sheet

How has thinking about the solar system changed over time? This activity is designed to make you think about the information in *Boy, Were We Wrong About the Solar System!* by Kathleen Kudlinski. Specifically, your group is responsible for becoming experts on what scientists thought about the solar system at a particular time and how their ideas changed.

Our time period is: _____ Pages: _____

Directions:

1. Reread out loud the section of *Boy, Were We Wrong About the Solar System!* that describes your time period.

2. Select someone to be the recorder for your group. Using details from the book, discuss the questions. Have the recorder write your group's answers.

During this time period, they thought…

_____

_____

_____

_____

_____

_____

Solar System Time Line Planning Sheet *(cont.)*

Boy, were they wrong! They realized…

_____

_____

_____

_____

_____

Why did the thinking change? Include specific inventors, inventions, and technology.

_____

_____

_____

_____

3. Work together to create a poster for the class time line that includes the information on this sheet. Make sure that you put the dates at the very top of the poster so that it will be easy to form a time line with your classmates.

Sample Solar System Time Line

This poster captures some of the changing scientific understandings of the solar system in the late 20th and early 21st centuries

Solar System Neighborhood Posters

We had decided early on in our planning process that we wanted students to do small-group work around the content of the unit. The state science content standards require students to recognize "that Earth is part of a system called 'the solar system' that includes the sun (a star), planets, and many moons" (Massachusetts Department of Elementary & Secondary Education 2006). We knew we wanted to embed this knowledge in a broader conversation about changing theories about the planets, so we decided to organize students into four small groups, with each group being responsible for becoming "experts" on the celestial bodies within a region (or neighborhood, as we called it) of our solar system.

The groups were assigned to the following neighborhoods: terrestial planets, asteroid belt, gas giants, and the kuiper belt. Students used the Solar System Model with *When Is a Planet Not a Planet?*, *13 Planets: The Latest View of the Solar System*, and *Next Stop Neptune* to research the following:

1. Provide a definition that describes this region of the solar system.

2. Describe the celestial bodies that are in this region of the solar system.

3. Review how scientists' thinking about this region of the solar system has changed over time.

4. What is unique about this region of the solar system? Show the evidence.

The groups were given the task of creating poster presentations that would include the answers to the questions above, two visuals, something that would show important details about the neighborhood they were studying, and a map of the solar system that highlights where the neighborhood is located within the solar system. Students were responsible for preparing the poster and for preparing to orally present their poster to their classmates. To support students, we created a sample poster for the sun; groups were able to use this poster as a mentor text for their own posters.

To guide their research, students in each group were given the same template for note-making. We opted for a specific note-making form that would be used for all four books and that would lead students towards the subtopics they needed to explore. Because students would soon be working on individual research on topics of their choice when writing their feature articles, which would necessitate more open-ended research, we felt that scaffolding and supporting the note-making process and modeling the connection between note-making and research questions was important. The resources provided on pages 180–190 show the directions students were given for their presentations, the note-making form they used to take notes on all of the core books, the peer note-making form they used to record their learning from other group presentations, and the rubric that was used to assess the presentations.

Name _____ Date _____

Neighborhood Group Poster Presentations

Directions: With your group members, you are responsible for learning about and teaching your classmates about one of the regions, or "neighborhoods," of the solar system. Follow the steps below.

Our solar system neighborhood is: _____

Your Goal: Create and present a poster that provides the following information about your solar system neighborhood:

1. Provide a definition that describes this neighborhood of the solar system.

2. Describe the celestial bodies that are in this neighborhood of the solar system.

3. Review how scientists' thinking about this neighborhood of the solar system has changed over time.

4. What is unique about this neighborhood of the solar system? Show the evidence.

5. Provide two visuals:

   • something that shows important details about your neighborhood

   • a map of the solar system that highlights where your neighborhood is located

Neighborhood Group Poster Presentations *(cont.)*

Steps for Creating Your Poster

1. Read the space texts that your group has been provided with and take notes about your neighborhood of the solar system. Use the note-making form.

2. As a group, discuss what you have found. Decide if you need to seek out more information.

3. Divide up the tasks of writing the text sections and creating the illustrations for your poster.

4. Write and illustrate!

5. Review one another's drafts to be sure that the writing is clear and the information is complete.

6. Revise your writing and illustration based on group members' feedback.

7. Create final copies of your writing and illustrations to glue onto your group's poster.

Neighborhood Group Poster
Presentations (cont.)

Steps for Planning Your Presentation

1. Each group member should speak during your poster presentation.

2. Divide up the task of reading and explaining the poster so that everyone will have a turn to speak.

3. Practice your presentation with your group members.

Name_____ Date _____

Note-Making Form for
Solar System Neighborhoods

Solar System Neighborhood: _____

Book Title: _____

Author: _____

Publishing Company: _____

City, State: _____ Date of Publication: _____

1. In the chart, record information from your reading that tells where
   your neighborhood is located within the solar system. Include page
   numbers of excellent maps, photographs, and information.

Information	Page Number(s)	New Questions I Have

Note-Making Form for
Solar System Neighborhoods (cont.)

2. Draw the solar system and circle your neighborhood.

Note-Making Form for
Solar System Neighborhoods (cont.)

3. Record information from your reading that defines the neighborhood. What is in it? Why are these celestial bodies grouped together?

Information	Page Number(s)	New Questions I Have

Note-Making Form for
Solar System Neighborhoods (cont.)

4. Record information from your reading that tells how scientists' thinking about this neighborhood has changed over time.

Information	Page Number(s)	New Questions I Have

Note-Making Form for
Solar System Neighborhoods *(cont.)*

5. Record information from your reading that provides interesting facts and unique features of your neighborhood.

Information	Page Number(s)	New Questions I Have

Name _____ Date _____

Peer Note-Making Form for Neighborhood Presentations

Directions: Circle the neighborhood this group is presenting. Then take notes to answer each question as the group is presenting.

terrestial planets	asteroid belt	gas giants
dwarf planets	kuiper belt	

1. Where is the neighborhood located within the solar system?

   _____

   _____

   _____

   _____

2. Define this neighborhood. What makes it unique?

   _____

   _____

   _____

   _____

   _____

   _____

Peer Note-Making Form for Neighborhood Presentations *(cont.)*

3. What celestial bodies are located within this neighborhood?

_____

_____

_____

_____

4. How has scientists' thinking about this neighborhood changed over time?

_____

_____

_____

_____

5. What was really interesting to you about the presentation or the neighborhood group?

_____

_____

_____

_____

Neighborhood Poster Presentation Rubric

Criteria	Excellent	Good	Satisfactory	Unsatisfactory
Definition and Celestial Bodies: How well have you defined your solar system neighborhood and the celestial bodies within it?	You have a thorough and specific definition of your neighborhood and many details about the celestial bodies within it, with proper scientific vocabulary.	You have a correct definition of your neighborhood and details about the celestial bodies within it, with proper scientific vocabulary.	You have a correct definition of your neighborhood, but not a lot of details about the celestial bodies within it or possibly a few mistakes.	You do not define the neighborhood or do not define it correctly.
Scientists' Thinking: How well have you discussed how scientists' thinking has changed over time?	You have thoroughly described what scientists used to think about your neighborhood, how their ideas changed over time, and what they now think.	You have described what scientists used to think about your neighborhood, how their ideas changed over time, and what they think now.	You have described what scientists used to think or what they think now, but not both. Or, you describe both but only very briefly, possibly with a few mistakes.	You have not defined what scientists used to think and what they think now, or you do so inaccurately.
Unique Details: How have you shared evidence of the unique details of your neighborhood?	You have thoroughly described evidence of many unique features of your neighborhood.	You have described evidence of the unique features of your neighborhood.	You have described some evidence of the unique features of your neighborhood, perhaps with some mistakes.	You do not have a section on the unique details of your neighborhood.
Two Visuals: Do the visuals show important details about your neighborhood and a map of the solar system that highlights your neighborhood location?	You have well-detailed visual illustrations that show important details and a specific and accurate map of the solar system that identifies your neighborhood.	You have clear visual illustrations that show important details and an accurate map of the solar system that identifies your neighborhood.	You have visual illustrations and a map of the solar system, but you may not have a lot of details included or possibly a few mistakes.	You may be missing one or both visuals and/or they have a lot of mistakes in information.
Presentation: How well have you shared the information on your poster?	Every member of your group played a role in presenting the information to the class and presented information clearly and confidently.	Every member of your group played a role in presenting the information to the class.	Some but not all members played a role in presenting the information to the class. Or, it was difficult to understand or hear the presentation.	One or two people dominated the presentation.
Writing Conventions: Have you written your information with proper sentence structure, spelling, grammar, and punctuation?	Your poster has accurate sentence structure, spelling, grammar, and punctuation.	Your poster has accurate sentence structure and mostly accurate spelling, grammar, and punctuation.	Your poster can be understood but has errors in spelling, grammar, and punctuation.	Your poster is difficult to understand because of many errors in spelling, grammar, and punctuation.

Exploring Earth's Orbit and Rotation: Day and Night, and Seasons

To launch the second phase of the unit focusing on Earth's orbit and rotation, students did some writing in a note-making form to consider what they knew already about Earth's place in space and the causes of day and night and the seasons. They each completed the Organizer for Group Work on Earth's Place in Space (page 193), first individually and then as a group. In this note-making form, we wanted students to connect what they had learned about Earth during the Terrestrial Planets group presentation with their own prior knowledge about Earth. We wanted to be able to assess their prior knowledge and to see their hypotheses about day and night and the seasons.

Seasons Poster and Day and Night, and the Seasons Skits

Once students compared and contrasted what they knew and shared their hypotheses, the class read *On Earth*. After that overview and a discussion comparing the information in the text with their notes, students were put into small groups to read *Sun Up, Sun Down: The Story of Day and Night*. They used the note-making form shown on pages 194–195 to record their findings.

After completing this Duet Model comparison, Catherine transitioned into the Solar System Model to explore Earth's revolution around the sun. She read aloud *The Reasons for Seasons* and played the digital texts described earlier in this chapter. She also divided the class into four groups and assigned one of the four Wendy Pfeffer titles focusing on the solstices and equinoxes to each group. For note-making, students completed the chart on page 196. To extend the discussion of seasonal changes, Catherine then asked the groups to prepare posters to share with the class. The groups reread, made notes, and then incorporated the following information into a poster display:

- What is the winter solstice? the vernal equinox? the summer solstice? the autumnal equinox?

- Describe the position of Earth relative to the sun at this time of the year.

- Describe some of the cultural traditions associated with the winter solstice, the vernal equinox, the summer solstice, and the autumnal equinox.

- What do the winter solstice, the vernal equinox, the summer solstice, and the autumnal equinox mean to you?

One group's poster of the summer solstice

Throughout the planning of this unit, we were mindful of the fact that understanding the orbit and rotation of Earth meant being able to conceptualize and visualize celestial movement. We suspected that students would need to enact the movement with their bodies to help support their understanding. This led us to design an assessment that incorporated dramatic interpretation. We decided to give students the task of working in small groups to design and perform a brief skit using dialog and props. Two of the groups had to design and perform skits based on what causes day and night, while the other two groups had to design and perform skits that demonstrated why seasons occur based on Earth's tilt and orbit. They received the assignment sheet shown on page 198. The rubric on page 199 was used to assess the performances. You will notice that as with all the assessments in the unit, we addressed content, content literacy, and language arts, focusing on the clarity and accuracy of the information presented orally and physically in the skits.

Name_____ Date _____

Note-Making Form for Group Work on Earth's Place in Space

Directions: Think about what you have learned about the solar system. Record your thoughts about Earth and its place in space. What is unique about Earth? What is the relationship between Earth and the other celestial bodies of the solar system?

My ideas:

_____
_____
_____
_____

Now, take some time to discuss your ideas with your group members. What new ideas came out of the group discussion? Make some notes about your group members' ideas.

Ideas from our group discussion:

_____
_____
_____
_____

What do I know about day and night?

_____
_____
_____

What do I know about the seasons?

_____
_____
_____

Name_____ Date _____

Note-Making Form for *Our Earth* and *Sun Up, Sun Down*

Directions: Use what you learned from *Our Earth* by G. Brian Karas and *Sun Up, Sun Down: The Story of Day and Night* by Jacqui Bailey, illustrated by Matthew Lilly, to answer the questions below.

Why is the sun important to life on Earth?

_____

_____

_____

_____

How does the appearance of the sun in the sky change throughout the day?

_____

_____

_____

Why do shadows change their length during the day?

_____

_____

_____

_____

Note-Making Form for *Our Earth* and *Sun Up, Sun Down* (cont.)

Draw and write what causes day and night.

_____

_____

_____

_____

Name_____ Date _____

Note-Making Form for Seasons
in the Northern Hemisphere

Directions: Draw diagrams that illustrate the position of Earth in relation to the sun at the seasonal markers for the Northern Hemispshere.

Winter Solstice	Spring Equinox
Summer Solstice	**Autumn Equinox**

Sample Note-Making Form for Seasons in the Northern Hemisphere

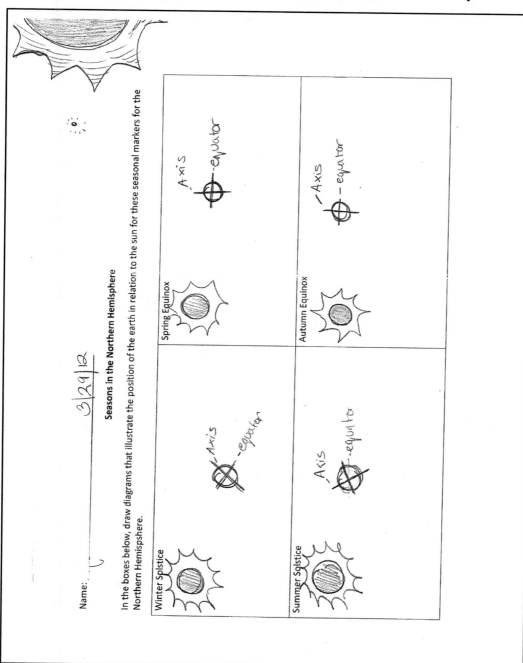

Name_____ Date_____

Earth's Place in Space:
Performing Orbit and Rotation

Our group is responsible for (circle one):   Day and Night   Seasons

Overview:

Why do we experience day and night and seasonal changes? Create a dramatic performance that will illustrate the science behind what we experience as day and night or the seasons. Your goal is to use movement and words to create a clear explanation of the scientific processes at work.

Step 1: Review and Discuss the Process

Review your notes about Earth's orbit and rotation and talk with your group members about your understanding of day and night or the seasons. Brainstorm ideas about how you would use a dramatic performance to illustrate why we experience day/night or the seasons. As you brainstorm, you should consider:

- How you will use movement to demonstrate the concepts;
- What you will say to explain the concept;
- How you could use props or materials to explain the concepts; and
- The role each group member will have in the performance.

Step 2: Write the Script

Work together to create a written script for your performance. While you do not have to follow an official script format, you should be sure to write down everything you will say, notes that will help you to remember how you will move, and a list of the props that you will need. Make arrangements to get the props that you will need either by asking your teacher if they are available in the classroom or by bringing them in from home.

Step 3: Rehearse

Run through your planned performance several times. Think carefully about how the talk and actions you have included will help your audience understand the science behind day and night or the seasons. Make any revisions that you feel are needed to make your explanation more clear.

Step 4: Perform

Skit Rubric

Criteria	Excellent	Good	Satisfactory	Unsatisfactory
Describing the Science in Words: How well have you described the science behind day/night or the seasons through the words of your performance?	You created a script that clearly explained the science of day/night or the seasons AND your explanation was entertaining for the audience.	You created a script that clearly explained the science of day and night or the seasons.	Your explanation was confusing at times, but overall, you were able to explain the science of day and night or seasons.	You included inaccurate information in your explanation or your explanation, was too confusing to understand.
Describing the Science through Movement: How well have you depicted the science behind day/night or the seasons through the movement your performance?	Your body movements throughout the performance were chosen to creatively help the audience to understand the science you were explaining.	Your body movements helped the audience to understand the science you were explaining.	The body movements that you used helped the audience to understand your explanation most of the time but were sometimes confusing.	The body movements that you used were inappropriate or distracting.
Use of Props: Have you selected props that make your explanation more clear?	You made creative choices for props that made your explanation much more easily understood.	You made good choices of props to help your audience understand your explanation.	Your props were at times distracting to the audience but for the most part helped your audience understand your explanation.	You did not use any props to aid in your explanation, or the props you used distracted the audience from your explanation.
Voice: Have you spoken with appropriate volume, clarity and tone throughout your performance?	Your audience can clearly hear your voices. You vary your tone of voice to match what you are saying and to keep your audience interested.	Your audience can clearly hear your voices. Your tones of voice are a good fit for what you have to say.	It is sometimes hard to hear your voices, or your tone of voice did not always match what you are saying.	It was very hard to hear you, or your tone of voice was not appropriate.

Exploring the Phases of the Moon

Following the performance of the skits, we moved into the third phase of our content exploration—learning about the phases of the moon. In this phase, we wanted students to move from firsthand observation and hypothesis to text and video exploration and finally to expression of their understandings in text and illustration.

Moon Journals

The first student-created texts were moon journals. The week before the unit began, Catherine distributed an observation form that prompted students to draw what the moon looked like to them when they stood in the same location at the same time over the course of a month. Catherine decided to have students begin to record their observations of the moon with the onset of the new moon. This would allow them to take notes with drawings and have a body of evidence before they formally began their study of the phases of the moon at the end of the unit.

Moon Phase Illustration and Chronological Narrative

Students began their exploration of the moon phases by reading their own moon journals for data and comparing and contrasting their drawings over the five-week period that they were collecting. After posing some theories about why the moon looks the way it does at certain times, students reconstructed the phases of the moon in small groups, using laminated cards with photographs and drawing on their journals as evidence. Next, Catherine began the Solar System Model exploration of digital texts depicting the different phases of the moon, as described earlier in this chapter, and concluded with Melissa Stewart's nonfiction book *Why Does the Moon Change Shape?* In order to document their thinking about the phases of the moon and the reason for the moon's changing appearance, students took notes using the Moon Phases Note-Making Form shown on pages 202–203.

Inspired by the many stunning illustrations of the moon that we found in the picture books we located for the unit, we hit upon the idea of having students create visual images of the moon phases to demonstrate their understandings. Their images would be accompanied by student-created text describing each moon phase and the science behind why we see the moon differently each day over the course of a month. We envisioned a museum display of the students' illustrations in the hallway, with the student-created texts as museum cards.

Students used their notes and the texts available to write a chronological narrative of the moon phases and the reasons for those moon phases and then created a series of illustrations. Students used the project procedures on pages 204–205 to create their narratives. Other books about the moon and the first moon landing were available in class to show the range of media that can be used to depict the moon. *One Giant Leap, Moonshot, The Flight of Apollo 11, Kitten's First Full Moon, Next Stop Neptune: Experiencing the Solar System, If You Decide to Go to the Moon, Ramadan Moon,* and *A Full Moon Is Rising: Poems* all introduced possibilities for creating images of the moon phases. Ultimately because of time constraints, it proved expedient for all students to use pencils to imitate the black and white gouache and colored pencil illustrations found in *Kitten's First Full Moon.* Next year when Catherine carries out this unit with her students, she will collaborate with the art teacher at her school to offer students a range of media and illustrative styles.

The rubric on page 206 was used for assessment of the narratives. We were looking to see if students could accurately draw and write about the moon phases in chronological order. By asking students to pay attention to their use of voice in their chronological narratives, we were reinforcing the importance of voice in nonfiction writing. Students had been immersed in well-written nonfiction trade books throughout the unit, and they were writing their own feature articles. We felt it was important to emphasize the importance of this quality in their writing about the moon phases, too.

Name_____ Date _____

Moon Phases Note-Making Form

Directions: Draw the moon in each of its phases and give the reasons for its appearance.

Moon phase	The moon looks like this	Reasons the moon looks this way
1. new moon		
2. waxing crescent		
3. first quarter		
4. waxing gibbous		

Moon Phases Note-Making Form *(cont.)*

Moon phase	The moon looks like this	Reasons the moon looks this way
5. full moon		
6. waning gibbous		
7. third quarter		
8. waning crescent		

Name_____ Date _____

What Are the Moon's Phases?
Chronological Narrative and Illustrations

Overview

What are the phases of the moon? Why does the moon appear to change shape at different points during the month? Answer these questions in a chronological narrative and a series of illustrations just as the authors and illustrators of the books we've explored in our space unit have done for other topics. Your narrative has to answer the following questions:

- What are the moon's phases?
- In what chronological order do they appear?
- What causes the moon to have these phases?
- How do Earth and the sun impact the shape the moon appears to have?

Your illustrations have to answer the following questions:

- What are the moon's phases?
- In what chronological order do they appear?

Step 1: Drafting

First, you will outline the moon's phases in chronological order. Next, you will turn that outline into a chronological narrative, starting with the new moon and ending again with the new moon. As you go through each of the moon's phases, explain why it looks the way it does during that phase and what is the role that Earth and the sun have in making it look that way.

What Are the Moon's Phases?
Chronological Narrative and Illustrations *(cont.)*

Step 2: Revising and Publishing the Narrative

After you have a first draft, look over your piece, and see if you have:

- Correct facts
- Correct chronological order
- Interesting voice or style that makes your audience want to read it or hear it

Once you have checked your piece for factual errors and added some "voice" to it, have a friend in class and your teacher look it over. Then, you can write your published version.

Step 3: Illustrating the Phases of the Moon

Look at picture book examples of some of the ways that artists have illustrated the moon using different media. Once you have selected a medium that you would like to use, such as watercolors, colored pencils, or cutout collage, you can begin creating your moon phase illustrations. As you work, make sure that you:

- Plan first in pencil
- Double-check the order of the moon phases
- Make sure you have the correct side of the moon lit for the waxing and waning phases
- Add a paragraph to your chronological narrative that discusses why you used the medium you did to illustrate the moon phases

Moon Phase Chronological Narrative and Illustrations Rubric

Criteria	Excellent	Good	Satisfactory	Unsatisfactory
Chronology of Moon Phases: How well have you depicted the order of the moon phases in your *narrative*?	You thoroughly and accurately detail the order of the moon phases.	You accurately detail the order of the moon phases.	You have several chronological errors.	You do not have the correct order of moon phases.
Chronology of Moon Phases: How well have you depicted the order of the moon phases in your *illustrations*?	You thoroughly and accurately detail the order of the moon phases.	You accurately detail the order of the moon phases.	You have several chronological errors.	You do not have the correct order of moon phases.
Causes for the Moon Phases: How well have you described in your narrative why we see the moon in different phases throughout the month?	You thoroughly describe the causes of the moon phases and how Earth and the sun impact how we see the moon during each phase.	You describe the causes of the moon phases and how Earth and sun impact how we see the moon during each phase.	You attempt to describe the causes of the moon phases but talk about only Earth or the sun and not both, or you have several errors.	You do not address what causes the moon to appear the way it does throughout the month.
Style in Writing: How well have you added voice to your chronological narrative?	Your narrative is filled with voice.	Your narrative has some voice.	You struggle to capture an engaging voice.	You just list the facts, without adding an engaging voice.
Writing Mechanics: Have you written your narrative with proper sentence structure, spelling, grammar, and punctuation?	Your narrative has accurate sentence structure, spelling, grammar, and punctuation.	Your narrative has accurate sentence structure and mostly accurate spelling, grammar, and punctuation.	Your narrative can be understood but has errors in spelling, grammar, and punctuation.	Your narrative is difficult to understand because of the many errors in spelling, grammar, and punctuation.

Sample Moon Illustration and Narrative

One student's moon illustration

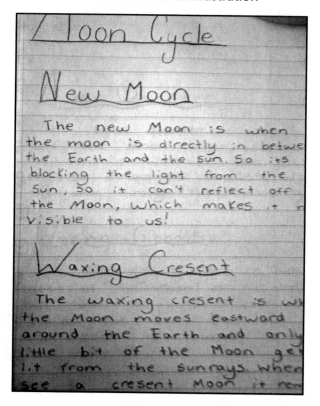

One student's first page of moon narrative

Writing Feature Articles

From the onset, it made a great deal of sense to us to construct this unit as an integrated science and language arts unit. One of Catherine's language arts requirements is that students compose an original feature article. Since this is a genre often used in popular science magazines and we knew that mentor texts for student writing would be readily available, the genre was a perfect fit for student writing in the unit. We decided to weave in students' work on the feature articles, using the Mountain Model throughout the unit of study. Since Catherine had much experience teaching students to write feature articles, we left the planning and assessing of this aspect of the unit in her capable hands.

Using writing workshop as an opportunity to extend students' study of the solar system, contextualize nonfiction writing, and honor individual students' personal interests proved to be a successful model. Students had guidance, structure, and support as they learned about the solar system, developed foundational knowledge, and acquired authentic questions about the universe and the solar system. As students worked and read across texts in each portion of the unit, they had opportunities to continually practice the kinds of reading, writing, and evidence-gathering that they would need to do individually for their feature articles. As Catherine modeled the components of a good feature article using mentor texts, students were in their solar system neighborhood groups researching the solar system. As they transitioned into the study of Earth's rotations and orbit, they began to read space-related feature articles. Because of their expanded content knowledge, they could consider the relative strengths and weaknesses of sample space-related feature articles and use those articles, as well as the nonfiction writing they were exposed to in the trade books, as models for their own writing.

The students started writing their feature articles by brainstorming a list in their writer's notebooks about all the space-related topics they knew and were interested in. Then they choose the one topic they were most interested in and wrote another list in order to narrow down that topic. For example, someone may have had Kuiper Belt in their original list, but their second list may have included Pluto, Haumea, space debris, etc. Finally, from that second list, they chose their specific topics and started researching. During their research using books, articles, and websites that Catherine and the school librarian helped them locate, they may have found that there was very little available information on their topic, in which case they chose another. Catherine found that the most challenging aspect for students was taking their notes and using them to write their own sentences and paragraphs in their own words. To support them in this process, she did whole-group modeling and individual coaching of strategies for students needing additional guidance.

Sample Feature Articles List

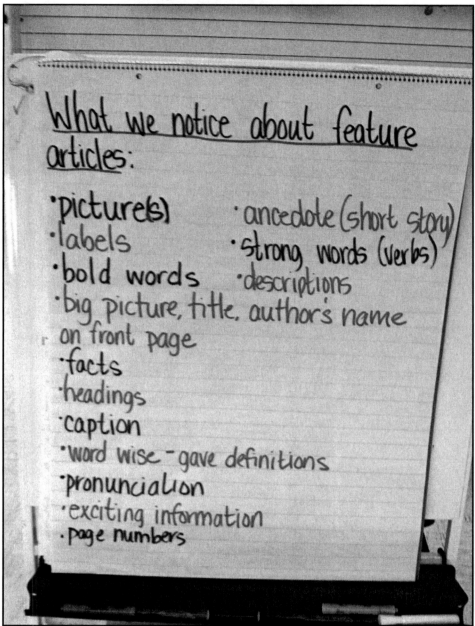

What we notice about feature articles:

- pictures(s)
- labels
- bold words
- big picture, title, author's name on front page
- facts
- headings
- caption
- word wise - gave definitions
- pronunciation
- exciting information
- page numbers
- anecdote (short story)
- strong words (verbs)
- descriptions

Student observations of the elements of feature writing

Review of Student-Created Texts

Throughout our planning process for student responses to text and student construction of texts, we were mindful of our initial content planning chart that outlined the state science and Common Core State Standards that we were hoping to meet.

On the following pages, you will find a chart summarizing the goals, texts, and student work aligned with the content standards of the unit.

Space Text Set: Student Responses to Texts

Unit Goals	Model and Texts	Responding to Texts	Student-Created Texts
Students will understand the celestial objects that comprise the solar system. Students will be able to describe how our knowledge of the solar system is constantly changing from new discoveries/ technologies by exploring previously held theories.	*Boy, Were We Wrong About the Solar System!* (Kudlinski 2008) Solar System Model: *13 Planets* (Aguilar 2011) *When Is a Planet Not a Planet?* (Scott 2008) *Next Stop, Neptune* (Jenkins and Jenkins 2004)	Note-making organizer for *Boy, Were We Wrong About the Solar System!*	Class time line Solar System Neighborhood posters and presentations

Standards
Recognize that Earth is part of a system called "the solar system" that includes the sun (a star), planets, and many moons. Earth is the third planet from the sun in our solar system
Reading Informational Text PreK–5, Key Ideas and Details 5.3 (CCSS)
Reading Informational Text PreK–5, Craft and Structure 5.6 (CCSS)
Reading Informational Text Grade 5, Integration of Knowledge and Ideas 5.7(CCSS)
Reading Informational Text PreK–5, Integration of Knowledge and Ideas 5.9 (CCSS)
Writing Standards PreK–5, Text Types and Purpose 5.2 (CCSS)
Writing Standards PreK–5, Research to Build & Present Knowledge 5.7 (CCSS)

Space Text Set: Student Responses to Texts *(cont.)*

Unit Goals	Model and Texts	Responding to Texts	Student-Created Texts
Students will understand how and why Earth orbits around the sun and rotates on its axis, and the result of those movements in terms of day and night, seasons, and location of the sun and moon in the sky.	Duet Model: *On Earth* (Karas 2004) *Sun Up, Sun Down: What Makes Day and Night* (Bailey 2004) Solar System Model: *The Reasons for Seasons* (Gibbons 1995) *A New Beginning: Celebrating the Spring Equinox* (Pfeffer 2008) *The Longest Day: Celebrating the Summer Solstice* (Pfeffer 2010) *We Gather Together: Celebrating the Harvest Season* (Pfeffer 2006) *The Longest Day: Celebrating the Winter Solstice* (Pfeffer 2003) Various digital texts	Note-making organizer for *Sun Up, Sun Down*	Posters explaining the winter solstice, spring equinox, summer solstice, autumnal equinox Skits about day and night and the seasons

Standards

Recognize that Earth revolves (orbits) the sun in a year's time and that Earth rotates on its axis once approximately every 24 hours. Make connections between the rotation of the earth and day and night, and the apparent movement of the sun, moon, and stars across the sky.

Reading Informational Text PreK–5, Craft and Structure 5.6 (CCSS)

Reading Informational Text Grade 5, Integration of Knowledge and Ideas 5.7 (CCSS)

Reading Informational Text PreK–5, Integration of Knowledge and Ideas 5.9 (CCSS)

Writing Standards PreK–5, Text Types and Purpose 5.2 (CCSS)

Writing Standards PreK–5, Research to Build & Present Knowledge 5.8 (CCSS)

Space Text Set: Student Responses to Texts (cont.)

Unit Goals	Models and Texts	Responding to Texts	Student-Created Texts
Students will be able to record and identify the moon's phases and talk about them.	Solar System Model: Moon journals Various digital texts *Why Does the Moon Change Shape?* (Stewart 2009)	Note-making organizer on moon phases for use across texts	Chronological narratives of the moon phases Illustrations of the moon phases
Standards			
Describe the changes that occur in the observable shape of the moon over the course of the month Reading Informational Text Grade 5, Integration of Knowledge and Ideas 5.7 (CCSS) Reading Informational Text PreK–5, Integration of Knowledge and Ideas 5.9 (CCSS) Writing Standards PreK–5, Text Types and Purpose 5.2 (CCSS) Writing Standards PreK–5, Research to Build & Present Knowledge 5.8 (CCSS)			

Unit Goals	Models and Texts	Responding to Texts	Student-Created Texts
Students will become more capable writers of informational text, using the various texts they read as mentor texts for their own writing and culminating in feature articles and other associated texts and presentations.	Mountain Model: General topics feature article samples Core texts from solar system exploration Space feature articles from children's magazines	Individual student notes	Individual feature articles in response to student-generated research questions about the universe or solar system.
Standards			
Reading Informational Text PreK–5, Key Ideas and Details 5.1 (CCSS) Reading Informational Text PreK–5, Craft and Structure 5.6 (CCSS) Reading Informational Text PreK–5, Integration of Knowledge and Ideas 5.9 (CCSS) Writing Standards PreK–5, Text Types and Purpose 5.2 (CCSS) Writing Standards PreK–5, Research to Build & Present Knowledge 5.7 (CCSS) Writing Standards PreK–5, Research to Build & Present Knowledge 5.8 (CCSS)			

Note: Bibliographic information for titles and websites listed in this chart can be found in the space text set in Chapter Ten.

Teacher Reflections on Teaching with Text Sets

At the conclusion of the unit, we had a chance to talk with Catherine about what she and her students had experienced during the solar system unit. She was very positive about the texts and the activities of the unit, noting how much the students enjoyed reading the texts and expressing that multiple exposures to the content through the multimodal, multigenre text set significantly expanded students' content knowledge.

Even more specifically, she reported watching her students gain confidence in their growing knowledge over the course of the unit. Compared with past experiences working on feature articles, she could see how the extensive experience with the content through multiple texts supported the students' writing processes:

> *Prior knowledge helped to support their topic choice. Without the in depth knowledge they had of the solar system their topics would not have had much depth. Their knowledge of the solar system, beyond the planets, was deeply enhanced during their neighborhood exploration. Their prior knowledge also helped support their research. They knew where to go to get the information they needed. Their experiences with the sources (both books and websites) used for the neighborhood project helped them know what sources would be best to use to research.*

(Catherine, personal communication)

Further reinforcement of students' pride and confidence in their own learning was visible during a special visit from a songwriter who specializes in science content. The artist sat with the students and invited them to participate in the process of composing a song by providing him with a topic and content for the song. Naturally, the students wanted to write a song about space.

> *The songwriter was telling the kids that he has written many songs about space in the past, including one about the planets. He told them that he had written a song called "9 Planets," but he had to rewrite it. He asked if they knew why. Immediately, their hands shot up. When he called on someone, the student explained that Pluto used to be known as a planet but is now a dwarf planet. He then explained to them that even before that, the song was called "10 Planets." Immediately, their hands flew up again—some saying it was Ceres, some saying Haumea, some saying Eris. Someone then added that they read a book called "13 Planets" and that there are many dwarf planets.*

(Catherine, personal communication)

We were pleased to hear that the students learned content and had fun doing it, but perhaps what pleased us most was hearing Catherine talk about how the unit helped her to transform her science instruction. Like many teachers, she felt that her science instruction was often fragmented by external demands, such as a heavy emphasis on language arts and mathematics instruction and a highly scheduled week with shorter designated science and social studies periods. Conceptualizing the unit as an integrated science and language arts unit allowed Catherine to use her allotted time frames differently. Merging the content areas opened up more time for science instruction. She could be certain that she was still covering both sets of standards and that she was doing so with more depth and greater opportunity for students to make connections within and across the content areas.

Our Reflections on the Unit

Our collaboration with Catherine occurred following our work on the immigration unit described in Chapter Six. This opportunity afforded us with a chance to reflect further upon and refine our approach to teaching with text sets. In particular, we thought more deeply about the following aspects of curriculum design with multimodal, multigenre text sets.

The development of this science unit strongly affirmed our belief that curriculum design needs to begin with a survey of current events and perspectives in the field. We were guided by current events along with our reading about ongoing explorations and new understandings. This allowed us to frame the unit around current (and continually evolving) views of the different types of celestial bodies in different regions of the solar system having distinct characteristics. This would have been an entirely different unit if we had not been listening to the news and reading as much as we could about the current state of the field.

In locating texts for this unit of study, we had a broader, diverse range of differentiation to cover with the reading material, reflecting a broader range of reading abilities than was found in the elementary classroom from Chapter Six. We faced the task of looking for complex ideas at different levels to reach the students' various reading abilities. Because the classroom was culturally and linguistically diverse, we also sought texts with strong multicultural representations. Juggling these variables was challenging but manageable because we have much experience locating texts. But it made us think about how important it is for us to support you as you seek to do the work of locating texts for the units that you teach.

In designing this unit, we had free reign to imagine many possibilities for student-created texts, so we focused on having students respond in very specific modalities, bringing in performance and visual texts in more sophisticated and independent ways than we did in the elementary unit. Across the unit, student products included varying visual displays with shorter accompanying explanatory text, a longer piece of expository text, a short dramatic performance, a museum display of artwork, and fortuitously and without our foreknowing, the composition of an original song. We hope that the incorporation of many modalities into student-composed texts for assessment helped students with their diverse learning styles to have many opportunities to show their learning and their strengths.

Finally, this unit highlighted the issue of scientific accuracy in texts. This is a lens that we always use to view nonfiction texts, a lens that has us checking to see if the texts we use are written by or have been vetted by content-area experts. We make sure to look for back or front matter that describes the authors, sources, and research processes; and turn again and again to lists of books that we know have been reviewed by experts in the field, such as the annual notable/outstanding book awards lists put out by the National Science Teachers Association and the National Council of Teachers of Social Studies.

In this unit, one book in particular generated some good discussion for us. *Sun Up, Sun Down: The Story of Day and Night* focuses specifically on the phenomenon that causes us to experience day and night. An important thing to note about this particular text is that the text begins by using language that actually reinforces commonly held misconceptions that the sun moves across the sky. Halfway through the text, this idea is refuted: "In fact, it was the Earth that had moved, but you'd have to have been in a spaceship to see it." We knew it would be important to highlight this point for students. We suggested that it might be a good idea for the teacher to facilitate a connection to the ideas in *Boy, Were We Wrong About the Solar System!*, reviewing a geocentric view versus a heliocentric view. A second point for discussion also arose from the book. The text implies that noon is the time at which the sun is highest in the sky. We had some questions about this, thinking about how the orbit of Earth around the sun leads to seasonal changes in the Northern and Southern Hemispheres, including changes in the time of sunrise and sunset. We suspected that the issue was more complex. Research led us to find that in fact there is "astronomical noon." Since sunrise and sunset change each day because of the tilt of Earth's axis, the sun is at its highest point at a slightly different time each day at midday. There's a great discussion of this on the NASA website (http://imagine.gsfc.nasa.gov/docs/ask_astro/answers/970714. html). Likely, since the focus of this particular book is on day and night, rather than on the orbit of Earth and seasonal changes, the author chose to simplify this discussion. This was a well-written text and appropriate for our purposes with its clear content focus, but these two areas needed attention to ensure that students accurately understood the science. These discussions reinforced the importance of careful selection of nonfiction texts and carefully reading the selected texts to identify places that may require scaffolding of student comprehension.

For us, the design of this unit encompassed all that we love most about teaching with text sets: engaging with exciting content; discovering new and wonderful children's books, magazines, and digital texts; creating the arrangement of texts to facilitate student content and literacy learning; and opening doors for students to express their learning in multimodal, multigenre projects.

Reflection Questions

1. How does reading this specific case study provide you with a deeper understanding of the benefits of teaching with text sets?

2. What new ideas did you generate in relation to your own teaching practices while reading this chapter?

3. After reading about this unit of study, what do you see as some of the challenges and opportunities of teaching with text sets?

Part III

Sample Text Sets and Models

#50688: Teaching with Text Sets

Exploring the Great Depression

This chapter provides a complete text set for the topic of the Great Depression. It details book titles, digital resources, and instructional suggestions. For an annotated list of these texts and digital resources, please see the Digital Resource CD (greatdepressionannotated.doc).

Texts

Nonfiction Picture Books

Christensen, Bonnie. 2009. *Woody Guthrie: Poet of the People*. Decorah, IA: Dragonfly Books.

McCarthy, Megan. 2008. *Seabiscuit: The Wonder Horse*. New York: Simon & Schuster Books for Young Readers.

Rappaport, Doreen. 2009. *Eleanor, Quiet No More*. White Plains, NY: Disney/Hyperion.

Winter, Jonah. 2011. *Born and Bred in the Great Depression*. New York: Schwartz & Wade Books.

Nonfiction

Appelt, Kathi, and J. C. Schmitzer. 2001. *Down Cut Shin Creek: The Packhorse Librarians of Kentucky.* New York: HarperCollins.

Blumenthal, Karen. 2002. *Six Days in October: The Stock Market Crash of 1929.* New York: Atheneum.

Bolden, Tanya. 2010. *FDR's Alphabet Soup: New Deal America, 1932–1939.* New York: Knopf.

Cooper, Michael. 2004. *Dust to Eat: Drought and Depression in the 1930s.* New York: Clarion Books.

Freedman, Russell. 2005. *Children of the Great Depression.* New York: Clarion Books.

Marrin, Albert. 2009. *Years of Dust: The Story of the Dust Bowl.* New York: Dutton Children's Books.

Nau, Thomas. 2007. *Walker Evans: Photographer of America.* New York: Roaring Brook.

Partridge, Elizabeth. 1998. *Restless Spirit: The Life and Work of Dorothea Lange.* New York: Viking.

———. 2002. *This Land Was Made for You and Me: The Life and Songs of Woody Guthrie.* New York: Viking.

Sandler, Martin. 2009. *The Dust Bowl Through the Lens: How Photography Revealed and Helped Remedy a National Disaster.* New York: Walker Books for Young Readers.

Stanley, Jerry. 1992. *Children of the Dust Bowl: The True Story of the School at Weedpatch Camp.* New York: Crown Publishing.

Fiction Picture Books

Birtha, Becky. 2010. *Lucky Beans.* Park Ridge, IL: Albert Whitman & Co.

Harper, Jo. 2005. *Finding Daddy: A Story of the Great Depression.* Madison, CT: Turtle Books.

Henson, Heather. 2008. *That Book Woman.* New York: Atheneum Books for Young Readers.

Hopkinson, Deborah. 2005. *Saving Strawberry Farm.* New York: Greenwillow Books.

———. 2006. *Sky Boys: How They Built the Empire State Building.* New York: Schwartz & Wade.

Lied, Kate. 2002. *Potato: A Tale from the Great Depression.* Washington, DC: National Geographic Society.

MacLachlan, Patricia. 1995. *What You Know First.* New York: Joanna Cotler Books.

Mitchell, Margaree King. 1993. *Uncle Jed's Barbershop.* New York: Simon and Schuster.

Rockliff, Mara. 2012. *My Heart Will Not Sit Down.* New York: Alfred A. Knopf.

Turner, Ann Warren. 1997. *Dust for Dinner.* New York: HarperTrophy.

Novels and Short Stories

Brown, Don. 2007. *The Train Jumper.* New York: Roaring Brook.

Cohen, Miriam. 2004. *Mimmy and Sophie: All Around the Town.* New York: Farrar, Straus & Giroux.

Curtis, Christopher Paul. 1999. *Bud, Not Buddy.* New York: Delacorte Press.

———. 2012. *The Mighty Miss Malone.* New York: Random House/Wendy Lamb Books.

Fusco, Kimberly Newton. 2010. *The Wonder of Charlie Anne.* New York: Alfred A. Knopf.

Giff, Patricia Reilly. 2011. *R My Name Is Rachel.* New York: Random House/Wendy Lamb Books.

Hale, Marian. 2007. *The Truth About Sparrows.* New York: Henry Holt.

Hesse, Karen. 1997. *Out of the Dust.* New York: Scholastic Press.

Larson, Kirby. 2011. *The Friendship Doll.* New York: Delacorte.

Peck, Richard. 1998. *A Long Way from Chicago: A Novel in Stories.* New York: Dial Books for Young Readers.

———. 2000. *A Year Down Yonder.* New York: Puffin Books.

Phelan, Matt. 2009. *Storm in the Barn.* Cambridge, MA: Candlewick.

Pinkney, Andrea Davis. 2012. *Bird in a Box.* New York: Little, Brown Books for Young Readers.

Ryan, Pam Muñoz. 2000. *Esperanza Rising.* New York: Scholastic.

Vanderpool, Clare. 2010. *Moon Over Manifest.* New York: Random House.

Periodicals

"The Big Crash." 2009. *Scholastic News*, 5/6 ed., October 19.

Calkins, Ruth Hutchinson. 2008. "Remembering the Depression." *Cobblestone*, March.

"Hard Times." 2010. *Junior Scholastic*, April 12.

Hayes, Nancy. 2008. "Firing, Not Hiring." *Cobblestone*, March.

Linnell, Kim. 2008. "Dandelions for Dinner." *Cobblestone*, March.

McKinley, Cynthia. 2008. "Eyes, Soul, Voice." *Cobblestone*, March.

Price, Sean. 2009. "Live from the Great Depression." *Scholastic News*, 5/6 ed., October 19.

"Riding the Rails." 2010. *Junior Scholastic*, April 12.

Digital Resources

American Memory Project of the Library of Congress
http://memory.loc.gov/ammem/fsahtml/fadocamer.html

Farm Security Administration, Library of Congress: America from the Great Depression to World War II
http://memory.loc.gov/ammem/fsowhome.html

Library of Congress: Themed Classroom Sets, Teaching the Great Depression
http://www.loc.gov/teachers/classroommaterials/themes/great-depression/

National Public Radio: Music of the Great Depression
http://www.npr.org/2009/10/23/113844245/remembering-the-great-depressions-sunny-side
http://www.npr.org/2008/11/15/96654742/a-depression-era-anthem-for-our-times

The New Deal Network
http://newdeal.feri.org/index.htm

The New York Times: The Great Depression
http://topics.nytimes.com/top/reference/timestopics/subjects/g/great_depression_1930s/index.html

PBS: American Experience, FDR
http://www.pbs.org/wgbh/americanexperience/films/fdr/

PBS: American Experience, Riding the Rails
http://www.pbs.org/wgbh/americanexperience/films/rails/

PBS: American Experience, Surviving the Dust Bowl
http://www.pbs.org/wgbh/americanexperience/films/dustbowl/

PBS: Jazz Documentary, Jazz in Time: The Great Depression
http://www.pbs.org/jazz/time/time_depression.htm

Scholastic: Great Depression Resources
http://www.scholastic.com/browse/search/teacher?query=great%20depression

Smithsonian Institution: Treasures from American History
http://americanhistory.si.edu/exhibitions/small_exhibition.cfm?key=1267&exkey=143&pagekey=246

Text Set Models

Duet

If teaching upper elementary or secondary students, you could use *That Book Woman* and *Down Cut Shin Creek: The Packhorse Librarians of Kentucky* to explore the impact of the Works Progress Administration (WPA) of the New Deal on rural families of Appalachia.

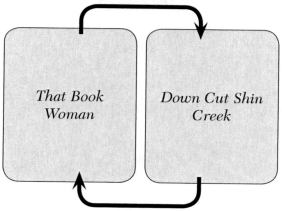

Great Depression Duet Model

In pairing a historical fiction picture book with a short nonfiction chapter book, we are asking students to consider the experience of one boy and his family with a packhorse librarian and contextualize it among the thousands of families who received reading material through the duration of the program. Students can explore how both the fiction and nonfiction personalize history. A comparison and contrast of David Small's illustrations with the primary source photographs in *Down Cut Shin Creek* is a simple way for students to compare and contrast historical information in fiction and nonfiction. Such explorations could prompt students to consider their own access to a school or public library and who funds those public resources.

Sunburst

Karen Hesse's Newbery Medal-winning verse novel *Out of the Dust* is a versatile text that can be explored with students in elementary and secondary classrooms. Through the novel, students will witness the struggle that thirteen-year-old Billie Jo, the protagonist, endures as she copes with the loss of her mother, the emotional distance of her father, and the unyielding desolation of the Dust Bowl.

Great Depression Sunburst Model

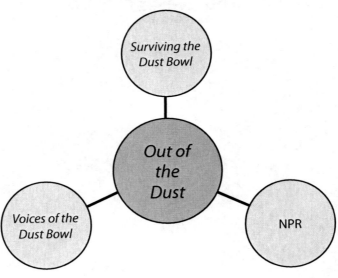

An exploration of this historical novel can be expanded upon through a variety of multimodal, multigenre resources. For instance, students can watch the PBS American Experience episode, "Surviving the Dust Bowl," available online at http://www.pbs.org/wgbh/americanexperience/films/dustbowl/. They can also listen to music from the time period, available from National Public Radio (http://www.npr.org/2009/10/23/113844245/remembering-the-great-depressions-sunny-side). Or, they can view photographs or listen to interviews, performances, and announcements from migrant farm labor camps, available from the Voices of the Dust Bowl collection from the Library of Congress (http://memory.loc.gov/). More primary sources are available at the Library of Congress Classroom Materials site at: http://www.loc.gov/teachers/classroommaterials/primarysourcesets/dust-bowl-migration/.

Tree Ring

If teaching secondary students, Russell Freedman's nonfiction chapter book *Children of the Great Depression* is an ideal core text for the Tree Ring. Freedman provides his readers with an extensive selected bibliography in narrative form.

Great Depression Tree Ring Model

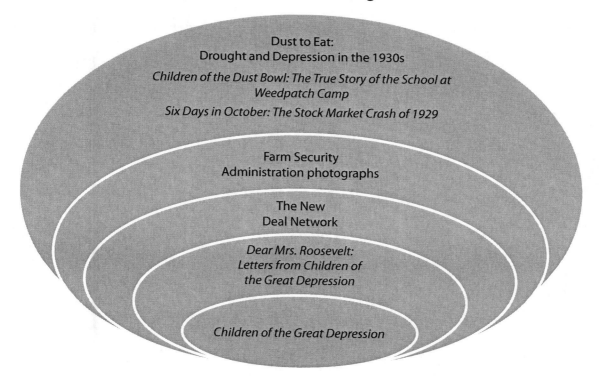

Dust to Eat:
Drought and Depression in the 1930s

Children of the Dust Bowl: The True Story of the School at Weedpatch Camp

Six Days in October: The Stock Market Crash of 1929

Farm Security
Administration photographs

The New
Deal Network

Dear Mrs. Roosevelt: Letters from Children of the Great Depression

Children of the Great Depression

When students have completed this survey book, you should make sure that they read all the back matter. Then, you can present them with excerpts from some of Freedman's research. One group could read excerpts from *Dear Mrs. Roosevelt: Letters from Children of the Great Depression*. Another group could be exploring The New Deal Network of the Franklin and Eleanor Roosevelt Institute, while still another group explores the Farm Security Administration photographs from the Library of Congress. Have students make connections between what Freedman included and excluded. Do they find sources he should have quoted? Do they see different versions of some of the pictures he selected? How would the inclusion of those pictures impact the text? Finally, have your students read some of the other books written for young people about this time period, such as *Children of the Dust Bowl: The Story of the School at Weedpatch Camp* (Stanley 1992) and *Six Days in October: The Stock Market Crash of 1929* (Blumenthal 2002).

solar System

If teaching secondary students, the following five middle grade historical novels are ideal for using in the Solar System Model: *Esperanza Rising*; *Bud, Not Buddy*; *The Mighty Miss Malone*; *Bird in a Box*; and *Moon Over Manifest*. Portions of these books are set in cities and in rural areas. In each novel, children struggle on their own or with the help of supportive adults to find their place in the America of the Great Depression. Some have families to fall back on; others do not. Taken together, these books begin to represent the diversity of the United States. Three of the books have African-American protagonists, another tells of a newly arrived Mexican immigrant, and the fifth involves a Caucasian.

Great Depression Solar System Model

By exploring these texts in small groups, students will have the chance to compare and contrast the experiences of the protagonists, explore popular culture of the time, and discover the ways in which native-born Americans and newly arrived immigrants reinvented themselves. The exploration of these five novels can be enhanced with the multimodal, multigenre resources identified in the text set as a whole at the start of this chapter and referred to in other text models more specifically.

Student Responses to Texts

Specific genre studies that lend themselves to this topic are:

- Historical fiction
- Nonfiction picture books
- Photo essays
- Oral histories/interviews
- Public art (murals, statues)

Great Depression Text Set: Student Responses to Texts

Subtopics, Genres, and Mentor Texts	Student-Created Texts
Biography Genre Study • *Woody Guthrie: Poet of the People* (Christensen 2009) • *This Land Was Made for You and Me: The Life and Songs of Woody Guthrie* (Partridge 2002)	Using these two books as mentor texts, have students research another figure from the Great Depression and use the individual's life as a way to reflect on the time period as a whole. Students could create individual picture book biographies or a class-collected biography.
Exploring Symbols of Hope • *Sky Boys: How They Built the Empire State Building* (Hopkinson 2006) • *Seabiscuit: The Wonder Horse* (McCarthy 2008) • Clips from *The Wizard of Oz* and *Snow White and the Seven Dwarfs* movies • Oz artifacts from the Smithsonian	Have students explore symbols of America today through words, images, and objects. What are appropriate symbols of our culture today? What is being made in America right now that makes people proud?
The New Deal • *FDR's Alphabet Soup: New Deal America, 1932–1939* (Bolden 2010) • Documents, Photos, and Files at the New Deal Network (http://newdeal.feri.org/index.htm)	In small groups, students negotiate a set of New Deal programs for America today, drawing on the success or failure of these programs as evidence. Federal Writers and Artists Programs of the WPA: Have students document your community today through photography, interviews, recipe collection, etc., using the different programs created during the New Deal as a model. Create a class book or host a museum night for the community. New Deal Community Map: Have students explore evidence of the New Deal in your neighborhood, community, city, or state, and build a 3-D map. What buildings or programs are still in use today?

Great Depression Text Set: Student Responses to Texts *(cont.)*

Subtopics, Genres, and Mentor Texts	Student-Created Texts
Historical Fiction Picture Book Study • *My Heart Will Not Sit Down* (Rockliff 2012) • *Lucky Beans* (Birtha 2010) • *What You Know First* (MacLachlan 1995) • *Mimmy and Sophie: All Around the Town* (Cohen 2004) • *Saving Strawberry Farm* (Hopkinson 2005)	After reading aloud these very different historical fiction picture books, have students research, write, and illustrate their own original stories set during the Great Depression. Stories can be based on actual or imagined events. Have students select the "right" medium for illustrating the mood of their story.
Period Music • "Brother, Can You Spare a Dime?" comparisons at National Public Radio (http://www.npr.org/2008/11/15/96654742/a-depression-era-anthem-for-our-times) • PBS Jazz Documentary by Ken Burns http://www.pbs.org/jazz/time/time_depression.htm	Someday people will view our time as a period in history. After examining some of the music of the Great Depression, have students in small groups put together time capsule collections of today's music. If they had to select five songs for future generations, which would they choose, and why? Students can present their songs and written or audio explanations of their selections in listening stations for one another.
The Power of the Lens • *Walker Evans: Photographer of America* (Nau 2007) • *Restless Spirit: The Life and Work of Dorothea Lange* (Partridge 1998) • *The Dust Bowl Through the Lens: How Photography Revealed and Helped Remedy a National Disaster* (Sandler 2009)	Have students create original photo essays based on topics of interest that are rooted in your community, using digital cameras.

Immigration

This chapter provides a complete text set for the topic of immigration. It details book titles, periodicals, digital resources, and instructional suggestions. For an annotated list of the texts and digital resources, please see the Digital Resource CD (immigrationannotated.doc).

Texts

Nonfiction Picture Books

Historic

Bauer, Marion Dane. 2007. *The Statue of Liberty*. Wonders of America series. New York: Aladdin.

Curlee, Lynn. 2003. *Liberty*. New York: Aladdin Paperbacks.

Firestone, Mary. 2007. *The Statue of Liberty*. American Symbols series. Mankato, MN: Picture Window Books.

Glaser, Linda. 2010. *Emma's Poem: The Voice of the Statue of Liberty*. Boston: Houghton Mifflin Books for Children.

Lawlor, Veronica. 1997. *I Was Dreaming to Come to America: Memories from the Ellis Island Oral History Project*. New York: Puffin Books.

Levine, Ellen. 2006. *If Your Name Was Changed at Ellis Island*. New York: Scholastic.

Maestro, Betsy. 1996. *Coming to America: The Story of Immigration*. New York: Scholastic, Inc.

Maestro, Betsy, and Guilio Maestro. 1989. *The Story of the Statue of Liberty.* New York: HarperCollins.

McGovern, Ann. 1999. *…If You Lived 100 Years Ago.* New York: Scholastic, Inc.

Mortensen, Lori. 2009a. *Angel Island.* American Symbols series. Mankato, MN: Picture Window Books.

———. 2009b. *Ellis Island.* American Symbols series. Mankato, MN: Picture Window Books.

Rappaport, Doreen. 2008. *Lady Liberty: A Biography.* Cambridge, MA: Candlewick Press.

Shea, Peggy Dietz. 2005. *Liberty Rising: The Story of the Statue of Liberty.* New York: Henry Holt and Company.

Yaccarino, Dan. 2011. *All the Way to America: The Story of a Big Italian Family and a Little Shovel.* New York: Alfred A. Knopf.

Nonfiction

Historic

Bausum, A. 2010. *Denied, Detained, Deported: Stories from the Dark Side of Immigration.* Washington, DC: National Geographic.

Bial, Raymond. 2002. *Tenement: Immigrant Life on the Lower East Side.* Boston: Houghton Mifflin Company.

———. 2009. *Ellis Island: Coming to the Land of Liberty.* Boston: Houghton Mifflin.

Freedman, Russell. 1980. *Immigrant Kids.* New York: Scholastic.

Granfield, Linda. 2001. *97 Orchard Street: Stories of Immigrant Life.* Toronto, ON: Tundra Books.

Hopkinson, Deborah. 2003. *Shutting Out the Sky: Life in the Tenements of New York 1880–1924.* New York: Orchard Books.

Hoobler, Dorothy, and Thomas Hoobler. 2003. *We Are Americans: Voices of the Immigrant Experience.* New York: Scholastic.

Jacobs, William Jay. 1990. *Ellis Island: New Hope in a New Land.* New York: Charles Scribner and Sons.

Landau, Elaine. 2008. *The Statue of Liberty.* True Books: American History series. Danbury, CT: Children's Press.

Wong, Li Keng. 2006. *Good Fortune: My Journey to Gold Mountain.* Atlanta: Peachtree.

Fiction Picture Books

Contemporary

Bunting, Eve. 1988. *How Many Days to America?: A Thanksgiving Story*. New York: Clarion.

———. 2004. *A Picnic in October*. New York: Harcourt Brace & Company.

Elvgren, Jennifer Riesmeyer. 2006. *Josias, Hold the Book*. Honesdale, PA: Boyds Mills Press.

Figueredo, D. H. 1999. *When This World Was New*. New York: Lee and Low Books.

Lainez, Rene Colato. 2010. *My Shoes and I*. Honesdale, PA: Boyds Mill Press.

McKissack, Patricia C. 2011. *Never Forgotten*. New York: Schwartz & Wade Books.

Recorvits, Helen. 2003. *My Name Is Yoon*. New York: Farrar, Straus & Giroux.

Simson, Lesley. 2011. *Yuvi's Candy Tree*. Minneapolis, MN: Kar-Ben Publishing.

Winter, Jeanette. 2009. *Nasreen's Secret School*. New York: Beach Lane Books.

Historic

Avi. 2003. *Silent Movie*. New York: Atheneum Books for Young Readers.

Bartone, Elisa. 1993. *Peppe the Lamplighter*. New York: Lothrop, Lee and Shepard Books.

Cohen, Barbara. 1998. *Molly's Pilgrim*. New York: Lothrop, Lee & Shepard Books.

Colon, Edie. 2011. *Goodbye, Havana! Hola, New York!* New York: Simon and Schuster.

Currier, Katrina Saltonstall. 2005. *Kai's Journey to Gold Mountain: An Angel Island Story*. San Francisco: Angel Island Association.

Hest, Amy. 2003. *When Jessie Came Across the Sea*. Cambridge, MA: Candlewick Press.

Hochain, Serge. 2004. *Building Liberty: A Statue Is Born*. Washington, DC: National Geographic.

Polacco, Patricia. 1998. *The Keeping Quilt*. New York: Simon and Schuster.

Ross, Alice. 1997. *The Copper Lady*. Minneapolis: Carolrhoda Books.

Russell, Barbara. T. 2006. *Maggie's Amerikay*. New York: Farrar, Straus & Giroux.

Say, Allen. 1993. *Grandfather's Journey*. Boston: Houghton Mifflin.

Tarbescu, Edith. 1998. *Annushka's Voyage*. New York: Clarion Books.

Woodruff, Elaine. 1999. *The Memory Coat*. New York: Scholastic.

Yolen, Jane. 2008. *Naming Liberty*. New York: Philomel.

Novels and Short Stories

Contemporary

Alvarez, Julia. 2009. *Return to Sender*. New York: Knopf.

Budhos, Marina. 2006. *Ask Me No Questions*. New York: Atheneum Books for Young Readers.

————. 2010. *Tell Us We're Home*. New York: Atheneum Books for Young Readers.

Ellis, Deborah. 2010. *No Safe Place*. Toronto, ON: Groundwood Books.

Gallo, Don, ed. 2007. *First Crossing: Stories of Teen Immigrants*. Cambridge, MA: Candlewick.

Jaramillo, Ann. 2008. *La Linea*. New York: RB/Square Fish.

Lai, Thannha. 2011. *Inside Out and Back Again*. New York: HarperCollins.

Lombard, Jenny. 2008. *Drita, My Homegirl*. New York: Puffin.

Manivong, Laura. 2010. *Escaping the Tiger*. New York: HarperCollins.

Mikaelson, Ben. 2003. *Red Midnight*. New York: Harper Trophy.

Na, An. 2002. *A Step from Heaven*. New York: Speak.

Sensai, N. H. 2010. *Shooting Kabul*. New York: Simon and Schuster Books for Young Readers.

Tan, Shaun. 2006. *The Arrival*. New York: Arthur Levine.

Testa, Maria. 2007. *Something About America*. Cambridge, MA: Candlewick.

Williams, Karen Lynn, and Khadra Mohammed. 2007. *Four Feet, Two Sandals*. Grand Rapids, MI: Wm. B. Eerdmans Publishing.

Historic

Auch, Mary Jane. (2002) 2004. *Ashes of Roses*. New York: Dell-Laurel-Leaf.

Avi. 1996. *Beyond the Western Sea*. Book One: The Escape from Home. New York: Avon.

Bartoletti, Susan Campbell. 2003. *My Name Is America: The Journal of Finn Reardon*. My Name Is America series. New York: Scholastic.

Frost, Helen. 2006. *The Braid*. New York: Farrar, Straus & Giroux.

Giff, Patricia Reilly. (2000) 2002. *Nory Ryan's Song*. New York: Dell Yearling.

————. 2003. *Maggie's Door*. New York: Wendy Lamb Books.

———. 2006. *A House of Tailors*. New York: Yearling.

Glaser, Linda. 2005. *Bridge to America*. Boston: Houghton Mifflin.

Harris, Carol Flynn. 2001. *A Place for Joey*. Honesdale, PA: Boyds Mill Press.

Hesse, Karen. 1993. *Letters from Rifka*. New York: Puffin.

Lasky, Kathryn. 1998. *Dreams in the Golden Country: The Diary of Zipporah Feldman, a Jewish Immigrant Girl*. Dear America series. New York: Scholastic.

———. 2003. *Hope in My Heart*. My America series. New York: Scholastic.

Napoli, Donna Jo. 2005. *The King of Mulberry Street*. New York: Wendy Lamb Books.

———. 2009. *Alligator Bayou*. New York: Wendy Lamb Books.

Pryer, Bonnie. 2010. *Iron Dragon: The Courageous Story of Lee Chin*. Minneapolis: Enslow.

Tal, Eve. 2005. *Double Crossing*. El Paso, TX: Cinco Puntos Press.

Wells, Rosemary, with Secundino Fernandez. 2010. *My Havana*. Somerville, MA: Candlewick Press.

Wolf, Linda Press. 2006. *The Night of the Burning: Devorah's Story*. New York: Farrar, Straus & Giroux.

Woodruff, Elvira. 2000. *The Orphan of Ellis Island*. New York: Scholastic Paperbacks.

Yep, Laurence. 2008. *The Dragon's Child: A Story of Angel Island*. New York: HarperCollins.

Poetry

Gunning, Monica. 2004. *America, My New Home*. Honesdale, PA: Boyd's Mill Press.

Mak, Kam. 2002. *My Chinatown: One Year in Poems*. New York: HarperCollins.

Periodicals

"A New Wave." 2010. *Kids Discover*, March.

Arnesen, Eric. 2006. "Putting Out the Unwelcome Mat." *Cobblestone*, April.

Bray, Ilona. 2011. "The Ghosts of Angel Island." *Appleseeds*, October.

Bubar, Joe. 2012. "The Debate over Immigration." *Junior Scholastic*, January 30.

"Changing Ellis Island." 2002. *Kids Discover*, May.

Jacobson, Bob. 2006. "Search for Ancestors." *Cobblestone*, February.

Kowalski, Kathiann. 2005. "Escaping the Empire." *Cobblestone*, May.

"Waves of Immigrants." 2010. *Kids Discover*, March.

Zubar, Shari Lynn. 2010. "Gateway to America." *Cobblestone*, July–August.

Digital Resources

Contemporary Immigration

U.S. Homeland Security, Annual Immigration Statistics
http://www.dhs.gov/files/statistics/immigration.shtm

The City/La Ciudad, Digital Resources on Latin American Immigration Now
http://www.pbs.org/itvs/thecity/index.html

PBS, The New Americans
http://www.pbs.org/independentlens/newamericans/

NPR, Weekend America, Immigration: One Thing
http://weekendamerica.publicradio.org/collections/coll_display.php?coll_id=20120

PBS, "In the Mix"
http://www.pbs.org/inthemix/shows/show_teen_immigrants.html

Smithsonian Institution Traveling Exhibit, "Becoming American: Teenagers and Immigration"
http://www.sites.si.edu/images/exhibits/Becoming%20American/index.htm

The Statue of Liberty

EarthCam®, View of the Statue of Liberty
http://www.earthcam.com/usa/newyork/statueofliberty/

The Statue of Liberty-Ellis Island Foundation Inc., Statue of Liberty Page
http://www.statueofliberty.org/Statue_of_Liberty.html

The Statue of Liberty National Park
http://www.nps.gov/stli/

Ellis Island

Ellis Island National Park
   http://www.nps.gov/elis/

The History Channel, Ellis Island
   http://www.history.com/minisites/ellisisland/

The Statue of Liberty-Ellis Island Foundation Inc., Ellis Island Page
   http://www.ellisisland.org/genealogy/ellis_island.asp

Angel Island

Angel Island Conservancy
   http://angelisland.org/

Angel Island Immigration Station Foundation
   http://www.aiisf.org

The Library of Congress, "The Chinese in California, 1850–1925"
   http://www.loc.gov/teachers/classroommaterials/connections/chinese-cal/history6.html

National Park Service, Golden Gate, Angel Island, 1846–1876
   http://www.nps.gov/goga/historyculture/angel-island.htm

Scholastic, Asian Pacific American Heritage, "Angel Island: Li Keng Wong's Story"
   http://teacher.scholastic.com/activities/asian-american/angel_island/index.htm

University of Illinois, Angel Island Photo Gallery
   http://www.english.illinois.edu/maps/poets/a_f/angel/gallery.htm

Historic Immigration

Digital History. Ethnic America
    http://www.digitalhistory.uh.edu/historyonline/ethnic_am.cfm

The Historical Society of Pennsylvania, Strangers in the Land of Strangers
    http://www2.hsp.org/exhibits/strangers/index.html

Lewis W. Hine—Ellis Island, George Eastman House, Still Photograph Archive
    http://www.geh.org/fm/lwhprints/htmlsrc/ellis-island_idx00001.html

Library of Congress: Immigration Resources for Teachers
    http://www.loc.gov/teachers/classroommaterials/themes/immigration/#

The Lower East Side Tenement Museum, New York City
    http://www.tenement.org/

New York Public Library Immigration Images
    http://digitalgallery.nypl.org/nypldigital/dgkeysearchresult.cfm?keyword=immigration+to
    +the+United+States

PBS, Becoming American: The Chinese Experience
    http://www.pbs.org/becomingamerican/index.html

PBS Kids, Big Apple History: From New York to Your Town
    http://pbskids.org/bigapplehistory/immigration/index-flash.html

PBS Teachers Immigration Resources and Activities (Grades 3–5)
    http://www.pbs.org/teachers/thismonth/immigration/index1.html

Scholastic, Immigration Activities and Resources
    http://teacher.scholastic.com/activities/immigration/

UCR/California Museum of Photography, The Golden Door: Immigration Images from the
    Keystone-Mast Collection
    http://www.cmp.ucr.edu/collections/permanent/projects/stereo/immigration/ellisisland.
    html

Text Set Models

Duet

Because of their versatility, *Lady Liberty: A Biography* and *Naming Liberty* is a successful Duet for elementary and secondary classrooms. With the younger grades, these texts would be foundational to the unit. For older students, these books as a Duet would be a wonderful scaffold for thinking about the historic period of immigration at the turn of the last century.

Immigration Duet Model

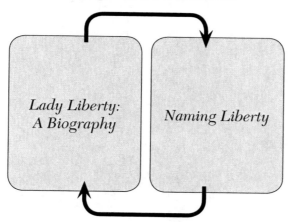

Each book is multigenre and written in verse. *Lady Liberty: A Biography* tells of the construction of the Statue of Liberty from the various points of view of people involved in its design, construction, and fundraising. The story is told through historical fiction verse vignettes coupled with glorious illustrations that spread across the gutter of the two-page spread. *Naming Liberty* also works concurrently in several genres. On the left side of each two-page spread is the fictional verse narrative of Gitl, a Russian girl waiting to escape the pogroms of Russia in the late 19th century. On the right side of each two-page spread is the nonfiction verse narrative of the design and construction of the Statue of Liberty. Each page has its own separate illustration. Both texts have valuable author's notes and back matter for classroom discussion and use. The texts introduce the origin of the Statue of Liberty and its status as a global icon and serve as mentor texts for writing verse fiction and nonfiction.

Sunburst

For a whole-class read or read-aloud, Laurence Yep's *The Dragon's Child: A Story of Angel Island* is ideal for exploring 19th and early 20th century Chinese immigration in elementary grades. The book is written as historical fiction through research Yep did of his family history, including extensive interviews with his grandfather conducted over many years by U.S. immigration officials, documenting his travels between China and the United States. Each chapter begins with a question and an answer drawn from one of the interviews. In the novel, protagonist Gim Lew Yep would rather stay home than immigrate to the United States, "the land of the Golden Mountain."

Immigration Sunburst Model

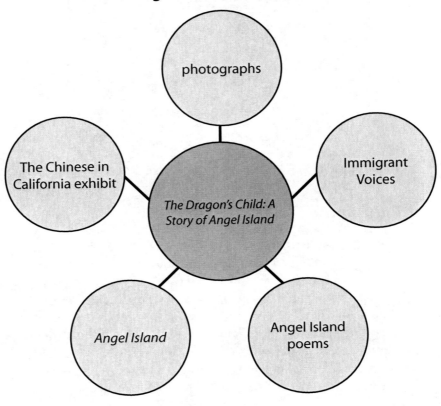

Many readers will learn for the first time about the role Chinese immigrants and Chinese Americans played in building the American West and the restrictions placed on Chinese immigration in the early part of the 20th century. Before, during, and after reading this riveting historical novel, students can explore other aspects of Chinese immigration. Using resources gathered by the University of Illinois (http://www.english.illinois.edu/maps/poets/a_f/angel/gallery.htm), you might want to print and laminate photographs of immigrants at Angel Island in the early 20th century in order to prompt inquiry and cultivate interest before reading the novel.

While reading the novel, students can read about historic and contemporary immigration to America's West Coast in "Immigrant Voices" on the Angel Island Immigration Station webpage and even contribute their own families' stories. Finally, once Gim is at Angel Island, you can share poems that were written on the walls of the Angel Island Immigration Station by detained Chinese immigrants and have students compare and contrast the experiences in the poems to those of Gim. Lori Mortensen's simple picture book *Angel Island* may be useful for orienting students more specifically to the process that immigrants underwent upon arrival and the reasons for the detainment. The digital exhibit, "The Chinese in California, 1850–1925" from the Library of Congress (http://www.loc.gov/teachers/classroommaterials/connections/chinese-cal/history6.html) has photographs and primary source materials that you also might want to share with your students.

When students are finished reading *The Dragon's Child: A Story of Angel Island*, you might want to have them explore the Scholastic Online Exhibit (http://teacher.scholastic.com/activities/asian-american/angel_island/index.htm) entitled "Angel Island: Li Keng Wong's Story" to compare and contrast a young girl's experience leaving her rural Chinese village to immigrate to America in 1933. Some students might choose to read Wong's biography, *Good Fortune: My Journey to Gold Mountain* (2006).

Tree Ring

For secondary students studying the historic period of European immigration in the late 19th and early 20th century, *Shutting Out the Sky: Life in the Tenements of New York 1880–1924* by Deborah Hopkinson, which follows the lives of five young people who immigrate to the United States from Europe as children or teenagers, is an ideal starting point. Rather than separate each person's experience into a different chapter, Hopkinson pulls them together in chapters that reflect the immigrant's chronological and psychological journey from the homeland to America.

Immigration Tree Ring Model

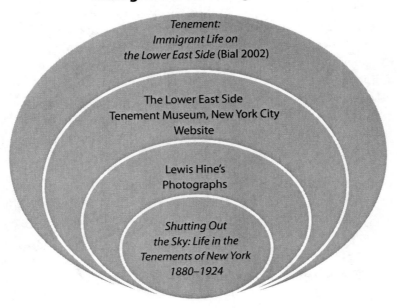

In her afterword, Hopkinson discusses some of her research strategies, including examining Lewis Hine's historic photographs, visiting the Lower East Side Tenement Museum in New York City, and listening to oral histories. You can provide your students with access to these same resources, and you can ask them to explore those resources before, during, and after they have completed *Shutting Out the Sky*. Students can be split into small groups to take virtual tours of different apartments, complete with audio, of 97 Orchard Street, the Tenement Museum (http://www.tenement.org). They can examine Hine's photographs at the New York Public Library (http://digitalgallery.nypl.org/nypldigital/dgkeysearchresult.cfm?keyword=lewis+hine+immigration+photos) or at the George Eastman House (http://www.geh.org/fm/lwhprints/htmlsrc/ellis-island_idx00001.html). If your local public library subscribes to the Ancestry.com database, you can take a field trip to your local library and have students listen to excerpts from the Ellis Island Oral History project as well.

Hopkinson also recommends books for young readers, including many of the historical novels and chapter book nonfiction included in this text set. Of particular interest is Raymond Bial's *Tenement: Immigrant Life on the Lower East Side*, a photo essay of 97 Orchard Street, the location of the Lower East Side Tenement Museum.

Solar System

Taken together, this collection of contemporary short stories, novels, and graphic fiction, present a range of experiences of immigration. In *Shooting Kabul* and *Ask Me No Questions*, September 11th looms, and in *Something About America*, the 1990s war in Kosovo. *First Crossing: Stories of Teen Immigrants*, a collection of short stories, presents a range of fictional teens from around the world adjusting to life in the United States. Shaun Tan's *The Arrival* is a wordless graphic novel that combines history and fantasy. Students will pore over the panels, experiencing the fear, discomfort, and joy of the acclimation of life in a new land.

Immigration Solar System Model

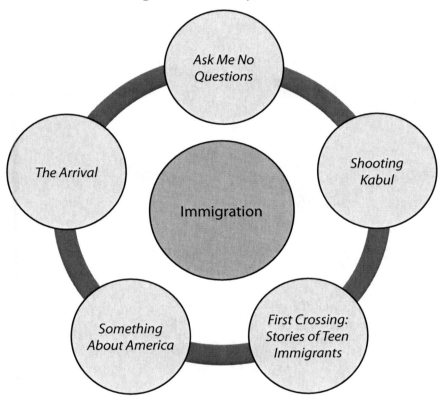

Reading these texts concurrently will allow students to consider the reasons why immigrants continue to seek a safe haven in the United States and the conflicting welcome they can often receive. By comparing and contrasting experiences of fictional immigrants from various parts of the world, students can see what common experiences are at the core of the transition from one homeland to another and the ways in which cultures continue to clash.

These books can be supported with a variety of multimodal, multigenre online texts, including the 2011 PBS Special The New Americans (http://www.pbs.org/independentlens/newamericans/), the traveling Smithsonian Institute exhibit "Becoming American: Teenagers and Immigration" (http://www.sites.si.edu/images/exhibits/Becoming%20American/index.htm), and particularly "In the Mix" (http://www.pbs.org/inthemix/shows/show_teen_immigrants.html), a PBS program produced by teenagers for teenagers.

Student Responses to Texts

Specific genre studies that lend themselves to this topic are:

- Historical fiction
- Nonfiction picture books
- Verse fiction/verse nonfiction
- Photographs
- Oral histories and interviews
- Contemporary realistic fiction

When teaching immigration, the texts types in the chart on pages 243–244 can be used as mentor texts for student writing and artistic production.

Immigration Text Set: Student Responses to Texts

Subtopics, Genres, and Mentor Texts	Student-Created Texts
Oral Histories of Immigrants • Primary sources available online and through http://www.Ancestry.com	New oral histories based on student-conducted interviews with immigrants (young and old). Students use audio or video resources to record interviews, which could be posted on a class blog or written and shared privately in a class book or an organized reading to which family and community members are invited Fictional short stories or letters to or from home based on these oral histories Music, fiction, or visual art in response to the oral histories, presented at a reading or performance for parents, peers, and community members
Letters or Diary Entries • Primary sources available online • *Letters from Rifka* (Hesse 1993)	Fictional letters from/to home Personal letters to family members
Verse Fiction/Nonfiction • *Naming Liberty* (Yolen 2008) • *Lady Liberty: A Biography* (Rappaport 2008)	Student-written fiction and nonfiction verse picture books about historic or contemporary immigration
Family History • *All the Way to America* (Yaccarino 2011) • *The Dragon's Child: A Story of Angel Island* (Yep 2008)	Student-researched histories of one side of their family, going back several generations Music, fiction, or visual art in response to their research, presented at a reading or performance for parents, peers, and community members
Things They Carried (Objects) • *All the Way to America: The Story of a Big Italian Family and a Little Shovel* (Yaccarino 2011) • *Annushka's Voyage* (Tarbescu 1998) • *The Memory Coat* (Woodruff 1999) • Photos of Ellis Island Treasury Room (online) • Historic photographs (online)	Immigration Museum Exhibit: Student-created replicas of the objects immigrants have brought to the United States (in the past or present) and museum cards providing context Family trunks

Immigration Text Set: Student Responses to Texts (cont.)

Subtopics, Genres, and Mentor Texts	Student-Created Texts
Contemporary Immigration Issues • Contemporary national and local newspapers and magazines • U.S. Immigration Service/Homeland Security websites • Websites of members of Congress, Governors, the White House • *Tell Us We're Home* (Budhos 2010) • *Ask Me No Questions* (Budhos 2006) • *No Safe Place* (Ellis 2010) • *First Crossing: Stories of Teen Immigrants* (Gallo 2007) • *La Linea* (Jaramillo 2008) • *Drita, My Homegirl* (Lombard 2008) • *Escaping the Tiger* (Manivong 2010) • *Red Midnight* (Mikaelson 2003) • *A Step from Heaven* (Na 2002) • *Shooting Kabul* (Sensai 2010)	Traditional research reports Student-written-and-produced class magazine devoted to issues related to contemporary immigration Podcast in which students read excerpts from their traditional newspaper or class magazine Student-created website devoted to different perspectives on immigration Music, fiction, or visual art in response to their research, presented at a reading or performance for parents, peers, and community members

chapter 10

Space

This chapter provides a complete text set for the topic of space. It details book titles, digital resources, and instructional suggestions. For an annotated list of the texts and digital resources, please see the Digital Resource CD (spaceannotated.doc).

Texts

Nonfiction Picture Books

Aguilar, David. 2011. *13 Planets: The Latest View of the Solar System*. Washington, DC: National Geographic.

Aldrin, Buzz, and Wendell Minor. 2009. *Look to the Stars*. New York: G. P. Putnam's Sons.

Bailey, Jacqui. 2004. *Sun Up, Sun Down: The Story of Day and Night*. North Mankato, MN: Picture Window Books.

Branley, Franklyn Mansfield. 1986. *What Makes Day and Night*. New York: HarperCollins.

———. 1991. *The Big Dipper*. New York: HarperCollins.

———. 2000. *The International Space Station*. New York: HarperCollins.

———. 2002a. *Mission to Mars*. New York: HarperCollins.

———. 2002b. *The Sun, Our Nearest Star*. New York: HarperCollins.

Burleigh, Robert. 2009. *One Giant Leap*. New York: Philomel Books.

Crelin, Bob. 2009. *Faces of the Moon*. Watertown, MA: Charlesbridge.

Floca, Brian. 2009. *Moonshot: The Flight of Apollo 11*. New York: Jackson/Atheneum Books for Young Readers.

Gibbons, Gail. 1995. *The Reasons for Seasons*. New York: Holiday House.

Jenkins, Alvin. 2004. *Next Stop Neptune: Experiencing the Solar System*. New York: Houghton Mifflin.

Karas, G. Brian. 2005. *On Earth*. New York: G. P. Putnam's Sons.

Kim, F. S. 2010. *Constellations*. Danbury, CT: Children's Press.

Kudlinski, Kathleen. 2008. *Boy, Were We Wrong About the Solar System!* New York: Dutton Children's Books.

McNulty, Faith. 2005. *If You Decide to Go the Moon*. New York: Scholastic Press.

Mortensen, Lori. 2010. *Come See the Earth Turn: The Story of Leon Foucault*. Berkeley, CA: Tricycle Press.

Pfeffer, Wendy. 2003. *The Shortest Day: Celebrating the Winter Solstice*. New York: Dutton Children's Books.

———. 2006. *We Gather Together: Celebrating the Harvest Season*. New York: Dutton Children's Books.

———. 2008. *A New Beginning: Celebrating the Spring Equinox*. New York: Dutton Children's Books.

———. 2010. *The Longest Day: Celebrating the Summer Solstice*. New York: Dutton Children's Books.

Rey, H. A. 2008. *Find the Constellations*. New York: Houghton Mifflin.

Ride, Sally, and Tam O'Shaughnessy. 1992. *Voyager: An Adventure to the Edge of the Solar System*. San Diego: Sally Ride Science.

———. 1999. *The Mystery of Mars*. New York: Crown Publishers.

Simon, Seymour. 1998. *Comets, Meteors, and Asteroids: Our Solar System*. New York: HarperCollins Publishers.

———. 2000. *Destination: Jupiter*. Washington, DC: Smithsonian/HarperCollins.

———. 2003. *Earth: Our Planet in Space.* New York: Simon and Schuster Books for Young Readers.

———. 2007. *Our Solar System.* Washington, DC: Smithsonian/HarperCollins.

———. 2006. *Destination: Space.* Washington, DC: Smithsonian/HarperCollins.

Sis, Peter. 2000. *Starry Messenger: Galileo Galilei.* New York: Foster/Farrar, Straus & Giroux.

Stewart, Melissa. 2009. *Why Does the Moon Change Shape?* New York: Marshall Cavendish.

Trammel, Howard K. 2010. *The Solar System.* Danbury, CT: Children's Press.

Nonfiction

Bell, Trudy E. 2008. *Earth's Journey Through Space.* New York: Chelsea House.

Berkowitz, Jacob. 2009. *Out of this World: The Amazing Search for an Alien Earth.* Toronto: Kids Can Press.

Chaikin, Andrew. 2009. *Mission Control, This Is Apollo: The Story of the First Voyages to the Moon.* New York: Viking Press.

Gaiter, Will. 2011. *The Night Sky: Month by Month.* New York: DK Publishing.

Jackson, Ellen. 2002. *Looking for Life in the Universe: The Search for Extraterrestrial Intelligence.* New York: Houghton Mifflin.

Ottaviani, Jim. 2009. *T-Minus: The Race to the Moon.* New York: Aladdin.

Rusch, Elizabeth. 2012. *The Mighty Mars Rovers: The Incredible Adventures of Spirit and Opportunity.* Boston: Houghton Mifflin.

Schyffert, Bea Uusma. 2003. *The Man Who Went to the Far Side of the Moon: The Story of Apollo 11 Astronaut Michael Collins.* San Francisco: Chronicle Books.

Scott, Elaine. 2007. *When Is a Planet Not a Planet? The Story of Pluto.* New York: Clarion Books.

———. 2008. *Mars and the Search for Life.* New York: Clarion Books.

———. 2011. *Space, Stars, and the Beginning of Time: What the Hubble Telescope Saw.* Boston: Clarion Books.

Siy, Alexandra. 2009. *Cars on Mars: Roving the Red Planet.* Watertown, MA: Charlesbridge.

Stone, Tanya Lee. 2009. *Almost Astronauts: 13 Women Who Dared to Dream.* Somerville, MA: Candlewick Press.

Stott, Carole, and Giles Sparrow. 2010. *Starfinder: The Complete Beginner's Guide to the Night Sky.* New York: DK Publishing.

Thimmesh, Catherine. 2006. *Team Moon: How 400,000 People Landed Apollo 11 on the Moon.* New York: Houghton Mifflin.

Wittenstein, Vicky O. 2010. *Planet Hunter: Geoff Marcy and the Search for Other Earths.* Honesdale, PA: Boyds Mills Press.

Wunsch, Susi Trautmann. 1998. *The Adventures of Sojourner: The Mission to Mars That Thrilled the World.* New York: Mikaya Press.

Fiction Picture Books

Bruchac, Joseph. 1992. *Thirteen Moons on Turtle's Back: A Native American Year of Moons.* New York: Philomel Books.

Dayrell, Elphinstone. 1968. *Why the Sun and the Moon Live in the Sky: An African Folktale.* New York: Houghton Mifflin.

Henkes, Kevin. 2004. *Kitten's First Full Moon.* New York: Greenwillow Books.

Hunter, Anne. 1996. *Possum's Harvest Moon.* New York: Houghton Mifflin.

Leedy, Loreen, and Andrew Schuerger. 2006. *Messages from Mars.* New York: Holiday House.

McCarty, Peter. 2006. *Moon Plane.* New York: Holt.

O'Brien, Patrick. 2009. *You Are the First Kid on Mars.* New York: Putnam.

Robert, Na'ima. 2009. *Ramadan Moon.* London: Frances Lincoln Children's Books.

Thurber, James. 1971. *Many Moons.* New York: Harcourt Brace.

Picture Book Poetry

Florian, Douglas. 2007. *Comets, Stars, the Moon, and Mars: Space Poems and Paintings.* New York: Harcourt.

Hopkins, Lee Bennett. 2009. *Sky Magic: Poems.* New York: Dutton Children's Books.

Singer, Marilyn. 2011. *A Full Moon Is Rising: Poems.* New York: Lee & Low Books.

Taylor, Joanne. 2002. *Full Moon Rising.* Toronto: Tundra Books.

Periodicals

Terrestrial Planets

Chiang, Mona. 2001. "Why Mars?" *Science World*, November 26.

David, Leonard. 2002. "Fourth Planet Odyssey." *Odyssey*, April.

Pasachoff, Jay. 2011. "Catch A Pass! (of Venus with the Sun)." *Odyssey*, May/June.

Gas Giants

Bortolotti, Dan. 2008. "10 Things You Didn't Know About." *Owl*, November.

"Gaseous Planets." 2001. *Monkey Shines on Health and Science*, September.

"Not-So-Bling Rings." 2010. *Astronomy*, May.

"Observing the Ringed Planet!" 2005. *Odyssey*, January.

Dwarf Planets

"Bye-Bye Pluto." 2006. *Weekly Reader*, December 8.

Crosswell, Ken. 2010. "How Cool Is Pluto?" *Highlights*, February.

Cutraro, Jennifer. 2008. "For Kids: Pluto, Plutoid: What's in a Name?" *Science News for Kids*, June 20.

Gramling. C. 2006. "Dwarf Planet Discord." *Science News for Kids*, October 11.

"New Moon Found." 2011. *Current Science*, November 25.

"New World Order." 2006. *Current Events*, September 15.

O'Meara, Stephen James. 2007. "Xena Gets the Ax!" *Odyssey*, February.

Stern, Alan. 2002. "NASA's Mission to Pluto and the Kuiper Belt." *Odyssey*, April.

Talcott, Richard. 2010. "How We'll Explore Pluto." *Astronomy*, July.

Kuiper Belt

Cowen, Ron. 2010. "On the Fringe." *Science News for Kids*, January 16.

"It's Chilly Out There!" 2010. *Odyssey*, April.

Regas, Dean. 2011. "The Search for More Plutos." *Astronomy*, July.

Sohn, Emily. 2007. "A Family in Space." *Science News for Kids*, March 21.

Stern, Alan. 2002. "Frontier at the Edge: The Kuiper Belt." *Odyssey*, April.

———. 2010. "Secrets of the Kuiper Belt." *Astronomy*, April.

Asteroid Belt

Barnes-Svarney, Patricia. 1995. "Closest Encounters." *Odyssey*, February.

"Meteorites: Where They Come From, How They Travel, and What They Do When They Get Here." 1992. *Science World*, September 4.

"Space Rocks." 2007. *Scholastic Super Science*, November/December.

Stephans, Robert. 2010. "Asteroid Maven." *Sky and Telescope*, October.

Goldilocks Zone (also known as Habitable Zone or Life Zone)

"Astro News: Dozens of Extrasolar Planets Discovered." 2012. *Astronomy*, January.

Bortolotti, Dan. 2011. "Searching for Another Earth." 2011. *Owl*, January/February.

Drake, Nadia. 2011. "Extrasolar Orb Occupies Just Right Spot for Life: Planet Hunters Add More Than 1,000 New Candidates." *Science News*, December 31.

Ornes, Stephen. 2011. "Distant 'Goldilocks' World." *Science News for Kids*, December 21.

Smith, Natalie. 2012. "Is Anybody Out There?" *Junior Scholastic*, March 14.

Villard, Ray. 2011. "Hunting for Earthlike Planets." *Astronomy*, April.

Day and Night

"Ask Astro: What's a Day?" 2011. *Astronomy*, September.

"The Day Earth Stood Still." 2010. *Current Science*, November 26.

"Discovering Planet Earth." 2005. *Ask*, September.

Greij, Eldon. 2010. "Biological Clocks: How Ingenious Internal Clocks Help Birds Anticipate Critical Life Events." *Birder's World*, April.

"Middle Earth Spins." *Current Science*, November 4.

"Night and Day." 2011. *Click*, November/December.

"Prove the Earth Spins at Night!" 2003. *Odyssey*, February.

"Reasons for the Seasons." 2010. *Junior Scholastic*, September 20.

Hubble Telescope

Coston, Barbara Carney. 2011. "Hubble—The Orbiting Telescope." *Hopscotch*, August/September.

Hammel, Heidi B. 2011. "Why We Should Build Webb: By Pushing Beyond Hubble's Limits, Webb Will Inspire a New Generation." *Sky and Telescope*, December.

Sohn, Emily. 2008. "For Kids: Hubble Trouble Doubled." *Science News for Kids*, October 24.

————. 2009. "For Kids: Hubble Lives On." *Science News for Kids*, January 21.

Mars Rover

Lackdwalla, Emily. 2011. "Face to Face with a Giant: NASA's New Rover Curiosity Will Take Mars Exploration to an Entirely New Level." *Sky and Telescope*, December.

"Mars Or Bust: A NASA Rover Heads Toward the Red Planet." 2012. *Junior Scholastic*, January.

Warren, Stephanie. 2012. "Mission to Mars." *Scholastic Math*, January 16.

Digital Resources

Websites

American Museum of Natural History
http://www.amnh.org/

American Museum of Natural History, Hayden Planetarium
http://www.haydenplanetarium.org/index.php

European Space Agency for Kids
http://www.esa.int/esaKIDSen/

Harvard-Smithsonian Center for Astrophysics
http://www.cfa.harvard.edu/education/

International Astronomical Union
http://www.iau.org/

MESSENGER: MErcury Surface, Space ENvironment, GEochemistry, and Ranging
http://messenger.jhuapl.edu/index.php

MicroObservatory Robotic Telescope Network
http://mo-www.harvard.edu/MicroObservatory/

NASA, Astronomy Picture of the Day's Educational Links
http://apod.nasa.gov/apod/lib/edlinks.html

NASA, For Educators
http://www.nasa.gov/audience/foreducators/index.html

National Geographic, Science and Space
http://science.nationalgeographic.com/science/space

PBS, Astronomy
http://www.pbs.org/topics/science-nature/astronomy/

Scholastic, Weekly Reader
http://www.weeklyreader.com/

Science for Kids
http://www.eurekalert.org/scienceforkids/

Science NetLinks
http://sciencenetlinks.com/

Science News for Kids
http://www.sciencenewsforkids.org/

Smithsonian Education
http://smithsonianeducation.org/index.html

Smithsonian National Air and Space Museum
http://www.nasm.si.edu/

The Space Place
http://spaceplace.nasa.gov/

Space Telescope Science Institute
http://oposite.stsci.edu/

StarChild: A Learning Center for Young Astronomers
http://starchild.gsfc.nasa.gov/docs/StarChild/StarChild.html

Thinkfinity, Verizon Foundation
http://www.thinkfinity.org/

WatchKnowLearn, Educational Videos on Space and Astronomy
http://www.watchknowlearn.org/Category.aspx?CategoryID=137

WorldWide Telescope Ambassadors
https://wwtambassadors.org/wwt/

Tablet Apps

AstroApp: Space Station and Space Shuttle Crew, NASA

Beyond Planet Earth Augmented Reality (AR) App, American Museum of Natural History

Britannica Kids: Solar System, Britannica

Hubble Top 100, European Space Agency (ESA) and NASA

Journey to the Exoplanets, Scientific American

Man In Space, Sky at Night Magazine

Mars Globe HD, Midnight Martian

Moon Globe HD, Midnight Martian

NASA App HD, NASA

Solar System for iPad, Touch Press

Solar Walk for iPad, Touch Press

Spaced (NASA, ESA)

Star Walk for iPad: Interactive Astronomy Guide, Vito Technology, Inc.

There's No Place Like Space, Ocean House Media

Text Set Models

Duet

To focus on the suspense, excitement, and achievement that are at the heart of the 1969 moon landing, we recommend pairing two nonfiction picture books, *One Giant Leap* and *Moonshot: The Flight of Apollo 11.* These books stand out among many titles published to commemorate the 40th anniversary of the moon landing through their literary qualities and their spectacular illustrations.

Space Duet Model

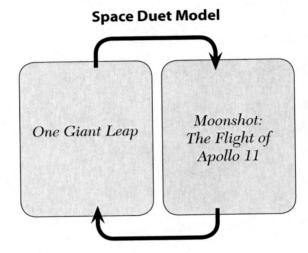

Since the books are very closely matched in content, you will want to guide your students to compare and contrast the choices made by the authors about how best to convey the trajectory of the voyage and how they chose to emphasize the pivotal moment of that first step. Additionally, you will want to discuss the structure of nonfiction narratives and how the authors use figurative language to tell the compelling story of the voyage. The illustrations in these books are also rich material for examination. Note the varying perspectives used by the illustrators to emphasize the scope of this accomplishment that forever changed our relationship with the vastness that is space. These dramatic picture books are appropriate for read-alouds in elementary and secondary classrooms.

Sunburst

Is there life beyond planet Earth? The exploration of the unknown is a topic of endless fascination. Capitalize on secondary students' interest in cutting edge astronomy with *Planet Hunter: Geoff Marcy and the Search for Other Earths.*

Space Sunburst Model

Highlighting the accomplishments of an astronomer who has devoted his career to perfecting methods of exploring the outer reaches of space, this text is ideal as the core text of a Sunburst Model as it is easily extended with a wide array of compelling multimodal, multigenre texts. Two other nonfiction books that provide complementary content are *Out of this World: The Amazing Search for an Alien Earth* and *Looking for Life in the Universe: The Search for Extraterrestrial Intelligence.* Students can examine how technologies for space exploration are ever changing by investigating The Space Place, NASA's website for young students (http://spaceplace.nasa.gov/). A fascinating tablet app on the topic is Journey of the Exoplanets from Scientific American and Farrar, Straus & Giroux. Students can listen to Neil deGrasse Tyson describe the known outer reaches of space at the Hayden Planetarium website (http://www.haydenplanetarium.org/tyson/tags/subjects/exoplanets).

Tree Ring

A Full Moon Is Rising is a collection of seventeen annotated poems set in different locations around the globe that celebrate the full moon. This text is ideal for use as a core text in the Tree Ring Model because the diverse topics touched upon in the poems naturally pique readers' interest and lead to further exploration and because of the comprehensive back and front matter included in the text.

Space Tree Ring Model

Comets,
Stars, the Moon, and Mars
and *Sky Magic*

Source
for poems in *A Full*
Moon Is Rising

A Full Moon
Is Rising

Students can start by exploring the resources that Singer lists in the source notes. As students examine the sources, guide them to revisit the poems to find evidence of how the sources influenced the author's composition of the poem. Compare the information provided in the source texts with the information as it is expressed in poetic form. Ask students to think about the selection process of the author—when might her content choices have been inquiry based, content based, or based on appreciation of beauty in the natural world? In this process, you will illuminate both research and writing processes. Following this examination, students can explore other volumes of poetry about space. A close content match, *Full Moon Rising* includes a poem for the full moon of each month. *Comets, Stars, the Moon, and Mars: Space Poems and Paintings* and *Sky Magic: Poems* takes a broader view, encompassing poems about all the celestial bodies in the sky.

Solar System

While we wrote this book, NASA's Mars Rover, Opportunity, was exploring the rim of Endeavor Crater on the planet Mars. Four core texts within a Solar System Model can be used to guide students' investigation of Mars and efforts to explore and eventually visit our nearest planet. We suggest juxtaposing three nonfiction texts with two works of fiction that speculate on currently known information about Mars.

Space Solar System Model

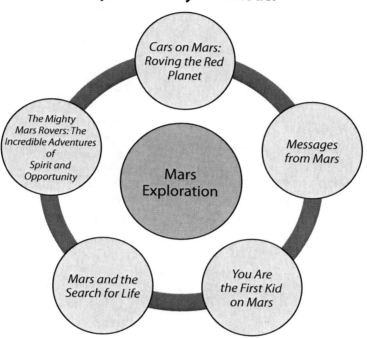

In *Mars and the Search for Life,* a nonfiction title appropriate for intermediate grades, Scott traces the history of scientific thinking about the planet and its composition, leading up to the present exploration of the planet. *Cars on Mars: Roving the Red Planet,* also a nonfiction text appropriate for intermediate grades, details the Rover missions with amazing photographic detail. *The Mighty Mars Rovers: The Incredible Adventures of Spirit and Opportunity,* part of the Scientists in the Field series, is a current and comprehensive photo essay overview of the Mars missions appropriate for a secondary audience. Following a reading of these texts, students can be introduced to two titles that imagine what it would be like to travel to Mars. *You Are the First Kid on Mars,* told in second person narration, features a young male protagonist who makes a four-month long journey to a colony on Mars where he participates in scientific research. In contrast to this solitary journey, *Messages from Mars* presents a busy class of multicultural students who send emails home describing their journey and scientific explorations.

Engage students in a critique of the accuracy of the speculative fiction using the information they learned from the nonfiction texts and additional resources. Be sure to visit the Mars for Kids section of NASA's Mars Exploration Program site (http://marsprogram .jpl.nasa.gov/participate/funzone/), which includes multimedia resources.

Student Responses to Texts

When studying space, the text types below might make sense for your students to construct.

Space Text Set: Student Responses to Texts

Subtopics, Genres, and Mentor Texts	Student-Created Texts
Narrative Nonfiction Picture Story Books • *One Giant Leap* (Burleigh 2009) • *Moonshot: The Flight of Apollo 11* (Floca 2009)	**Narrative nonfiction storybooks:** Students research and retell another climactic moment in space exploration, using narrative devices and figurative language (similes, metaphors, alliteration) used in these two books.
Life on Mars? • Episodes of *My Favorite Martian* • Excerpts from Orson Wells' recording of *War of the Worlds* • *You Are the First Kid on Mars* (O'Brien 2009) • *Mars and the Search for Life* (Scott 2008) • *Cars on Mars: Roving the Red Planet* (Siy 2009) • *The Mighty Mars Rovers: The Incredible Adventures of Spirit and Opportunity* (Rusch 2012) • *Looking for Life in the Universe: The Search for Extraterrestrial Intelligence* (Jackson 2002)	**Speculative fiction short stories:** Students write and illustrate speculative picture books or short stories, using factual information they have learned as well as the different ways that Martians have been represented over time. Some may choose to record their stories using the Orson Wells narration of *War of the Worlds* as a mentor text.
Defining a Planet • *When Is a Planet Not a Planet? The Story of Pluto* (Scott 2007) • *13 Planets: The Latest View of the Solar System* (Aguilar 2011) • International Astronomical Union website • NASA website • American Museum of Natural History, Hayden Planetarium website	**The Definition of a Planet/Business Letter:** Students compare and contrast different definitions of planets, arguing for and against qualities that should be included or excluded in the definition, and share their working definitions of a planet in business letters sent to the International Astronomical Union (IAU).
Exploring Space • *Cars on Mars: Roving the Red Planet* (Siy 2009) • *The Mighty Mars Rovers: The Incredible Adventures of Spirit and Opportunity* (Rusch 2012) • *Planet Hunter: Geoff Marcy and the Search for Other Earths* (Wittenstein 2010) • NASA website • American Museum of Natural History, Hayden Planetarium website • National Air and Space Museum of the Smithsonian Institute website	**Digital multimedia presentations:** Students create presentations on different instruments used for space exploration in the present as well as the past, and future missions currently in research stages.

Honeybees

This chapter provides a complete text set for the topic of honeybees. It details book titles, digital resources, and instructional suggestions. For an annotated list of the texts and digital resources, please see the Digital Resource CD (honeybeesannotated.doc).

Texts

Nonfiction Picture Books

Ashley, Susan. 2004. *Bees*. Delran, NJ: Weekly Reader Early Learning.

Bullard, Lisa. 2011. *Busy Animals: Learning About Animals in Autumn*. Mankato, MN: Picture Window Books.

Cole, Joanna. 1996. *The Magic School Bus Inside a Beehive*. New York: Scholastic.

Dawson, Emily. 2011. *How Bees Make Honey*. Mankato, MN: Amicus Publishing.

Fujiwara, Yukimo. 2006. *Honey, A Gift from Nature*. La Jolla, CA: Kane/Miller Publishing.

Gibbons, Gail. 1997. *The Honey Makers*. New York: Mulberry Books.

Glaser, Linda. 2003. *Brilliant Bees*. Minneapolis, MN: Lerner Publishing.

Heiligman, Deborah. 2002. *Honeybees*. Washington, DC: National Geographic Society.

Loewen, Nancy. 2004. *Busy Buzzers: Bees in Your Backyard*. North Mankato, MN: Picture Window Books.

Micucci, Charles. 1995. *The Life and Times of the Honeybee*. New York: Houghton Mifflin.

Milton, Joyce. 2003. *Honeybees*. New York: Grosset & Dunlap.

Mortensen, Lori. 2009. *In the Trees, Honeybees*. Nevada City, CA: Dawn Publications.

Nelson, Robin. 2012. *From Flower to Honey*. Minneapolis, MN: Lerner Publications.

Rockwell, Anne. 2005. *Honey in a Hive*. New York: HarperCollins Publishing.

Rotner, Shelley, and Anne Woodhull. 2010. *The Buzz on Bees: Why Are They Disappearing?* New York: Holiday House.

Sayre, April Pulley. 2006. *The Bumblebee Queen*. Watertown, MA: Charlesbridge Publishing.

Stewart, Melissa. 2009. *How Do Bees Make Honey?* Tarrytown, NY: Marshall Cavendish Benchmark.

Nonfiction

Becker, Helaine. 2009. *The Insecto-Files: Amazing Insect Science and Bug Facts You'll Never Believe*. Toronto: Maple Tree Press.

Buchmann, Stephen. 2010. *Honeybees: Letters from the Hive*. New York: Delacorte Press.

Burns, Loree Griffin. 2010. *The Hive Detectives: Chronicle of a Honey Bee Catastrophe*. Boston: Houghton Mifflin Books for Children.

Jango-Cohen, Judith. 2007. *Bees*. Tarrytown, NY: Marshall Cavendish Benchmark.

Solway, Andrew. 2003. *Classifying Insects*. North Mankato, MN: Heinemann Library.

Fiction Picture Books

Buchman, Stephan, and Diana Cohn. 2007. *The Bee Tree*. El Paso, TX: Cinco Puntos Press.

Cheng, Andrea. 2002. *When the Bees Fly Home*. Gardiner, ME: Tilbury House.

Formento, Alison. 2012. *These Bees Count!* Park Ridge, IL: Albert Whitman.

High, Linda O. 1998. *Beekeepers*. Honesdale, PA: Boyds Mills Press.

Kessler, Christina. 2006. *The Best Beekeeper of Lalibela: A Tale from Africa*. New York: Holiday House.

Krebs, Laurie. 2008. *The Beeman*. Cambridge, MA: Barefoot Books.

Morales, Melita. 2011. *Jam & Honey*. Berkeley, CA: Tricycle Press.

Nargi, Lela. 2011. *The Honeybee Man*. New York: Schwartz & Wade Books.

Ofanansky, Allison. 2011. *What's the Buzz? Honey for a Sweet New Year.* Minneapolis, MN: Kar-Ben Publishing.

Polacco, Patricia. 1993. *The Bee Tree.* New York: Philomel Books.

Stockton, Frank. 2003. *The Bee-man of Orn.* Somerville, MA: Candlewick Press.

Wilson, J. V. 2011. *Bumblebee.* London: Frances Lincoln Children's Books.

Novels and Short Stories

Hosler, Jay. 2000. *Clan Apis.* Columbus, OK: Active Synapse.

Johnson, Emily Rhoads. 2000. *Write Me if You Dare!* Alpine, TX: Front Street Books.

Picture Book Poetry

Florian, Douglas. 2012. *UnBEElieveables: Honeybee Poems and Paintings.* La Jolla, CA: Beach Lane Books.

Periodicals

"A Honeybee's Body." 2011. *Weekly Reader*, May/June.

Abbink, Emily. 2010a. "Beeswax = Big Business." *Dig*, April.

———. 2010b. "Honey without the Sting: These Hives Belong to the Bee God." *Dig*, April.

Adams, Jacqueline. 2009. "Nests that Please Bees." *Science World*, September 21.

Anderson-Stojanovic, Virginia, R. 2010. "Bees in a Basket? Does the Hole Have the Answer?" *Dig*, April.

Andujar, Michelle. 2008. "To Bee or Not to Bee: Mass Disappearance of Bats and Bees!" *Skipping Stones*, May/August.

Baker, Lily. 2010. "Bees: the Superheroes of the Insect World!" *New Moon Girls*, November/December.

Bryant, Vaughn M. 2010. "Ready, Aim, Fire!" *Dig*, April.

———. 2012. "For the Love of Honey." *Calliope*, January.

"Busy bees." 2008. *National Geographic Young Explorer*, May.

"The Buzz about Backyard Bees: You Can't Get Honey That's More Local than from Your Own City Backyard!" 2009. *Natural Life*, November/December.

Chandler, Phil. 2009. "Keeping the Bees: Use This Less-Expensive Method to Raise Bees That Will Pollinate Your Crops and Provide Tasty Honey Fresh from the Comb." *Mother Earth News*, October/November.

Fraser, Stephen. 2005. "Sweet Truth: The Secret Life of Honeybees." *Current Science*, September 23.

Graber, Cynthia. 2008. "The Case of the Disappearing Bees." *Ask*, September.

Hennessey, Gail Skroback. 2010. "Sweet Buzz: Here's One Way to Satisfy a 'Sweet Tooth'!" *Dig*, April.

"Honeybee Colonies Collapsing." 2007. *Current Science*, May 4.

Khvoroff, D. Louise. 2009. "Fuzzy, Buzzing, Dynamos." *Fun for Kidz*, May/June.

Lannom, Gloria W. 2010. "China's Oldest Sweetener: These People Sure Loved the Sweet Stuff." *Dig*, April.

McDowell, C. Forrest. 2010. "Save our Bees! Save our Foods and Flowers!" *Skipping Stones*, May/June.

Schmitt, Donna. 2009. "The Honey Factory." *Fun for Kidz*, May/June.

Smith, Natalie. 2010. "Bees Feel the Sting." *Scholastic News*, April 26.

Tourneret, Eric. 2009. "The Honey Collectors." *Geographical*, August.

Walters, Jennifer Marino. 2009. "New Buzz on Bees." *Scholastic News*, October 26.

Digital Resources

Websites

American Beekeeping Federation
http://abfnet.org/

Apimondia
http://www.apimondia.com/en

Bee Culture
http://www.beeculture.com/index.cfm

Beehoo
http://beehoo.com/

Beesource
http://www.beesource.com/

U.S. Environmental Protection Agency on Colony Collapse Disorder
http://www.epa.gov/pesticides/about/intheworks/honeybee.htm

International Bee Research Association
http://www.ibra.org.uk/

National Geographic for Kids, Honeybee Mystery
http://kids.nationalgeographic.com/kids/stories/animalsnature/honey-bee-mystery/

National Honey Board
http://www.honey.com/

National Public Radio (NPR), Study Links Honeybee Deaths to Fungus, Insect Virus
http://www.npr.org/templates/story/story.php?storyId=130405226

National Public Radio (NPR), The Buzz On Bees: Coping with Vanishing Colonies
http://www.npr.org/templates/story/story.php?storyId=111658438

New York City Beekeeping
http://www.nycbeekeeping.com/

PBS, Nature: Silence of the Bees
http://www.pbs.org/wnet/nature/episodes/silence-of-the-bees/introduction/38/

United States Department of Agriculture's Bee Research Laboratory
http://www.ars.usda.gov/main/site_main.htm?modecode=12-75-05-00

United States Department of Agriculture, Honey Bees Colony and Collapse Disorder
http://www.ars.usda.gov/News/docs.htm?docid=15572

University of Minnesota Bee Lab
http://beelab.umn.edu/

Text Set Models

Duet

Although they are small creatures, honeybees play a vital role in our ecosystems. Two nonfiction survey texts that are good fits for the Duet Model are *The Life and Times of the Honeybee* and *Honey in a Hive*.

Honeybees Duet Model

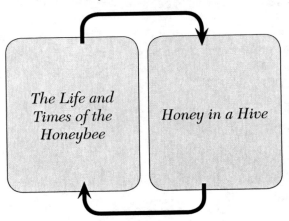

While covering similar content, these two authors use very different organizational formats. *The Life and Times of the Honeybee* comprises subtitled spreads with very specific areas of focus, such as "The Busy Days of a House Bee," and "A Honey Flower Menu." This multigenre text incorporates diagrams and sequenced images. *Honey in a Hive*, in contrast, is a chronological narrative of the honeymaking process. Students in elementary grades can compare and contrast the content of these books and discuss the effectiveness of these very different organizational structures.

Sunburst

Beekeeping in the city? Yes! Primary and intermediate grade students will be enthralled by the fictional story found in *Honeybee Man* of Fred who keeps bees in Brooklyn. This fictional text is an excellent vehicle for nonfiction explorations of honeybees and their role in an ecosystem in the Sunburst Model.

Honeybees Sunburst Model

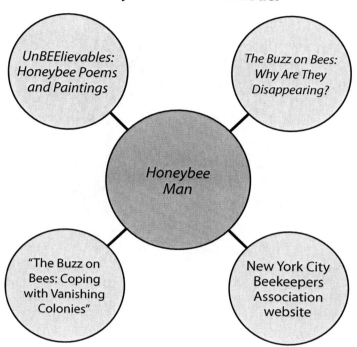

Having been introduced to the processes of pollination and honeymaking, students can further explore these concepts through a collection of related multimodal, multigenre texts. Complementary texts include *The Buzz on Bees: Why Are They Disappearing?*, which introduces the mystery of Colony Collapse Disorder to younger readers; the website of the New York City Beekeepers Association (http://www.nycbeekeeping.com/); a podcast of an NPR story "The Buzz on Bees: Coping with Vanishing Colonies" (http://www.npr.org) that discusses urban beekeeping; and the wonderful collection of annotated nonfiction poems *UnBEElievables: Honeybee Poems and Paintings*.

Tree Ring

Because of the depth of content coverage that students can achieve, the Tree Ring Model is an excellent way to explore the phenomenon of Colony Collapse Disorder. *The Hive Detectives: Chronicle of a Honey Bee Catastrophe*, part of the highly acclaimed Scientists in the Field series, published by Houghton Mifflin, traces the efforts of beekeepers and scientists to determine what is the root cause (or causes) of the disappearance of the honeybees.

Honeybees Tree Ring Model

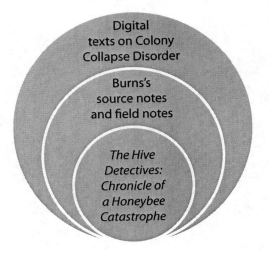

The breadth and depth of coverage in this text along with source material provided by the author both in the text and on her website, make this text well suited for exploration in the Tree Ring Model. After reading *The Hive Detectives: Chronicle of a Honey Bee Catastrophe*, secondary students could begin to explore the texts and resources that Burns consulted during the process of writing this text. These sources can be found both in the back matter of the book and on Burns's website (http://www.loreeburns.com/research/trips#bee_research). As part of her research process, Burns joined scientists as they engaged in fieldwork. Students can read about their field studies in Burns's blog, also accessible through the website. Following this exploration of Burn's sources, students branch out to read other texts on the topic of Colony Collapse Disorder.

In *The Hive Detectives: Chronicle of a Honey Bee Catastrophe*, Burns introduces various theories and perspectives on the phenomenon. Be sure to guide students to additional texts that explore these theories and perspectives. For example, students can watch the PBS documentary video, *The Silence of the Bees* (http://www.pbs.org/wnet/nature/episodes/silence-of-the-bees/full-episode/251/), listen to an NPR podcast on a parasitic fly affecting honeybee populations (http://www.npr.org/2012/01/06/144794041/parasitic-fly-threatens-honey-bee-populations), track the current work of the scientists followed in *The Hive Detectives: Chronicle of a Honey Bee Catastrophe* using an online search engine, and read an op-ed piece in *The New York Times* (http://www.nytimes.com/2010/03/25/opinion/25harder.html).

Solar System

The topic of honeybees can be further elaborated into subtopics, such as colony life, pollination, honeymaking, and beekeeping, to name a few that are appropriate for elementary and secondary students to explore. As an example of the Solar System Model, we suggest an exploration of survey books in small groups responsible for different topics. Each group will review the same set of core texts but will focus on locating information about their particular subtopic.

Honeybees Solar System Model

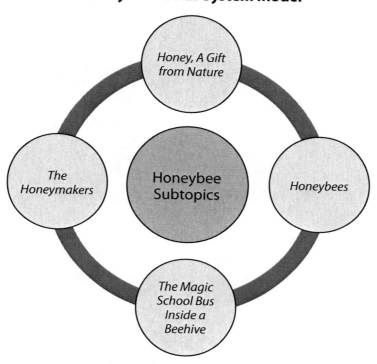

Four survey texts appropriate for this activity are *Honey, A Gift From Nature,* a nonfiction narrative first published in Japan in which a young girl describes the work of her father, a beekeeper; *Honeybees* part of National Geographic's Jump Into Science series and a chronological narrative in second person voice; *The Honeymakers,* a more detailed chronological narrative of the honeymaking processes; and *The Magic School Bus Inside a Beehive,* which blends factual information about bees in the context of a fantastical journey inside a beehive. These texts should be supplemented with the many wonderful multimedia digital resources listed in the text set.

Student Responses to Texts

When studying honeybees, the text types in this chart might make sense for your students to construct.

Honeybee Text Set: Student Responses to Texts

Subtopics, Genres, and Mentor Texts	Student-Created Texts
Bees: Friend or Foe? • *Honeybees* (Heiligman 2002) • The *Honeymakers* (Gibbons 1997) • *The Magic School Bus Inside a Beehive* (Cole 1996)	**First person vignettes:** Students can write from the perspective of the honeybee, using details from the texts to challenge people's common perceptions of them. Why are people so afraid of them?
The Latest on Colony Collapse Disorder • *The Hive Detectives: Chronicle of a Honey Bee Catastrophe* (Burns 2010) • *The Buzz on Bees: Why Are They Disappearing?* (Rotner and Woodhull 2010) • Various articles for young people listed in digital resources • American Bee Keeping Federation website • United States Environmental Protection Agency website • International Bee Research Association website	**Class magazine:** Students write articles detailing the latest research from scientists on bee populations and Colony Collapse Disorder.
Bee Poetry • *UnBEElievables: Honeybee Poems and Paintings* (Florian 2012) • *Honeybees* (Heiligman 2002) • *The Honeymakers* (Gibbons 1997) • *The Magic School Bus Inside a Beehive* (Cole 1996) • Various articles for young people listed in digital resources • National Geographic for Kids website, Honeybee Mystery	**Class or individual book of poetry:** Students can research honeybees and write a series of bee poems, using Florian's book as a mentor text.
Making Honey • *The Life and Times of the Honey Bee* (Micucci 1995) • *Honey in a Hive* (Rockwell 2005) • *The Magic School Bus Inside a Beehive* (Cole 1996) • *The Honeymakers* (Gibbons 1997) • National Geographic for Kids website, Honeybee Mystery	**Paintings, drawings, graphic fiction or nonfiction picture books:** Have students write and illustrate how bees make honey.
Bees in Your Community: Original Research • Student-conducted interviews with local beekeepers, scientists, farmers, and gardeners • *The Hive Detectives: Chronicle of a Honey Bee Catastrophe* (Burns 2010) • *The Buzz on Bees: Why Are They Disappearing?* (Rotner and Woodhull 2010)	**Community public service announcement:** Create a podcast to share on your school website educating students and families about the importance of bees in the local ecosystem. You may want to include clips from interviews as part of the podcast.

References Cited

Allan, Karen Kuelthau, Mary C. McMackin, Erika Thulin Dawes, and Stephanie A. Spadorcia. 2009. *Learning to Write with Purpose: Effective Instruction in Grades 4–8*. New York: Guilford Press.

Beck, Isabel L., Margaret G. McKeown, and Linda Kucana. 2002. *Bringing Words to Life: Robust Vocabulary Instruction*. New York: Guilford Press.

Common Core State Standards. 2010. "Key Points in English Language Arts." *Common Core State Standards Initiative*. Accessed May 22, 2012. http://www.corestandards.org/about-the-standards/key-points-in-english-language-arts.

The Cornell Lab of Ornithology. "All About Birds." Accessed June 13, 2012. http://www.allaboutbirds.org/Page.aspx?pid=1189.

Crafton, Linda K. 1991. *Whole Language: Getting Started…Moving Forward*. Katonah, NY: Richard C. Owen Publishers, Inc.

Daniels, Harvey. 2002. *Literature Circles: Voice and Choice in Book Clubs & Reading Groups*. Portland, ME; Stenhouse Publishers.

Echevarría, Jana, Mary Ellen Vogt, and Deborah Short. 2007. *Making Content Comprehensible for English Language Learners: The SIOP Model*. 3rd ed. Boston: Allyn & Bacon.

Fountas, Irene, and Gay Su Pinnell. 1996. *Guided Reading: Good First Teaching for all Children*. Portsmouth, NH: Heinemann.

Frost, Robert. (1913) 1991. *A Boy's Will and North of Boston*. Edited by Stanley Applebaum and Shane Weller. New York: Dover Publications.

Frost, Robert. "Stopping by Woods on a Snowy Evening," Poetry Foundation video, 1:26. Produced by David Grubin Productions and WGBH/Boston. Accessed June 13, 2012. http://www.poetryfoundation.org/features/video/18.

Graves, Michael F. 2005. *The Vocabulary Book: Learning & Instruction*. New York: Teachers College Press.

Hartman, Douglas K., and Jeanette A. Hartman. 1993. "Reading Across Texts: Expanding the Role of the Reader." *The Reading Teacher* 47 (3): 202–211.

Library of Congress. 1903. "Emigrants [i.e., immigrants] Landing at Ellis Island." Filmed July 9, 1903. Short film, 2:23. Filmed by Thomas A. Edison. http://hdl.loc.gov/loc.mbrsmi/lcmp002.m2a10987.

Library of Congress. "Using Primary Sources." Accessed June 13, 2012. http://www.loc.gov/teachers/usingprimarysources/.

Massachusetts Department of Elementary & Secondary Education. "Massachusetts Curriculum Frameworks." Last modified February 22, 2011. Accessed June 13, 2012. http://www.doe.mass.edu/frameworks/current.html.

Mathis, Janelle, B. 2002. "Picture Book Text Sets: A Novel Approach to Understanding Theme." *The Clearing House* 75 (3): 127–131.

Moje, Elizabeth Birr. 2008. "Foregrounding the Disciplines in Secondary Literacy Teaching and Learning: A Call for Change." *Journal of Adolescent & Adult Literacy* 52 (2): 96–107.

Monthey, Wanda. 2011. "An Overview of the SMARTER Balanced Assessment Consortium." SMARTER Balanced Assessment Consortium. Accessed June 13, 2012. http://www.renniecenter.org/event_pages/110412_SMARTER_BalancedOverview.pdf.

NASA. "NASA TV." Last modified March 9, 2012. Accessed June 13, 2012. http://www.nasa.gov/multimedia/nasatv/.

National Reading Panel. 2000. "Teaching Children to Read: An Evidence-Based Assessment of the Scientific Research Literature on Reading and Its Implications for Reading Instruction." National Institute of Child Health & Human Development. Bethesda, MD: National Institutes of Health. Accessed June 4, 2012. http://www.nichd.nih.gov/publications/nrp/smallbook.cfm.

Nichols, Maria. 2009. *Expanding Comprehension with Multigenre Text Sets*. New York: Scholastic.

NPR Music. 2008. "A Depression-Era Anthem for Our Times." NPR. http://www.npr.org/2008/11/15/96654742/a-depression-era-anthem-for-our-times.

Opitz, Michael F. 1998. "Text Sets: One Way to Flex Your Grouping—In First Grade, Too!" *The Reading Teacher* 51 (7): 622–624.

Pappas, Christine C., Barbara Z. Kiefer, and Linda S. Levstik. 1998. *An Integrated Language Perspective in the Elementary School: An Action Approach.* 3rd ed. Boston: Allyn & Bacon.

The American Presidency Project. "Audio/Video: Franklin D. Roosevelt" Accessed June 13, 2012. http://www.presidency.ucsb.edu/medialist.php?presid=32.

Tyson, Neil deGrasse. 2007. *Death by Black Hole and Other Cosmic Quandries.* New York: W. W. Norton & Company.

———. 2009a. "Conversations." Interview with Enrique Cerna. Seattle: KCTS 9 Television. http://www.youtube.com/watch?v=PrTTta55i5Q.

———. 2009b. *The Pluto Files: The Rise and Fall of America's Favorite Planet.* New York: W. W. Norton & Company.

———. 2011. "Discovery of Earth-like planet 'thrilling.'" Interview with Rebecca Jarvis and Chris Wragge. *The Early Show.* New York: CBS Interactive Inc. http://www.cbsnews .com/8301-502303_162-57337329/discovery-of-earth-like-planet-thrilling/.

Ward, Barbara A., and Terrell A. Young. 2008. "Text Sets: Making Connections Between and Across Books." *Reading Horizons* 48 (3): 215–226.

Recommended Multimodal Resources

Multimodal Resources in History/Social Studies

Ancient History

Multimodal Interactive Overview of Ancient Civilizations, British Museum, London
http://www.ancientcivilizations.co.uk/home_set.html

Multimodal Young Explorers, British Museum, London
http://www.britishmuseum.org/explore/young_explorers1.aspx

NOVA: Ancient Worlds Multimedia Site, Public Broadcasting Service (PBS)
http://www.pbs.org/wgbh/nova/ancient/

Europe

Greece

Ancient Greece, British Broadcasting Company (BBC), London
http://www.bbc.co.uk/history/ancient/greeks/

Ancient Greece, British Museum, London
http://www.ancientgreece.co.uk/

Ancient Greece, Rome, Heilbrunn Timeline of Art History, The Metropolitan Museum of Art, New York City
http://www.metmuseum.org/toah/ht/?period=04&region=eusb

The Greeks: Crucible of Civilization, Public Broadcasting System (PBS)
http://www.pbs.org/empires/thegreeks/htmlver/

NOVA: Secrets of the Parthenon, Public Broadcasting System (PBS)
http://video.pbs.org/video/980040228/

Odysseus Project, Hellenic Ministry of Culture
http://odysseus.culture.gr/index_en.html

Rome

Ancient History, Romans, British Broadcasting Company (BBC), London
http://www.bbc.co.uk/history/ancient/romans/

Ancient Rome, British Museum, London
http://www.britishmuseum.org/explore/cultures/europe/ancient_rome.aspx

Musei Capitolini, Rome (English version of website)
http://en.museicapitolini.org/

NOVA: Watering Ancient Rome, Public Broadcasting Service (PBS)
http://www.pbs.org/wgbh/nova/ancient/roman-aqueducts.html

Pompeii, The Discovery Channel
http://dsc.discovery.com/tv/pompeii/

Pompeii: Unraveling Ancient Mysteries, HMH School Publishers
http://www.harcourtschool.com/activity/pompeii/

The Roman Empire in the First Century, Public Broadcasting System (PBS)
http://www.pbs.org/empires/romans/

Secrets of the Dead: Lost Ships of Rome, Public Broadcasting Service (PBS)
http://video.pbs.org/video/1645539777

Asia

Asia for Educators, Columbia University
http://afe.easia.columbia.edu/tps/4000bce.htm

Mesopotamia/Iraq

Iraq's Ancient Past, Penn Museum, Philadelphia
http://www.penn.museum/sites/iraq/

Mesopotamia, The British Museum, London
http://www.mesopotamia.co.uk/

A Tour of Iraq's Ancient Sites, *The New York Times*
  http://atwar.blogs.nytimes.com/2011/01/02/a-tour-of-iraqs-ancient-sites/

China

Ancient China, The British Museum, London
  http://www.ancientchina.co.uk/menu.html

Freer/Sackler, The Smithsonian's Museum of Asian Art, Washington, DC
  http://www.asia.si.edu/collections/chinese.asp

Periods and Dynasties in Ancient China, Heilbrunn Timeline of Art History, The
  Metropolitan Museum of Art, New York
  Neolithic: http://www.metmuseum.org/toah/hd/cneo/hd_cneo.htm
  Bronze (Shang and Zhou):http://www.metmuseum.org/toah/hd/shzh/hd_shzh.htm
  Qin: http://www.metmuseum.org/toah/hd/qind/hd_qind.htm

Secrets of the Dead: China's Terracotta Warriors, Public Broadcasting Service (PBS)
  http://www.pbs.org/wnet/secrets/episodes/chinas-terracotta-warriors-watch-the-full-
  episode/844/

India

The Government Museum of Art and History, Chandigarh, India
  http://chdmuseum.nic.in/

Chhatrapati Shivaji Maharaj Vastu Sangrahalaya
  http://themuseummumbai.com/home.aspx

Ancient India, British Broadcasting Company (BBC), London
  http://www.bbc.co.uk/history/ancient/india/

Ancient India,The British Museum, London
  http://www.ancientindia.co.uk/

South Asian Art and Culture, Heilbrunn Timeline of Art History, The Metropolitan
  Museum of Art, New York
  http://www.metmuseum.org/toah/hd/sasa/hd_sasa.htm

The Story of India, Public Broadcasting Service (PBS), Washington
  http://www.pbs.org/thestoryofindia/about/episode_summaries/

Japan

National Museum of Japanese History
  http://www.rekihaku.ac.jp/english/index.html

Periods in Ancient Japan, Heilbrunn Timeline of Art History, The Metropolitan Museum
of Art, New York
  Neolithic: http://www.metmuseum.org/toah/ht/?period=02&region=eaj
  Jomon to Yayoi: http://www.metmuseum.org/toah/ht/?period=04&region=eaj

Africa

Egypt

Ancient History, Egyptians, British Broadcasting Company, London
  http://www.bbc.co.uk/history/ancient/egyptians/

Ancient Egypt, British Museum, London
  http://www.ancientegypt.co.uk/

Ancient Egypt, Museum of Science, Boston
  http://www.mos.org/quest/index.php

Collection of NOVA Digital Resources, Public Broadcasting Service (PBS)
  http://www.pbs.org/wgbh/nova/search/results/page/1?q=ancient+egypt&x=0&y=0

Egyptian Art, Heilbrunn Timeline of Art History, The Metropolitan Museum of Art, New
York City
  http://www.metmuseum.org/toah/hi/te_index.asp?i=14

Egyptian Museum and Papyrus Collection, Berlin
  http://www.egyptian-museum-berlin.com/index.php

Americas

Art of the Ancient Americas, Los Angeles County Museum of Art, Los Angeles
  http://www.lacma.org/art/collection/art-ancient-americas

Ancient Americas, The Field Museum, Chicago
  http://archive.fieldmuseum.org/ancientamericas/

Ancient Americas, Michael C. Carlos Museum of Emory University and Memorial Art
Gallery of the University of Rochester, Atlanta and Rochester
  http://carlos.emory.edu/ODYSSEY/AA/aafront.htm

Music in the Ancient Andes, Heilbrunn Timeline of Art History, The Metropolitan
Museum of Art, New York
  http://www.metmuseum.org/toah/hd/muan/hd_muan.htm

NOVA: America's Bog People, Public Broadcasting Service (PBS)
  http://www.pbs.org/wgbh/nova/ancient/americas-bog-people.html

NOVA: Ancient Clovis Cache, Public Broadcasting Service (PBS)
  http://www.pbs.org/wgbh/nova/ancient/ancient-clovis-cache.html

Medieval History

Creating French Culture: Treasures from the Bibliothèque Nationale de France, Library of Congress
http://www.loc.gov/exhibits/bnf/

Medieval Art, Heilbrunn Timeline of Art History, The Metropolitan Museum of Art, New York
http://www.metmuseum.org/toah/hi/te_index.asp?i=15

Middle Ages, British History, British Broadcasting Service, London
http://www.bbc.co.uk/history/british/middle_ages/

Medieval and Renaissance Illuminated Manuscripts from Western Europe, New York Public Library, New York
http://digitalgallery.nypl.org/nypldigital/explore/dgexplore.cfm?col_id=173

Medieval and Renaissance Manuscripts, Morgan Library, New York
http://www.themorgan.org/collections/collectionsMedRen.asp

Normans, British History, British Broadcasting Service, London
http://www.bbc.co.uk/history/british/normans/

NOVA: Building the Great Cathedrals, Public Broadcasting Service (PBS)
http://www.pbs.org/wgbh/nova/ancient/building-gothic-cathedrals.html

NOVA: China's Age of Invention, Public Broadcasting Service (PBS)
http://www.pbs.org/wgbh/nova/ancient/song-dynasty.html

NOVA: Medieval Siege, Public Broadcasting Service (PBS)
http://www.pbs.org/wgbh/nova/lostempires/trebuchet/

NOVA: Who Were the Vikings? Public Broadcasting Service (PBS)
http://www.pbs.org/wgbh/nova/ancient/who-were-vikings.html

Mystery of the Black Death, Secrets of the Dead, Public Broadcasting Service (PBS)
http://www.pbs.org/wnet/secrets/previous_seasons/case_plague/index.html

The Silk Road, American Museum of Natural History, New York
http://www.amnh.org/

Treasures of Islamic Manuscript Paintings, Morgan Library, New York
http://www.themorgan.org/collections/works/islamic/default.asp

Native American History

The American Experience: The Transcontinental Railroad, Native Americans, Public
Broadcasting Service (PBS)
http://www.pbs.org/wgbh/americanexperience/features/interview/tcrr-interview/

The American Experience: We Shall Remain, Public Broadcasting Service (PBS)
http://www.pbs.org/wgbh/amex/weshallremain/

Indian Country Today Media Network
http://indiancountrytodaymedianetwork.com/

National Museum of the American Indian, Smithsonian Institution, Washington DC, and
New York
http://nmai.si.edu/home/

Native American Public Telecommunications
http://www.nativetelecom.org/

Native Americans, Library of Congress, Washington
http://www.loc.gov/teachers/classroommaterials/themes/native-americans/

Early Modern History

Civil War and Revolution, British Broadcasting Company (BBC), London
http://www.bbc.co.uk/history/british/civil_war_revolution/

Enlightenment, The British Museum, London
http://www.britishmuseum.org/explore/galleries/themes/room_1_enlightenment.aspx

Islam: Empire of Faith, Public Broadcasting System (PBS)
http://www.pbs.org/empires/islam/index.html

Leonardo da Vinci, British Broadcasting Company (BBC), London
http://www.bbc.co.uk/science/leonardo/

The Mughal Dynasty, Public Broadcasting System (PBS)
http://www.pbs.org/treasuresoftheworld/taj_mahal/tlevel_1/t1_mughal.html

Tudors, British Broadcasting Company (BBC), London
http://www.bbc.co.uk/history/british/tudors/

Renaissance

Architecture in Renaissance Italy, Heilbrunn Timeline of Art History, The Metropolitan Museum of Art, New York
http://www.metmuseum.org/toah/hd/itar/hd_itar.htm

The Myth of the Renaissance in Europe, British Broadcasting Company (BBC), London
http://www.bbc.co.uk/history/british/tudors/renaissance_europe_01.shtml

Renaissance Europe, Explore/World Cultures, The British Museum, London
http://www.britishmuseum.org/explore/cultures/europe/renaissance_europe.aspx

Age of Exploration

Empire and Sea Power, British Broadcasting Company (BBC), London
http://www.bbc.co.uk/history/british/empire_seapower/

Europe and the Age of Exploration, Heilbrunn Timeline of Art History, The Metropolitan Museum of Art, New York
http://www.metmuseum.org/toah/hd/expl/hd_expl.htm

The Great Exchange, The Mariners' Museum
http://ageofex.marinersmuseum.org/index.php?type=webpage&id=6

Colonial American History and the American Revolution

Adams National Historic Site
http://www.nps.gov/adam/index.htm

The American Revolution, The History Channel
http://www.history.com/topics/american-revolution

The American Revolution Center, Philadelphia
http://www.americanrevolutioncenter.org/

Ben Franklin, Public Broadcasting Service (PBS)
http://www.pbs.org/benfranklin/

Boston National Historic Park, National Park Service
http://www.nps.gov/bost/index.htm

Colonial and Early America, Library of Congress
http://www.loc.gov/teachers/classroommaterials/themes/colonial-america/

The Coming of the American Revolution, Massachusetts Historical Society
http://www.masshist.org/revolution/

Connecticut Historical Society
http://www.chs.org/

George Washington, Mt. Vernon Historic Site
  http://www.mountvernon.org/

Georgia Historical Society
  http://www.georgiahistory.com/

Images of the American Revolution, Teaching with Documents, The National Archives
  http://www.archives.gov/education/lessons/revolution-images/

Liberty! The American Revolution, Public Broadcasting Service (PBS)
  http://www.pbs.org/ktca/liberty/

Library of Congress: Jamestown Settlement
  http://www.loc.gov/teachers/classroommaterials/primarysourcesets/jamestown/

Maine Historical Society
  http://www.mainehistory.org/

Maryland Historical Society
  http://www.mdhs.org/

Massachusetts Historical Society
  http://www.masshist.org/

New Hampshire Historical Society
  http://www.nhhistory.org/

New Jersey Historical Society
  http://www.jerseyhistory.org/

New York Historical Society Museum and Library
  http://www.nyhistory.org/

North Carolina Museum of History
  http://ncmuseumofhistory.org/

Patrick Henry, Red Hill Historic Site
  http://www.redhill.org/index.html

Paul Revere House
  http://www.paulreverehouse.org/

Historical Society of Pennsylvania
  http://hsp.org/

Preservation Virginia: Jamestown Rediscovery
  http://www.apva.org/rediscovery/page.php?page_id=1

Rhode Island Historical Society
  http://www.rihs.org/

South Carolina Historical Society
http://www.southcarolinahistoricalsociety.org/

Thomas Jefferson, Monticello Historic Site
http://www.monticello.org/

Vermont Historical Society
http://www.vermonthistory.org/

Virginia Historical Society
http://www.vahistorical.org/

Williamsburg, Virginia
http://www.history.org

"Within These Walls" Exhibit of Colonial House, 200 Years of History, American History Museum, Smithsonian
http://americanhistory.si.edu/house/

The Civil War

"'1861': A Social History of the Civil War," National Public Radio
http://www.npr.org/2012/03/09/146936196/1861-a-social-history-of-the-civil-war

Abolition of the Slave Trade, Schomberg Center, New York Public Library
http://abolition.nypl.org/home/

Abraham Lincoln Home, National Historic Site
http://www.nps.gov/liho/index.htm

Abraham Lincoln Papers, Library of Congress
http://memory.loc.gov/ammem/alhtml/malhome.html

Abraham Lincoln Presidential Library and Museum
http://www.alplm.org/

African-American Soldiers in the Civil War, The History Channel
http://www.history.com/topics/african-american-soldiers-in-the-civil-war

African-American Soldiers during the Civil War, The Library of Congress
http://www.loc.gov/teachers/classroommaterials/presentationsandactivities/presentations/timeline/civilwar/aasoldrs/

The American Experience: Abraham and Mary Lincoln: A House Divided, Public Broadcasting Service (PBS)
http://www.pbs.org/wgbh/americanexperience/films/lincolns/

Britain's Abolition, British Broadcasting Service, London
http://www.bbc.co.uk/history/british/abolition/

The Civil War: 150 Years, National Park Service
http://www.nps.gov/features/waso/cw150th/index.html

Civil War Exhibits of the Smithsonian Institution
http://civilwar150.si.edu/

The Civil War, National Portrait Gallery, Smithsonian Institution
http://npg.si.edu/exhibit/cw/npgcivilwar.html

The Civil War, Public Broadcasting Service (PBS)
http://www.pbs.org/civilwar/

American Civil War (1861–1865), *The New York Times*
http://topics.nytimes.com/topics/reference/timestopics/subjects/c/civil_war_us/index.html

Discovering the Civil War, National Archives, Washington, DC
http://www.archives.gov/exhibits/civil-war/

Ford's Theatre, House Where Lincoln Died, National Historic Site
http://www.nps.gov/foth/index.htm

Library of Congress, African-American Odyssey: Free Blacks in the Antebellum Period
http://memory.loc.gov/ammem/aaohtml/exhibit/aopart2.html

Library of Congress, African-American Odyssey: Slavery—The Peculiar Institution
http://memory.loc.gov/ammem/aaohtml/exhibit/aopart1.html

Library of Congress: Civil War Music: When Johnny Comes Marching Home
http://www.loc.gov/teachers/classroommaterials/primarysourcesets/civil-war-music/

National Geographic Underground Railroad Site
http://www.nationalgeographic.com/railroad/

National Underground Railroad Freedom Center
http://www.undergroundrailroad.com/

The New York Historical Society: Slavery in New York
http://www.slaveryinnewyork.org/tour_galleries.htm

Slavery and the Making of America: PBS Online Resources
http://www.pbs.org/wnet/slavery/

Slavery in the North
http://www.slavenorth.com/slavenorth.htm

"Unknown No More: Identifying a Civil War Soldier," National Public Radio
http://www.npr.org/2012/04/11/150288978/unknown-no-more-identifying-a-civil-war-soldier

Women in the Civil War
http://www.history.com/topics/women-in-the-civil-war

Industrialization

The African-American Mosaic, Chicago: Destination for the Great Migration, Library of Congress
http://www.loc.gov/exhibits/african/afam011.html

"Great Migration: The African-American Exodus North," National Public Radio
http://www.npr.org/templates/story/story.php?storyId=129827444

The Industrial Revolution in the United States, Library of Congress
http://www.loc.gov/teachers/classroommaterials/primarysourcesets/industrial-revolution/

Jacob Laurence: The Migration Series, The Phillips Collection
http://www.phillipscollection.org/migration_series/index.cfm

Teaching with Documents: Photographs of Lewis Hine: Documentation of Child Labor, National Archives
http://www.archives.gov/education/lessons/hine-photos/

Lowell National Historic Park, National Park Service
http://www.nps.gov/lowe/index.htm

Victorian Britain: Children in Factories, British Broadcasting Service (BBC)
http://www.bbc.co.uk/schools/primaryhistory/victorian_britain/children_in_factories/

"Who Made America? Francis Cabot Lowell," Public Broadcasting Service (PBS)
http://www.pbs.org/wgbh/theymadeamerica/whomade/lowell_hi.html

Modern World History

Apartheid Museum, Johannesburg, South Africa
http://www.apartheidmuseum.org/

Faces of the Mexican Revolution, The Getty Museum, Los Angeles
http://blogs.getty.edu/iris/faces-of-the-mexican-revolution/

Fashioning Fashion: European Dress in Detail, 1700–1915, Los Angeles County Museum of Art (LACMA)
http://www.lacma.org/art/exhibition/fashioning-fashion-european-dress-detail-1700–1915

The Industrial Revolution and the Changing Face of Britain, The British Museum, London
http://www.britishmuseum.org/research/online_research_catalogues/paper_money/the_industrial_revolution.aspx

Revolution! The Atlantic World Reborn, New-York Historical Society Museum and Library
http://www.nyhistory.org/exhibitions/revolution-the-atlantic-world-reborn

Russian Revolution, Lenin Museum, Moscow, Russia
http://www.stel.ru/museum/Russian_revolution_1917.htm

The Wealth of Africa: Colonialism and Independence, The British Museum, London
http://www.britishmuseum.org/explore/online_tours/africa/the_wealth_of_africa
/colonialism_and_independence.aspx

World War I

Experiencing War: Stories from the Veterans History Project, World War I: The Great War, Library of Congress
http://www.loc.gov/vets/stories/ex-war-wwi.html

The Great War and the Shaping of the 20th Century, Public Broadcasting Service (PBS)
http://www.pbs.org/greatwar/

World War I, British Broadcasting Service (BBC), London
http://www.bbc.co.uk/history/worldwars/wwone/

World War I, The History Channel
http://www.history.com/topics/world-war-i

World War I (1914–18), *The New York Times*
http://topics.nytimes.com/topics/reference/timestopics/subjects/w/world_war_i_/index
.html

World War I: Their Stories, British Broadcasting Company (BBC), London
http://www.bbc.co.uk/schools/worldwarone/

World War I Web Guide, Library of Congress
http://www.loc.gov/rr/program/bib/wwi/wwi.html

World War II

America on the Homefront, National Archives
http://www.archives.gov/northeast/boston/exhibits/homefront/

Children of World War II, British Broadcasting Company (BBC), London
http://www.bbc.co.uk/schools/primaryhistory/world_war2/

Experiencing War: Stories from the Veterans History Project, World War II, Library of Congress
http://www.loc.gov/vets/stories/wwiilist.html

Japanese American Internment During World War II, Library of Congress
http://www.loc.gov/teachers/classroommaterials/primarysourcesets/internment/

Manzanar National Historic Site, National Park Service
http://www.nps.gov/manz/index.htm

The National World War II Museum, New Orleans
http://www.nationalww2museum.org/index.html

Official Site: Navajo Code Talkers Foundation, Arizona
http://www.navajocodetalkers.org/

Perilous Fight: America's World War II in Color, Public Broadcasting Service (PBS)
http://www.pbs.org/perilousfight/

U.S. Rationing during World War II, Smithsonian Institution, Education Department
http://www.smithsonianeducation.org/idealabs/wwii/

World War II Aviation, National Air and Space Museum, Smithsonian Institution
http://airandspace.si.edu/exhibitions/gal205/

World War II, British Broadcasting Service (BBC), London
http://www.bbc.co.uk/history/worldwars/wwtwo/

World War II Records, National Archives
http://www.archives.gov/research/military/ww2/index.html

World War II Remembered, Scholastic
http://teacher.scholastic.com/activities/wwii/index.htm

World War II School Radio, British Broadcasting Company (BBC), London
http://www.bbc.co.uk/learning/schoolradio/subjects/history/ww2clips

World War II, The History Channel
http://www.history.com/topics/world-war-ii

World War II (1939–45), *The New York Times*
http://topics.nytimes.com/top/reference/timestopics/subjects/w/world_war_ii_/index.html

World War II Web Guide, Library of Congress
http://www.loc.gov/rr/program/bib/WW2/WW2bib.html

The Holocaust

Anne Frank House, Amsterdam
http://www.annefrank.org/

Auschwitz Birkenau: German Nazi Concentration and Extermination Camp (1940–1945): UNESCO
http://whc.unesco.org/en/list/31/

The Holocaust, The History Channel
http://www.history.com/topics/the-holocaust

Jewish Museum, Berlin
http://www.jmberlin.de/main/EN/homepage-EN.php

Los Angeles Museum of the Holocaust, Los Angeles
http://www.lamoth.org/

Museum of Jewish Heritage: A Living Memorial to the Holocaust, New York
http://www.mjhnyc.org/

Simon Wiesenthal Center, Los Angeles
http://www.wiesenthal.com/site/pp.asp?c=lsKWLbPJLnF&b=6212365

United States Holocaust Memorial Museum, Washington, DC
http://www.ushmm.org/

Yad Vashem, World Holocaust Center, Jerusalem
http://www.yadvashem.org/

The Civil Rights Movement

1955–1956: The Story of the Montgomery Bus Boycott, *The Montgomery Advertiser*
http://www.montgomeryboycott.com/frontpage.htm

African American Museum in Philadelphia
http://aampmuseum.org/

American Experience: Freedom Riders, Public Broadcasting Service (PBS)
http://www.pbs.org/wgbh/americanexperience/freedomriders/

Birmingham Civil Rights Institute, Birmingham
http://www.bcri.org/index.html

Historic Places of the Civil Rights Movement, National Park Service
http://www.nps.gov/nr/travel/civilrights/

The International Civil Rights Center and Museum, Greensboro, NC
http://www.sitinmovement.org/

The King Center, Atlanta
http://www.thekingcenter.org/

Martin Luther King Jr. National Historic Site, National Park Service
http://www.nps.gov/malu/index.htm

National Civil Rights Museum, Memphis
http://www.civilrightsmuseum.org/

Separate Is Not Equal, Brown v. Board of Education, National Museum of American
History, Smithsonian Institution
http://americanhistory.si.edu/brown/index.html

Stories of Freedom and Justice, National Museum of American History, Smithsonian Institution
http://americanhistory.si.edu/freedomandjustice/learning_resources.html

Multimodal Resources in Science

General

American Museum of Natural History, New York
http://www.amnh.org/

Annenberg Foundation, Science Teaching Resources
http://www.learner.org/resources/browse.html?discipline=6&grade=0

Field Museum, Chicago
http://fieldmuseum.org/

The Franklin Institute
http://www2.fi.edu/

The National Academies
http://www.nationalacademies.org/

National Geographic
http://www.nationalgeographic.com/

National Geographic Kids
http://kids.nationalgeographic.com/kids/?source=NavKidsHome

National Museum of Natural History, Smithsonian Institution, Washington, DC
http://www.mnh.si.edu/

National Science Foundation
http://www.nsf.gov/

Natural History Museum of Los Angeles
http://www.nhm.org/site/

ScienceEducation.Gov
http://www.scienceeducation.gov/

TERC
http://www.terc.edu/

Earth and Space Science

Adler Planetarium, Chicago
http://www.adlerplanetarium.org/

Geological Society of America, Education and Outreach
http://www.geosociety.org/educate/

Harvard-Smithsonian Center for Astrophysics, Education and Outreach
http://www.cfa.harvard.edu/education/

NASA Education
http://www.nasa.gov/audience/foreducators/index.html

National Oceanic and Atmospheric Administration of the U.S. Department of Commerce, Office of Education
http://www.oesd.noaa.gov/

NOVA: Deadly Volcanoes, Public Broadcasting Service (PBS)
http://www.pbs.org/wgbh/nova/earth/deadly-volcanoes.html

NOVA: Volcano's Deadly Warning, Public Broadcasting Service (PBS)
http://www.pbs.org/wgbh/nova/volcano/

Rose Center for Earth and Space, American Museum of Natural History, New York
http://www.amnh.org/rose/

Savage Earth, Out of the Inferno: Volcanoes, Public Broadcasting Service (PBS)
http://www.pbs.org/wnet/savageearth/volcanoes/index.html

United States Geological Service Education Resources
http://education.usgs.gov/index.html

Volcano Interactives, Annenberg Foundation
http://www.learner.org/interactives/volcanoes/

Volcano World, Oregon State University, Corvalis
http://volcano.oregonstate.edu/

Life Sciences

National Aquarium, Baltimore
http://www.aqua.org/

National Zoological Park, Smithsonian Institution
http://nationalzoo.si.edu/

New England Aquarium, Boston
http://www.neaq.org/index.php

San Diego Zoo, San Diego
http://www.sandiegozoo.org/

Let's Go Outside!, United States Fish and Wildlife Service, Department of the Interior, Education
http://www.fws.gov/letsgooutside/

Wildlife Conservation Society
http://www.wcs.org/

Woods Hole National Oceanographic Institution, K–12 Resources
http://www.whoi.edu/main/k-12

Physical Science

Einstein Archives Online, Jerusalem
http://www.alberteinstein.info/

Physics Games, Public Broadcasting System (PBS)
http://pbskids.org/games/physics.html

Engineering and Technology

Engineering Is Elementary, Museum of Science, Boston
http://www.mos.org/eie/engineering_children.php

National Air and Space Museum, Smithsonian Institution
http://airandspace.si.edu/

Multimodal Resources in Literature

Children's Book Council, New York
http://www.cbcbooks.org/

Children's Literature Center, Library of Congress, Washington, DC
http://www.loc.gov/rr/child/

Children's Poet Laureate, Poetry Foundation
http://www.poetryfoundation.org/children/poet-laureate

The Cooperative Children's Book Center, University of Wisconsin–Madison
http://www.education.wisc.edu/ccbc/

International Children's Digital Library
http://en.childrenslibrary.org/

National Ambassador for Young People's Literature, Library of Congress, Washington, DC
http://www.read.gov/cfb/ambassador/

National Center for the Book, Library of Congress, Washington, DC
http://www.read.gov/cfb/

Poetry 180, Library of Congress, Washington, DC
http://www.loc.gov/poetry/180/

The Poetry Foundation
http://www.poetryfoundation.org/

Teachingbooks.net (by subscription; check your school or local library)
http://www.teachingbooks.net

Multimodal Resources in Art

The Art Institute of Chicago
http://www.artic.edu/aic/

Asian Art Museum, San Francisco
http://www.asianart.org/

The Barnes Foundation, Philadelphia
http://www.barnesfoundation.org/

The British Museum, London
http://www.britishmuseum.org

Centre Pompidou, Paris
http://www.centrepompidou.fr/

Cooper-Hewitt, National Design Museum, Smithsonian Institution, New York
http://www.cooperhewitt.org/

Denver Art Museum, Denver, CO
http://www.denverartmuseum.org/

The de Young Fine Arts Museum of San Francisco, San Francisco
http://deyoung.famsf.org/

Freer and Sackler, The Smithsonian's Museum of Asian Art, Smithsonian Institution, Washington, DC
http://www.asia.si.edu/

The Frick Collection, New York
http://www.frick.org/

The Getty, Los Angeles
http://www.getty.edu/index.html

The Guggenheim, Bilbao, Spain
http://www.guggenheim.org/bilbao/

The Guggenheim, New York
http://www.guggenheim.org/

The Isabella Stewart Gardner Museum, Boston
http://www.gardnermuseum.org/

Legion of Honor Fine Arts Museums of San Francisco, San Francisco
http://legionofhonor.famsf.org/

Los Angeles County Museum of Art
http://www.lacma.org/

The Louvre, Paris
http://www.louvre.fr/en

Metropolitan Museum of Art, New York
http://www.metmuseum.org

The Morgan Library and Museum, New York
http://www.themorgan.org/home.asp

Musée d'Orsay, Paris
http://www.musee-orsay.fr/en/home.html

Museo Nacional del Prado, Madrid
http://www.museodelprado.es/en/

The Museum of Fine Arts, Boston
http://www.mfa.org/

The Museum of Modern Art, New York
http://www.moma.org/

National Gallery, London
http://www.nationalgallery.org.uk/

The National Gallery of Art, Washington, D.C.
http://www.nga.gov/

National Museum of African Art, Smithsonian Institution, Washington, DC
http://www.nmafa.si.edu/

National Museum of Korea, Korea
http://www.museum.go.kr/main/index/index002.jsp

National Museum of Mexican Art, Chicago
http://nationalmuseumofmexicanart.org/

National Palace Museum, Taipei
http://www.npm.gov.tw/en/home.htm

The National Portrait Gallery, Smithsonian Institution, Washington, DC
http://www.npg.si.edu/

New Mexico Museum of Art, Santa Fe, NM
http://www.nmartmuseum.org/

The Peabody Essex Museum, Salem, MA
http://www.pem.org/

The Philadelphia Museum of Art
http://www.philamuseum.org/

The Phillips Collection, Washington, DC
http://www.phillipscollection.org/

Phoenix Art Museum, Phoenix, AZ
http://www.phxart.org/index.php

Polo Museale Fiorentino, The Uffizi Gallery, The Accademia, and Palatina, Florence
http://www.uffizi.firenze.it/en/index.php

Rijks Museum, Amsterdam
http://www.rijksmuseum.nl/

Seattle Art Museum, Seattle, WA
http://www.seattleartmuseum.org/default.asp

Smithsonian American Art Museum, Smithsonian Institution, Washington, DC
http://americanart.si.edu/

The State Hermitage Museum, St. Petersburg, Russia
http://www.hermitagemuseum.org/html_En/index.html

The Tate, London
http://www.tate.org.uk/

The Vatican Museums, Vatican City
http://mv.vatican.va/3_EN/pages/MV_Home.html

The Victoria and Albert Museum, London
http://www.vam.ac.uk/

Trees Text Set

For an annotated list of these texts, please see the Digital Resource CD (treesannotated.doc)

Nonfiction Picture Books

Appelbaum, Diana. 1993. *Giants in the Land*. New York: Houghton Mifflin.

Bang, Molly, and Penny Chisholm. 2009. *Living Sunlight: How Plants Bring the Earth to Life*. New York: Blue Sky Press.

Bulla, Clyde Robert. (1960) 2001. *A Tree Is a Plant*. Let's Read and Find Out series. New York: HarperCollins.

Burns, Diane L. 1995. *Trees, Leaves, and Bark*. Portland, OR: North Word Press.

Collard, Sneed. 2000. *The Forest in the Clouds*. Watertown, MA: Charlesbridge.

Chin, Jason. 2009. *Redwoods*. New York: Flash Point.

Davies, Jacqueline. 2004. *The Boy Who Drew Birds: A Story of John James Audubon*. New York: Houghton Mifflin.

DePalma, Mary Newall. 2005. *A Grand Old Tree*. New York: Arthur A. Levine.

Dorros, Arthur. 1999. *Rain Forest Secrets*. New York: Scholastic.

Dunphy, Madeleine. 2006. *Here Is the Tropical Rain Forest*. Berkeley, CA: Web of Life Children's Books.

George, Jean Craighead. 2008. *The Wolves Are Back*. New York: Dutton.

Gerber, Carole. 2006. *Leaf Jumpers*. Watertown, MA: Charlesbridge.

————. 2008. *Winter Trees*. Watertown, MA: Charlesbridge.

Gibbons, Gail. 1997. *Nature's Green Umbrella: Tropical Rain Forests*. New York: HarperCollins Publishing.

————. 2002. *Tell Me Tree: All About Trees for Kids*. New York: Little, Brown.

Guiberson, Brenda. 2010. *Life in the Boreal Forest*. New York: Henry Holt.

Johnson, Jen Cullerton. 2010. *Seeds of Change: Planting a Path to Peace*. New York: Lee and Low.

Johnson, Rebecca. 2001a. *A Walk in the Boreal Forest*. Biomes of North America series. Minneapolis: Carolrhoda Books, Inc.

————. 2001b. *A Walk in the Deciduous Forest*. Biomes of North America series. Minneapolis: Carolrhoda Books, Inc.

————. 2001c. *A Walk in the Rain Forest*. Biomes of North America series. Minneapolis: Carolrhoda Books, Inc.

Lasky, Kathryn. 1997. *The Most Beautiful Roof in the World: Exploring the Rainforest Canopy*. New York: Harcourt, Brace & Co.

————. 2006. *John Muir: America's First Environmentalist*. Somerville, MA: Candlewick Press.

Locker, Thomas. 2003. *John Muir, America's Naturalist*. Golden, CO: Fulcrum Publishing.

Napoli, Donna Jo. 2010. *Mama Miti: Wangari Maathai and the Trees of Kenya*. New York: Simon & Schuster Books for Young Readers.

Nivola, Claire. 2008. *Planting the Trees of Kenya: The Story of Wangari Maathai*. New York: Farrar, Straus & Giroux.

Pascoe, Elaine. 2003. *The Ecosystem of a Fallen Tree*. Focus on Science series. New York: Rosen Publishing.

Patent, Dorothy Henshaw. 1996. *Children Save the Rain Forest*. New York: Cobblehill Books.

————. 2004. *Garden of the Spirit Bear: Life in the Great Northern Rain Forest*. New York: Clarion.

Pfeffer, Wendy. 1997. *A Log's Life*. New York: Simon and Shuster.

Rosenstock, Barb. 2012. *The Camping Trip That Changed America: Theodore Roosevelt, John Muir, and Our National Parks*. New York: Dial Books for Young Readers.

Salas, Laura Purdie. 2007. *Temperate Deciduous Forests: Lands of Falling Leaves.* Amazing Science: Ecosystems series. North Mankato, MN: Picture Window Books.

Sayre, April Pulley. 2008. *Trout Are Made of Trees.* Watertown, MA: Charlesbridge.

Serafini, Frank. 2008. *Looking Closely Through the Forest.* Looking Closely series. Tonawanda, NY: Kids Can Press.

Trumbore, Cindy, and Susan Roth. 2011. *The Mangrove Tree: Planting Trees to Feed Families.* New York: Lee & Low Books.

Winter, Jeanette. 2008. *Wangari's Trees of Peace: A True Story of Africa.* New York: Harcourt.

Yolen, Jane. 1997. *Welcome to the Green House.* New York: Putnam and Grosset.

Nonfiction

Collard, Sneed. 1997. *Monteverde: Science and Scientists in a Costa Rican Cloud Forest.* London: Franklin Watts.

Franklin, Yvonne. 2010. *Forests.* Science Readers: Biomes and Ecosystems series. Huntington Beach, CA: Teacher Created Materials.

Goldstein, Natalie. 2011. *John Muir.* Conservation Heroes series. New York: Chelsea House Publishing.

Montgomery, Sy. 2006. *Quest for the Tree Kangaroo.* Scientists in the Field series. Boston: Houghton Mifflin.

Sherman, Pat. 2011. *John James Audubon.* Conservation Heroes series. New York: Chelsea House Publishing.

Sobol, Richard. 2008. *Breakfast in the Rain Forest: A Visit with Mountain Gorillas.* Cambridge, MA: Candlewick.

Fiction Picture Books

Cherry, Lynne. (1990) 2000. *The Great Kapok Tree: A Tale of the Amazon Rain Forest.* Boston: Sandpiper.

———. 2004. *The Sea, the Storm and the Mangrove Tangle.* New York: Farrar, Straus & Giroux.

Foggo, Cheryl. 2011. *Dear Baobab.* Toronto: Second Story Press.

Galbraith, Kathryn. 2010. *Arbor Day Square.* Atlanta: Peachtree Publishers.

Hopkinson, Deborah. 2004. *Apples to Oregon: Being the (Slightly) True Narrative of How a Brave Pioneer Father Brought Apples, Peaches, Pears, Plums, Grapes, and Cherries (and Children) Across the Plains.* New York: Atheneum Books for Young Readers.

McPhail, David. 2008. The Searcher and Old Tree. Watertown, MA: Charlesbridge Publishing.

Muldrow, Diane. 2010. *We Planted a Tree.* New York: Golden Book, Random House.

Pearson, Debora. 2006. *Leo's Tree.* Toronto: Annick Press.

Rawlinson, Julia. 2006. *Fletcher and the Falling Leaves.* New York: Greenwillow Books.

Smith, Lane. 2011. *Grandpa Green.* New York: Roaring Brook Press.

Stein, David Ezra. 2007. *Leaves.* New York: G. P. Putnam's Sons.

Williams, Karen Lynn. 2005. *Circles of Hope.* Grand Rapids, MI: Eerdmans Books for Young Readers.

Novels and Short Stories

Cisneros, Sandra. 1991. *The House on Mango Street.* New York: Vintage Books.

French, S. Terrell. 2011. *Operation Redwood.* New York: Amulet Books.

Rocklin, Joanne. 2011. *One Day and One Amazing Morning on Orange Street.* New York: Amulet Books.

Picture Book Poetry

Florian, Douglas. 2010. *Poetrees.* San Diego, CA: Beach Lane Books.

George, Kristine O'Connell. 1998. *Old Elm Speaks: Tree Poems.* New York: Clarion Books.

Lindbergh, Reeve. 1990. *Johnny Appleseed: A Poem.* Boston: Little, Brown.

Periodicals

"A Tree's Life." 2011. *National Geographic Young Explorer*, October.

Aplet, Greg, and Evan Hierpe. 2011. "The Future of Forests." *Mother Earth News*, June/July.

Bourne, Joel K. 2009. "Redwoods: The Super Trees." *National Geographic*, October.

"Chestnut Trees Could Temper Climate Change." *USA Today*, Junior Edition, June 2010: 7.

Churchman, Deborah. 2004. "Amazing Trees." *Ranger Rick*, June.

Cowan, Mary Morton. 2005. "Working the Woods." *Faces*, September.

Creegan, Elizabeth. 2009. "Growing Trees for Kenya." *Highlights for Children*, March.

Derr, Aron. 2010. "Rebuilding Years." *Boys' Life*, March.

Ferrara, Jan. 2011. "Wangari Maathai: Trees for Peace." *Faces*, February.

Goodsell, David. 2011. "Trees Lose Leaves—Why?" *Fun for Kidz*, September/October.

Hoffman, Kate. 2010–2011. "Conifers." *Ranger Rick*, December/January.

The Horn Book Magazine
    http://www.hbook.com/

Kelley, Stephanie. 2011a. "King of the Trees." *Fun for Kidz*, March/April.

———. 2011b. "Types of Trees." *Fun for Kidz*, March/April.

"Life in a Tropical Rain Forest." 2009. *Weekly Reader*, Edition 2, March.

"Looking at Leaves." 2011. *Click*, September.

Manhein, Bhavani. 2008. "The Cedar: A Many Splendored Tree." *Skipping Stones*,
    November/December.

Prescott, Lyle. 1997. "The Busy Life of a Rotting Log." *Ranger Rick*, July.

Ramaley, Shirley Ann. 2011. "Learning from Trees." *Fun for Kidz*, March/April.

Royer, Amber. 2011. "The Incredible Edible Tree." *Odyssey*, April.

School Library Journal
    http://www.schoollibraryjournal.com/

Siegelman, Sharon. 2004. "We Need Trees." *Weekly Reader*, Edition K, April.

Sweeney, Debora, and Judy Rounds. 2011. "Winter Birch Trees." *Arts & Activities*,
    December.

Wetzel, Carol. 2011. "Why Can Trees Live So Long?" *Odyssey*, April.

"Whose Leaf?" 2011. *Click*, September.

Witze, Alexandra. 2011. "Rain Tips Balance Between Forest and Savanna: Amount of Tree
    Cover Can Shift Suddenly and Abruptly." *Science News*, Nov 5.

Digital Resources

Websites

Arbor Day Foundation, Rain Forest Rescue Program
    http://www.arborday.org/programs/rainforest

Discover the Forest (U.S. Forest Service)
    http://www.discovertheforest.org/index.php

Finding My Forest
    http://www.findingmyforest.org/

Food and Agriculture Organization (FAO) of the United Nations
    http://www.fao.org/forestry/education/en/

Forest Education Initiative
    http://www.foresteducation.org/

The Green Belt Movement
    http://www.greenbeltmovement.org/index.php

Idaho Forest Products Commission
    http://www.idahoforests.org/index.html

Junior Forester Program—City of Cambridge, Massachusetts
    http://www.cambridgema.gov/theworks/ourservices/urbanforestry/
    programsandvolunteering/juniorforesterprogram.aspx

Lexington Tree Inventory 2004–2010
    http://ci.lexington.ma.us/committees/treeinventory.cfm

MCTI—Mobile Community Tree Inventory
    http://www.umass.edu/urbantree/mcti/

NASA Maps of Mangrove Forests
    http://earthobservatory.nasa.gov/IOTD/view.php?id=47427
    http://www.nasa.gov/topics/earth/features/scarcer-forests.html

National Forest Foundation
    http://www.nationalforests.org/

National Wildlife Federation, KIDS
    http://www.nwf.org/kids.aspx

Natural Inquirer: A Middle School Science Education Journal
    http://www.naturalinquirer.org/

Nature Explore, A National Arbor Day Foundation Program for Children
    http://www.arborday.org/explore/

NPR Story on Mangrove Trees in Fiji
    http://www.npr.org/templates/story/story.php?storyId=10983906

Oceans for Youth Foundation: Mangrove Video
    http://www.oceansforyouth.org/mangroves.html

Sierra Club
    http://www.sierraclub.org

U.S. Department of Agriculture, Forest Service, Conservation Education
    http://www.fs.usda.gov/conservationeducation

U.S. Environmental Protection Agency, Students
    http://www.epa.gov/students/index.html

U.S. National Park Service Interpretation and Education
    http://www.nps.gov/learn/

U.S. National Park Service WebRangers
    http://www.webrangers.us/

World Land Trust—Wildlife Webcams
    http://www.worldlandtrust.org/webcams

Tablet Apps

Audubon Trees—A Field Guide to North American Trees
    http://itunes.apple.com/us/app/audubon-trees-field-guide/id334843956?mt=8

Britannica Kids: Rainforests
    http://itunes.apple.com/us/app/britannica-kids-rainforests/id419396614?mt=8

Leafsnap
    http://itunes.apple.com/us/app/leafsnap/id430649829?mt=8

NatureFind
    http://itunes.apple.com/us/app/naturefind/id335373871?mt=8

Contents of the Digital Resource CD

Page	Title	Filename
Chapter 2 Resources		
44	Unit Planning Chart Template	unitplanning.pdf unitplanning.doc
Chapter 3 Resources		
51	Text Set Chart	textsetchart.pdf textsetchart.doc
Chapter 5 Resources		
103–104	Sample Note-Making Form: Trees Duet Model	notemakingtrees.pdf
Chapter 6 Resources		
126	Unit Planning Chart: Coming to America	comingamerica.pdf
139–142	Coming to America Notes	americanotes.pdf
143	Coming to America Project Planner	americaplanner.pdf
146	Book Comparison Chart	bookcompare.pdf

Page	Title	Filename
Chapter 7 Resources		
174	Solar System Maps Planning Sheet	solarsystemplanner.pdf
176–177	Solar System Time Line Planning Sheet	solarsystemtimeline.pdf
180–182	Neighborhood Group Poster Presentations	groupposter.pdf
183–187	Note-Making Form for Solar System Neighborhoods	noteformsolarsystem.pdf
188–189	Peer Note-Making Form for Neighborhood Presentations	peersolarsystem.pdf
190	Neighborhood Poster Presentations Rubric	solarsystemrubric.pdf
193	Note-Making Form for Group Work on Earth's Place in Space	placeinspaceform.pdf
194–195	Note-Making Form for *Our Earth* and *Sun Up, Sun Down*	notemakingsolarsystem.pdf
196	Note-Making Form for Seasons in the Northern Hemisphere	notemakingseasons.pdf
198	Earth's Place in Space: Performing Orbit and Rotation	placeinspace.pdf
199	Skit Rubric	skitrubric.pdf
202–203	Moon Phases Note-Making Form	moonphasesnoteform.pdf
204–205	What Are the Moon's Phases? Chronological Narrative and Illustrations	whataremoonphases.pdf
206	Moon Phase Chronological Narrative and Illustrations Rubric	moonphaserubric.pdf

Page	Title	Filename
Chapter 8–11 Resources		
N/A	The Great Depression Annotated Text Set	greatdepressionannotated.doc
N/A	Immigration Annotated Text Set	immigrationannotated.doc
N/A	Space Annotated Text Set	spaceannotated.doc
N/A	Honeybees Annotated Text Set	honeybeesannotated.doc
Appendices		
272–291	Recommended Multimodal Resources	multimodal.pdf
N/A	Trees Annotated Text Set	treesannotated.doc

Notes

Notes

Notes